INDEPENDENT
MONTHLY
LITERARY
MAGAZINE

REVISTA
LITERÁRIA
INDEPENDENTE
MENSAL

ADELAIDE

Independent Monthly Literary Magazine
Revista Literária Independente Mensal
Year IV, Number 20, January 2019
Ano IV, Número 20, janeiro de 2019

ISBN-13: 978-1-949180-81-7
ISBN-10: 1-949180-81-6

Adelaide Literary Magazine is an independent international monthly publication, based in New York and Lisbon. Founded by Stevan V. Nikolic and Adelaide Franco Nikolic in 2015, the magazine's aim is to publish quality poetry, fiction, nonfiction, artwork, and photography, as well as interviews, articles, and book reviews, written in English and Portuguese. We seek to publish outstanding literary fiction, nonfiction, and poetry, and to promote the writers we publish, helping both new, emerging, and established authors reach a wider literary audience.

A Revista Literária Adelaide é uma publicação mensal internacional e independente, localizada em Nova Iorque e Lisboa. Fundada por Stevan V. Nikolic e Adelaide Franco Nikolic em 2015, o objectivo da revista é publicar poesia, ficção, não-ficção, arte e fotografia de qualidade assim como entrevistas, artigos e críticas literárias, escritas em inglês e português. Pretendemos publicar ficção, não-ficção e poesia excepcionais assim como promover os escritores que publicamos, ajudando os autores novos e emergentes a atingir uma audiência literária mais vasta.

(http://adelaidemagazine.org)

Published by: Adelaide Books, New York
244 Fifth Avenue, Suite D27
New York NY, 10001
e-mail: info@adelaidemagazine.org
phone: (917) 477 8984
http://adelaidebooks.org

FOUNDERS / FUNDADORES
Stevan V. Nikolic & Adelaide Franco Nikolic

EDITOR IN CHIEF / EDITOR-CHEFE
Stevan V. Nikolic
editor@adelaidemagazine.org

MANAGING DIRECTOR / DIRECTORA EXECUTIVA
Adelaide Franco Nikolic

GRAPHIC & WEB DESIGN
Adelaide Books LLC New York

CONTRIBUTING AUTHORS IN THIS ISSUE

Sue Brennan, Kayle Nochomovitz, Mark Jacobs, Michael Paul Hogan, Omar Essa, Jack Coey, Thomas Kearnes, Kobina Wright Limitless, Erin Bank, Pavel Sokolov, Maria Frangakis, Jenny Hayes, Jenny Butler, Andy Spisak, Tammy Huffman, Tali Treece, Fred Miller, Dan Elasky, Nicole Reinholdt, Linda L. Dunlap, Terry Engel, Dr. Raymond Fenech, Lisa Reily, Thomas Dexter Kerr, Emily Wilford, Caleb Bouchard, Leslie Tucker, Brianna Heisey, Cristopher Major, Robert Steward, Mark Jamieson, Emily Brummett, Dane Myers, Louis Gallo, Aditya Shankar, Jamel Hall, Clark Holtzman, Doug Sutton-Ramspeck, Judith Simon Prager, Daniel King, Glen Armstrong, Christina Petrides, William Schoedel, Alexa Tirapelli, Sugar Tobey, Tim Suermondt, Mia Condic, Mark Young, Penney Knightly, Jonathan Andrew Perez, Ann Pedone, Keith Carver, Mary Shanley, Kevin Keane

CONTENTS / CONTEÚDOS

POETRY

NEW TITLES

Editor's Notes

STEVAN V. NIKOLIC

THE POINT WITHIN A CIRCLE

One of the trade secrets of medieval operative stonemasons was "proving of the square" by use of the "point within a circle". Indeed, if we make a circle, then draw the line through its center cutting the circle in half, at any point of the circumference which we would connect with these two points and where line cuts the circle, we would form an angle of the square.

The point within a circle is one of the most powerful symbols in many esoteric teachings. Its importance is not only in antiquity, which we may trace, but also in many rich meanings, which we may read from it. As Manly Hall, in his book The Secret Teachings of All Ages, stated: "The keys to all knowledge are contained in the dot, the line and the circle. The dot is universal consciousness, the line is universal intelligence, and the circle is universal force - the threefold, unknowable Cause to all known existence."

Although undefined in geometry, a point can be described as indicating location with no size.

Nothing exists without a center. From the nucleus of an atom, the center of planet Earth, the Sun in the solar system to the black hole in the center of the Galaxy, everything has a center. Even the abstract idea has a center because we consider it "pointless" if there is not a center holding it together. The fixed point is called the center of a circle. At times, it is synonymous with the circumference, just as circumference (distance around the circle) is often equated with the circular movement. It is very often an emblem of the Sun, or it stands for Heaven, perfection, or Eternity. Psychological study asserts that the discovery of the circle in humans arrives at the age when the child discovers himself ("I am"), and distinguishes himself from others. According to Swiss psychiatrist, Carl Gustav Jung (1875-1961), "a circle represents the ultimate state of Oneness". To the ancient Greek philosophers, the circle was the symbol of the number One, since it was the source of all subsequent shapes. They called it MONAD, from Greek "monas" (oneness).

A circle, understood as a circumference, is a symbol of adequate limitation and of the inner unity of all matter and universal harmony. Enclosing beings, objects, or figures within a circumference has a double meaning: from within, it implies limitation and definition; from without, it represents the defense of the content of a circle against disintegration and chaos.

Origins of the point within a circle, as is the case with many other ancient symbols, are lost in the mists of antiquity. A point within a circle was the Egyptian, Chinese and Mayan Glyph for "light". In many ancient myths and modern scientific theories about the beginning of the Universe, the universal creation process begins with the expansion from a Divine Center, or from the Big Bang, as in the very first words of God in Genesis "Let there be Light". On early Egyptian monuments the circle could be found with two letters in the center of it and bordered by two parallel serpents symbolizing wisdom and power. According to some scholars, the letters in the center stand for "beginning" and "end", indicative of God or Creator. Some other similar Egyptian symbols known to us are ANANTA (meaning "eternity") – a serpent in the form of a circle biting its tale, and CRUX ANSATA - a cross within a circle, symbolizing eternal life.

In Hindu mythology, Brahma speaks aloud the word AHM -"I AM", a word made of the first, middle and last letters of the Sanskrit alphabet, which represents the circle's three parts: the center, the radius, and the circumference. The point represents our own spiritual center or God within us; the radius - our mental and rational limits of understanding of God and the circle the sphere of our material existence. We can find the "point within a circle" as a symbol of "Phallus" in some old Indian legends. In many countries around the world, remains of ancient temples consisting of stones placed in circle can be found, with a single stone in the center. Although, the explanations of the real purpose of these temples are still controversial, these are usually connected with Sun worship practices in some cultures. The best-known examples are Druidic Temples in Great Britain.

In the Kabala, the point represents YOD, the creative knowledge of God, and the circle thespace in which He creates. The two parallel lines are symbols of justice and mercy of God. They are equal and upright because they are regulated by His perfect Wisdom. Christian theologian Lucian (c.240-312) wrote in the third century: "God makes himself known to the world; he fills up the whole circle of the universe, but makes his particular abode in the center, which is the soul of the just".

This symbol appeared in the Masonic ritual work, most likely, early in the 18th Century. The first Masonic record mentioning a point within a circle was Prichard's "Masonry Dissected". Today, it is mentioned, either in the lecture of the First degree, or in the opening of the Third degree in most of the Rituals. By tracing the development of this symbol through different cultures around the world from time immemorial, we learn of various understandings of its meaning. There are three elements constantly present in all of the stories: God, Man and the Universe.

When we think about God, we often refer to Him as Creator of all things, Great Architect of the Universe, the One with many names, Divine Omnipresence or Ultimate Cause of Everything. If one would have to present graphically or to draw a picture that would represent God or the Ultimate Cause, and be understood and accepted as such by all human beings what would that picture look like? Is it possible to express the infinite nature of God by drawing a point within a circle on a blank sheet of paper? Many accept this possibility because they perceive Him as being the center of existence, with the whole existence emanating from His creative power. One can understand it as God or as the Big Bang, but it is still there and still the Absolute Force, or Power or Spirit that created the Universe- the point within a circle.

Is there any better way visually to present the Universe than by using a point within a circle? Throughout the ages this has been the prime choice of Philosophers, Magicians, Artists, Alchemists, and Scientists. The origin of the word Universe is Latin "unus versum" - meaning "one turn". The human mind is incapable of fully comprehending time and space without the help of this symbol, which exists because of man's effort to visualize more perfectly immeasurable and infinite that Universe represents.

Finally, we come to a Human being, the point within its own circle of existence. This circle is one's family, neighbors, fellow workmen, Brothers or Sisters in the Lodge, community; all that surrounds one in the warm light of the Summer Solstice and cold light of the Winter Solstice, represented by two parallel lines. But then, a person is the eternal circle itself, trying to place in the center and keep in balance, the hidden point within, which then creates the puzzle, how can one draw a circle whose center is everywhere and circumference nowhere?

HELPING DAD
by Sue Brennan

The holiday wasn't going well, and finding out that Dad couldn't swim after we'd jumped off the boat wasn't the half of it. Mick and Andy had already swum off— bastards—and there I was playing the older responsible brother, yet again. Poor old Dad, at the arse-end of his second divorce, practically skint, his goggles askew, his roots growing out.

Oh God, his hair.

"When did he start dying his hair?" Mick had whispered to me, horrified, at the airport.

"Fucked if I know," I'd whispered back. "Maybe it was when Lynn told him she suddenly realised she was still young and didn't want to be stuck with an old man like him."

"Shit, did she really?"

I'd nodded sadly, recalling the last six months of Skype calls. Never knowing what mood he was going to be in—elated that he was free of the money-grabbing bitch; despair at facing another divorce and a lonely old age; hopeful that his new fitness regime and, apparently, attention to grooming, would win her back; excitement at being back on the dating scene—was emotional

Russian roulette every time I called. The most annoying part though, was that after each call I was expected to relay the information—word-by-word, mood-by-mood—to each brother.

"Why don't you just call him yourself?" I suggested to them. "I've got a life too, you know." Actually, I didn't.

"Eldest son duty mate," Mick said. "Sorry."

Apparently my duties as the eldest also included paying for Dad's flight's from Sydney to Phuket and back, organising accommodation for the four of us, paying for and sharing a twin room with Dad for ten nights, and now, teaching him how to swim.

"Dad!" I was treading water lightly, adjusting my goggles to make sure that what I was seeing was actually my father drowning and not just some weird old dude thing. Shit, he was going down. I swam over, he wasn't that far away, maybe six meters, grabbed hold of his arm and pulled him up.

"Dad! Dad...you've got flippers on... just move your legs like you're walking!"

But he was panicking, so I flipped him round onto his back and floated him over to a reefy area we'd been told by the crew to be careful of.

"Okay, okay, put your feet down. Here we go. You're good, Dad, you're good."

I knew he was going to be alright. I just had to wait for him to figure that out.

#

The Full Moon, a three-star resort, was populated by Germans mostly, and a smattering of Canadians, Brits and Australians. Mick flew over from Hong Kong where he'd been living for the last ten years working for a bank and making big bucks. Andy came down from Chang Mai on holiday from his English teaching job. For me, this was the end of a six month holiday cum what-the-hell-am-I-doing-with-my-life ramble throughout South East Asia. I was going to fly back in ten days with Dad and try to work out how to live in Australia again after almost two decades in the UK.

The first thing that went wrong was that Mick decided to bring his girlfriend of two minutes with him. When I arrived at the resort on the Wednesday afternoon, he and Andy were arguing over whose fault it was that there were now three people sharing a bungalow with twin beds when two of those people wanted to have lots of sex.

"Look, I just thought we'd get another room," Mick explained. "How was I to know the place would be booked out?"

Jessica, the girlfriend, was sitting at the bar by the pool with a glass of something colourful, looking out at the ocean with all the interest of someone reading yesterday's newspaper.

"Why don't you stay in my bungalow to-night, Andy?" I suggested. "Dad arrives tomor-row and then we'll sort something out for you guys. Maybe find another hotel?"

"Perfect!" Mick said, satisfied. "Now come and meet the most delectable little wench this side of the equator."

"Yeah, perfect," Andy drawled.

Several hours and much, much beer later, Jessica was passed out in one bungalow and the three of us were sitting on the balcony of the one next to it. Mick and Andy were talking about

rugby, something that I couldn't ever get too worked up about, so I was texting my ex-girlfriend back in Edinburgh. She'd already found someone else and was pushing the let's-still-be-friends thing a little by asking me whether it was too soon to move in with him.

- Well???

- Shit, why r u asking me this?

- Because u know me!!!

- Can't believe yr asking me if yr new bf should move into the fucking flat u shared with me! just more proof of how insanely self-obsessed u r

I was waiting for her response when I no-ticed that Andy and Mick had stopped talking and were looking at me with amusement.

"What?"

"The look on your face. Man!" Mick laughed. "Glad it's not me on the other end of that phone."

I switched it off and looked around for an-other beer.

"We've finished 'em all," Andy reported.

"Probably for the best. Got to get up early to get to the airport tomorrow."

"Yeah, about that," Andy said, and I knew, I just fucking knew what was coming. "We don't all—"

"Yes, we do all have to go get him," I snapped back. "And by all I mean not Jessica.

"Jeez, bro, chill."

"This is about him, about us, just being there for him, alright? This holiday. It's the least you can...it's the least we can do."

"Alright, alright, alright, alright."

#

So we all turned up at the airport the next day hungover and pissed off with each other, while Jessica, charged with finding another hotel, slumbered the morning away. When we got back to the resort, she was sitting on the balcony in a bikini eating pineapple on a stick. Mick grabbed the bamboo guard, leapt up and took a bite of it, kissed her, and whispered something in her ear. She looked at Dad, gave a small wave and said, "Hi, Mr. Howlett."

"Oh, don't call me that, sweetheart. It's Martin. Marty." I swear he sucked his stomach in. "I wouldn't mind a bite of that pineapple, too."

"Dad, no," Andy groaned under his breath.

"I'll get you your own pineapple, Dad," I said, stomping up the stairs to our bungalow and throwing his suitcase inside. When I came out I said to Jessica, "How'd you go this morning? Find a hotel?"

She didn't even try to pretend that she had looked and couldn't find anything, or that she'd woken late, but was about to go just as we turned up. That she even gave a shit. She just looked at Mick and shrugged.

"Hey, bro," he called over to me, "why don't you just go and look for one now? It's still early."

"Me? Why the hell should I go look for one?"

"Well, you made the booking."

"What? That doesn't even make—"

"Andy then. Hey? Why don't you go?"

Andy looked up from his phone in disbelief. "Why the fuck should—"

"Hey, language, language," Dad interrupted. "Listen, I heard about the problem," he said,

actually using air quotes. "Why don't I just sleep out here on the balcony and you boys take the beds inside."

"No," I stated. "Not going to happen. You'd get eaten alive anyway. Look Mick, it's your problem. Sort it out. If you can't be arsed, then it's you, Andy and Jessica all in there together. Come on, Dad."

"What? Where're we going?" he asked, following me along the path.

"To get some lunch. Get some fucking pineapple on a fucking stick."

#

He kept panting and looking up at the sky. His grip around my waist had slowly eased, but was still pretty tight.

"Come on, Dad. You're alright."

He looked at me, shaking his head then back up at the sky. I lifted the goggles from his eyes, releasing the seal, and pushed them up onto his forehead.

"It's all good, all good," I said in what I hoped was a soothing tone, and he did seem to settle, making whoo sounds as he exhaled. Anyone would think he was giving birth.

"See? See? You're doing alright now, aren't you?"

He moved a little so that I wasn't carrying his entire weight.

"Ah, there we go," I said as he found his footing on the reef and stood independently, just holding onto my arm. We looked at each other and managed a small laugh.

"You didn't think to tell us you couldn't swim?"

"Well, I did it a bit when I was younger, you know. But living in the country all this time... guess I'm out of practice."

About ten meters away, the boat bobbed gently on the surface of the ocean. A few people were climbing up the side of the boat in order to jump off again. One of the crew sat on the side with one leg dangling over the edge, taking photos with a phone and urging them on.

"You reckon you can remember how to do it? I can take you back to the boat if you like."

"Give me a minute. Where're the others?"

Good question. Where were Andy and Mick when you needed them? They didn't even think to watch out for Dad when we all jumped in. Just swam off to the other side of the boat. They hadn't been there for me when the restaurant I'd poured everything into—and I mean everything —collapsed. I'd lost the lot: my job; my partner in business and in life, Rosalind; my flat; my self-respect. Meanwhile, Mick was raking it in in Hong Kong, and Andy was screwing his way through Thailand.

Just because we were brothers didn't mean shit.

#

By the time we finished lunch and our pineapple, and I'd shown Dad the basic layout of the small town that encircled the resort, Mick and Andy were three beers in and the best of mates. They'd done a quick TripAdvisor search of the area and found a resort further down the beach that had a vacancy. They were just waiting for Jessica to finish her nap.

"Nap?" I asked. "Didn't she get up at midday?"

"Could do with one myself guys," Dad said. "Shall we reconvene at, say, five-ish?"

He disappeared into our bungalow. I climbed up onto the balcony of the one next to it, grabbed a beer and looked out at the ocean.

"He alright?" Mick asked.

"Yeah, he's good."

"You alright?"

"What do you mean?" I turned around to look at him. Through the window behind him I could see the slender form of Jessica lying on the bed, facing away from me.

"You seem kind of stressed."

'Yeah, well, you know.'

"I mean, we're on holiday, you know?"

"Yeah, I know that. Jesus, I've been on holiday for the last six months."

"I know. And you seem kind of stressed."

"Stop saying that. I just... I've got a lot to... I don't know what..."

"What are you going to do when you get back to Sydney?" Andy asked.

"Thought about opening another restaurant. A small place. Got an idea."

"What about...what's her name - ?"

"Nel?"

"Yeah. That still a thing?"

Nel. God, what a mistake that was. After it all fell apart and Rosalind and I broke up, I ended up with Nel who'd been one of my waitresses at the restaurant. I felt sorry for her, even though she easily got another waitressing job. Met in a pub for a drink, she was nice and listened to me rave on, ended up at her place and moved in the next day. Not much to build a relationship on, in retrospect.

"No. No, that's over."

"How long did that last then?"

"Don't know, four months? Something like that. Anyway, you're a fine one to talk," I said with a nod in Jessica's direction.

"That?" He smiled and shook his head.

"And you?" I nodded towards Andy.

"I've got something going on with one of the teachers at work, I think. Canadian."

"You think something's going on, or that she's Canadian?" I asked.

He told us, in fairly graphic detail, about the sexual tension since she arrived six months ago and the final culmination, shall we say, out the back of the school just before he flew down here. That explained the constant texting. Mick saw this as an opening to tell his story about meeting and bedding Jessica, both events happening in under three hours, if he can be believed. And he can. According to him, Hong Kong was full of 'Chinese chicks like her looking to fuck white guys like me' and he was never, ever going to leave. Or marry one of them.

I couldn't help but think that, with regards

to romance, relationships and women in general, the Howlett men weren't doing too well.

#

The little reception desk at the resort was littered with faded brochures for various local companies offering half-day and full-day diving and snorkelling trips. Every second shop in town was a travel agent selling the same trip for more or less the same price. There was no way we were not going to go snorkelling. So we went snorkelling, and now here I was perched on the side of a reef with my sixty-three year old father, the sun beating down on both of our balding heads.

"My goggles filled up with water," he said. "Couldn't see a damn thing."

"Yeah, they've got to be on fairly tight. Give me a look."

"Took a great big mouthful of water through this pipe as soon as I put my head in, too."

"Takes a bit of practice. Here, try this now."

He put the goggles on over his eyes and stuck the snorkel in his mouth.

"Why don't you just have a little practice? Here, watch me." I bent forward, stuck my head in the water and breathed loudly through the snorkel.

"See? You do it," I said, after spitting the mouthpiece out. He did so, his face barely touching the water, one hand still gripping my arm tightly. He took a few breaths and came back up.

"How was that?" he said with the snorkel in his mouth, so it sounded like, "ow wah jat?"

"Good, good," I said and laughed. "Now you've just got to get your head in the water."

He stuck his face in again and I pushed his head gently under, feeling the grip he had on my arm tighten and then relax as he realised he

could actually breathe. I was just wondering whether I should prise his fingers off me when I noticed a person swimming our way. Dad suddenly jerked up out of the water, lost his balance on the reef and put his full weight on me so that I was in danger of losing my footing as well. As I steadied us, the swimmer came up in front of us, removed the snorkel from his mouth and said, "You know you shouldn't stand on the reef."

He sounded American.

"Yeah, fuck off."

#

The place that Mick and Jessica moved up to was much nicer than The Full Moon, so we wandered up there the second night to have dinner at their rooftop restaurant. Dad looked up from the menu and said, "Bit better than our place, hey?"

"Yeah, and there's a day-spa and another bar down on the beach and you should see our room," Jessica said, technicolour cocktail in hand. "The bathroom's bigger than the whole bungalow you guys are in." It was the most I'd heard her say. She tended to just sit with her hand on Andy's knee, or tickle the back of his neck, looking completely bored.

"Well, it's not like we need a huge bathroom, is it Dad?" I said, not wanting to make her feel uncomfortable, but, what the hell?

"Need?" Mick said. "Nobody needs a huge bathroom. It's want, bro, want."

Two days and I'd just about had it with Mick, flashing his money and his hot, young girlfriend around.

"What's all this 'bro' shit anyway?" I asked. "How old are you?"

"Younger than you, bro," he said, grinning at me and Andy, who wasn't looking anyway.

"Alright you guys, I'm paying tonight,

okay?" Dad announced. "Order whatever you like."

He looked proudly around the table.

"Cheers, Dad," Andy said without looking up from his phone.

"Nice one, Dad," Mick agreed, and Jessica nodded her approval.

"Hang on," I said. "Guys, this is supposed to be us shouting Dad for a holiday, right?"

"Hey, if he wants to—" Andy started.

"You can't afford this, Dad," I whispered, leaning into his ear. "It's going to be expensive, you know?"

"I'll just whack it on the card," he said, loud enough for everyone to hear.

"Yeah, but you have to pay off the card eventually."

"Let him do it," said Mick.

"Why?" I countered. "If it comes to paying—if anyone should be paying—it should be you."

"Sure, I'll pay," he shrugged. "You want me to pay, I'll pay."

"No," Dad interrupted. "It's my way of saying thank you to you guys for getting me out here and for supporting me when...when I..."

He looked as though he was about to cry, and that was the moment the waitress chose to approach the table. I looked at her and shook my head. She rolled her eyes and wandered away.

Andy looked up from his phone, alarmed. "Hey, Dad," he said. "You're cool. Don't worry about it. You don't need to pay for anything, alright? We get the gesture. We get it."

Dad nodded, his eyes closed.

"Yeah, Mr. Howlett," Jessica, the girlfriend of sixty fucking seconds, said. "Let us take care of you now."

Dad opened his eyes, smiled around the table and threw his hands open in a gesture of grateful defeat.

"Yeah, but hang on," I said. "You guys aren't paying for anything! You guys aren't doing anything, haven't done anything. And Jessica, sorry, it's so nice to meet you and all, but—"

"Whoa," Mick cut in. "She's just being nice."

"Yeah, yeah I know. She's very nice. You're very nice Jessica, but my point is: what are you guys actually doing?"

"They're here," Dad said sternly, looking directly at me. "You're all here and that's enough. For me, that means something. Means the world."

"Right," said Andy, laying his phone on the table. "That's that sorted. Let's order."

"Yes, let's order," Dad said happily, looking around the restaurant. "Let's get that lovely girl back over here."

Mick and Andy teased him about getting back in the saddle, and I caught Jessica glaring at me across the table. I suppressed the urge to stick my tongue out at her. The waitress saw Dad

waving, two hands in the air as though he were drowning, and strolled casually over to the table. Orders were placed and menus collected. The conversation turned from young Thai waitresses to the next day's already-paid-for-by-me half-day snorkelling trip. Something else that I was just whacking on the card.

#

"Alright," Dad said with some confidence, "I think I'm ready." He released his grip on me and adjusted the goggles and mouthpiece.

"Just head over there past the boat," I pointed. "That's where the others are."

He nodded, squatted down until his head was submerged and pushed off from the reef.

His held his arms out in front of him, body sitting nicely on top of the water, flippers doing all the work. He had the feel of it now.

I sorted myself out and started to follow him. When I was alongside the boat, I stopped and trod water, did a 180 turn to look back at the shore, the tiny jetty we'd pulled out from not too far away, the rest of the ocean stretching to the horizon. I could hear voices, faintly. Couldn't hear what they were saying exactly, something like, 'You made it!' I could hear people being happy.

He was fine. They were all fine.

END

About the Author:

Sue Brennan is an Australian writer of poetry and fiction. She was shortlisted for the Alan Marshall Short Story Award (2016, 2018) and the Polestar Literary Award (2016). She has had poetry included in the Poetry D'Amour Anthology (2016, 2017, 2018). Her short stories have been published in Scarp, and one will be included in the forthcoming collection by Real Works Press. She is currently working on a novel.

THE GODDESS OF KINK
by Kayle Nochomovitz

She was barely swaying her hips, but she had every guy on the edge of his seat. Even the bartender had stopped pouring drinks, and just stood there, hand on the counter, mouth open. This girl was just like my girlfriend Jennifer, come to think of it. Jennifer could be doing absolutely nothing but walking down the street or just sitting in a classroom and somehow be the center of attention. But Jennifer's legs would have given out; this, she wouldn't have handled. Jasmine though, the dancer, slid to her knees. Slipped a honey finger between her lips and teased it from the base of her neck all the way to her satin crotch. Only the night before, I lay in Jennifer's bed, whispered goodnight into the fullness of her sepia curls, and wondered how on earth I would ever figure out what to do about her. Jennifer, my love, my agony. She would never have believed where I was now. I swear, Jasmine was looking directly at me.

I was here because Jeff, my newest friend, a fraternity guy, had convinced me. I'm not the fraternity type, but Jeff was different from what I'd pictured. We met in a Civil War Reconstruction seminar; we're both history majors, and we both plan to write theses related to the legacy of slavery. Despite what I knew about his sensibility, Jeff told me over coffee in the student union before class, "Sometimes you need to do something you would never imagine yourself doing." This came on the heels of me telling him that I wasn't sure what to do about my problems with Jennifer. He said, "Just go, okay? Take a break from thinking so much. You need to let loose. It'll help, you'll see."

My inexperience must have been pinned to my sleeve, because my neighbor, who had introduced himself as Tink, figured I needed fortifying. He was a wiry man with red skin. He cleared his throat and leaned towards me, cupping his hand and overpowering me with the stench of baked-into-clothing-cigarettes.

"She's new," Tink said, pointing at Jasmine. "Only started dancing a couple of weeks ago, but look at her."

"An absolute natural," I said.

Tink faced the stage and nodded earnestly, not grasping my humor.

At the end of her dance, Jasmine made her way around the room, getting twenties, I couldn't believe, in exchange for a few more juicy seconds of gyrating. At the edge of the stage, less than a foot from Tink and me, her skin shimmered like chocolate cream, the color of the bubbles once vanilla ice cream hits a root beer float. She was tiny. And hot as a muscle.

Tink grinned. His tongue flicked between his lips, lizard-like. Then Jasmine was in his lap, throwing her firm little breasts toward him. With her so close, I was overwhelmed. She was like the naughty doll that you dream about. Her lips were full and pouty. Perfect. She pursed them, like she might kiss Tink. He held his palms out to the sides, laughing, his small eyes flashing. When Jasmine had finished, he beckoned her close, slipped her some green, and whispered something in her ear. She came over to me, but didn't straddle my thighs. Instead, she handed me a red ticket and crooked her index finger, beckoning me to follow.

I looked over at Tink. He gave me a thumbs -up sign, which to be honest, was kind of nauseating.

#

I don't know what got into me, because usually, I don't go for this stuff. Well, not this exactly. I'd be lying if I didn't admit that the first time I saw Jennifer three months ago I didn't first notice her beautiful, plentiful breasts, which were hiding like two water balloons under her charcoal sweater as she stood in the quad. But I also noticed other things. Like her endless, slender, if not a little colt-like, jean-clad legs, and her clear skin, pale and tinged with pink from the autumn air, so that it set off the dark flickers in her eyes. But mostly, I noticed Jennifer's intelligence. Anna Karenina was lodged under her arm.

"How is that?" I asked her, after working up the nerve to go talk to her. "I've never read it."

She placed her long fingers on my forearm. "Oh, you have to. It's incredible."

"Oh yeah?"

"It's tragic, really. To see how trapped she is. I mean, she's desperate, she does what she can, but there's no way she can be happy."

Jennifer's hand lifted off my sleeve. I didn't want the conversation to be over. "Sounds intense," I said.

She smiled. "You can borrow it, if you want."

#

Jasmine led me through a small hallway in the back of the club, and then into a narrow, mirrored room with red velvet couches against its walls. No door, just a curtain, which she closed. Probably since I was standing awkwardly in the tiny space, she touched me on the shoulder with her fingertips to show me where to sit. My heart started to pound as she threw one of her tiny, meaty thighs over my lap.

"Shhh, relax," Jasmine cooed. She must have sensed my nervousness.

"Thanks."

She kind of stroked my arm, very lightly, while I took a deep breath and tried to remember who I was. Jeff was right. I was relieved to be away from everything for a little while. But I didn't have to lose hold of myself completely. Even as a thirteen-year-old kid, pumped with hormones and lying wide-eyed under the basketball-printed comforter of my childhood, I never fantasized about the goddess of kink floating in through my window or emerging from under my bed or anything. Then again, Jasmine was exquisite. She had amber colored eyes and the slenderest of wrists. I could easily have encircled her tiny waist with one of my hands.

To my surprise, Jasmine reached for my face. Before I had time to protest, she had removed my glasses and set them down next to me on the bench.

I started to say that I was blind without them, but she brought two fingers to my lips and whispered, "No, much better this way."

I didn't really agree, because I'm myopic enough that it makes me panicky, but I guessed it didn't really matter in there anyway, because how far did I need to see when she was basically on top of me. And she wasn't playing. Deftly, considering how little room she had to maneuver, she turned around, put her hands on her knees and bent over, so that her peach of an ass was right in my face, her silver thong just barely covering what needed to be covered. I didn't know what to think, or what to do. Of course, my male parts noticed everything in front of me. More than anything I wanted to touch her. On the other hand, I was embarrassed. It had taken weeks of courting Jennifer before I even got her shirt off. And I wasn't sure I minded that.

Jasmine turned back around, sucked on two fingertips, and gave me a sugary smile. I winced at the thought of how many times she'd done this, how many guys she'd brought back here. I wished she would stop smiling at me like that, like she had something figured out that I didn't. Just then she slithered closer so that her purple pasties were only an inch away from my chest. She glanced at herself in the mirrored wall to my left. A sick feeling washed over me. When we walked down the sidewalk together, to my annoyance, Jennifer was always stealing looks of herself in storefront windows.

Jasmine raised herself up. "What's wrong?"

She stared at me, trying to penetrate me with her eyes. There was another similarity: the stare. Jennifer's giraffe-like lashes. That way she had of making it absolutely impossible not to look back.

It was funny to think about Jennifer in there, but I tried to picture it: the thong, the high heels, her breasts bouncing. Last night, when she got out of the shower, her hair was wet and hung in slick dark curls. I had sworn to myself that last night was the night. I was going to say something. Because Jennifer had basically just agreed to go out on a date with our philosophy professor, and believe me, it wasn't the first outing of its kind. This one just happened to come in the form of a sandy-haired six-foot Brit in his early thirties.

"It's not a date," Jennifer said, pouting. "We're just going to have coffee and talk about Heidegger."

I retained my composure. Better to save my anger.

"I don't understand what the problem is, Brian. We've been through this before, about my socializing. I need to take advantage of opportunities. It doesn't mean anything."

I wished Jennifer could observe herself deep in conversation with a man, or with anyone, for that matter. Because it was always the same. Man, woman, LGBT or Q, the recipient of her gaze was always sucked in. I hated to admit it, but I was no different. For the gazillionth time, I wondered how I'd actually managed to snag her. Maybe I was just more pathetic than the rest. More willing to give up all of my spare time. "It does mean something," I said. "At least Professor Stone thinks it does."

Jenifer's nostrils flared. I never spoke to her that way.

"You can't be mad," I said. "You know I'm right."

"You are not," she insisted.

I should have walked away right then, but I made my first mistake: I hesitated. Holding her towel in place, Jennifer reached out and grabbed my wrist with her other arm. I waited for words to come out of my mouth which would direct, decide something. Then I made my second mistake: I let myself look into her eyes. They were shiny and wet, bloodshot. I fought it, but probably not as hard as I could, because I knew then that it was all over. Again. Anything but Jennifer's tears, convincing me that maybe, just maybe, I was all wrong. After all, we had a future to think about — although granted, a misty one — where she and I would sit in a cafe in some European capital and discuss Kafka over wine, then come home and dance our way through our apartment, on our time: three o'clock in the morning, or the middle of a weekday afternoon.

I knew the image was false, but then why was I so relieved as we embraced? Probably because I knew something that was true: if we broke up, Jennifer and I would both graduate and she would go off into the world without me. Hopefully back to Connecticut and her family, where she was safe and secure, and, let's face it, untouched. But who was I kidding? There were Brits in Connecticut also. And Connecticut would never suffice for Jennifer. She'd be off to some far-away place the first chance she got, hair flying. She seemed that far already.

My hand fumbled around on the seat next to me. My glasses weren't there.

Jasmine didn't seem to notice. "Should I dance more?" she asked, and seemed a little startled when I said no. But I didn't need another showgirl.

Jasmine placed her hands on my pecs. I pulled them off and started to get up. That's when she stepped back. We both heard a crunch. Her satin pump had instantly shattered both lenses. For a second she looked like I was going to hit her. Then she dropped to the floor, where the broken pieces lay, and started to sweep them up with her hands.

She looked up at me, pleading. "Please don't say anything to anyone. I'll pay for them, I swear."

Her lips quivered. All of a sudden, I could see what she must have looked like as a six-year-old, wanting something. I could also see what she would look like ten years from now, when tiny creases had begun to surround those golden eyes. I saw that thing that would always be with her, that thing that was her, whoever she really was. My chest began to hurt. I took a deep breath. Jennifer, safe behind a film of tears, had never showed me anything so real. Jennifer and I were over, I realized. What was the point of continuing? It was never going to go anywhere.

"I don't want your money," I told Jasmine. "Why don't you tell me your name? Your real one, that is."

She looked away, her eyes wild, like a frightened stag. I took hold of Jasmine's wrist, but she wouldn't look at me. I think I'd seen something that she hadn't wanted me to see.

"Please," I said.

Her face darkened like a camera shutter closing. "I'm sorry. I can't do that."

"At least take this then," I said, and pressed two carefully folded twenties into her palm. She looked down at the money and thanked me without smiling. Then she turned and walked away. But I couldn't let her go. I just wanted to whisk her out of there.

Jasmine headed toward the door in the corner of the club through which she and all the other dancers had emerged.

"Wait," I called after her. I picked up my pace. "Don't go."

As she got near the door, I grabbed hold of her arm again. From out of nowhere, a heavyset guy with dark eyes and greasy black hair shoved my shoulder. "Hey man, what do you think you're doing?"

"Nothing," I stuttered. "I just want to talk to her."

The next thing I knew, his fist met my cheekbone. It wasn't hard enough to knock me down, but hard enough for me to know that I didn't want him to. My hand rose up to touch my face, where a welt was already blooming.

#

The club was in Providence, and I had to get back to Boston, but the idea of doing sixty plus on I-95 at night without my eyeglasses quickly lost its appeal. Instead, I wandered through downtown until I found a not-too-seedy bar. After four glasses of whisky, I staggered back to my car in the club parking lot, where I imagined I'd pass out and figure it all out, including how exactly I would end things with Jennifer when I saw her.

My vision was blurry, but I could still make out the figures of Jasmine and her manager/ pimp/boyfriend as the steel club door opened into the parking lot. To my horror, Jasmine was still in her dancing outfit, her stockinged legs and high heels visible beneath the dark shawl draped over shoulders. My jaw throbbed. If it were me, I would never have wanted her to walk out into the cold like that. But the guy had his arm around her, and as he squeezed her towards him, she laughed, and put her head on his shoulder.

###

About the Author:

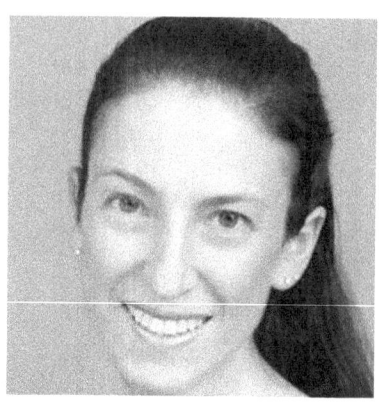

Kayle Nochomovitz is currently pursuing an MFA in Creative Writing at City College in Harlem, NY. Kayle is a trained portrait painter, yoga teacher and licensed massage therapist who has turned her creative talents to fiction. She lives in Riverdale, NY with her husband, three children and two step-children, ranging in age from 21 months to 16 years.

APPROXIMATE

by Mark Jacobs

"So how much does Beth tell you about me?"

"You know us, Edna. We talk."

"About my sex life?"

"We talk about a lot of things. It's what keeps us going."

Meeting her best friend's husband at a sherry bar. That was novel. Edna was into novel; into it, in fact, in a big way. Segunda Vez was supposed to feel like Madrid, evoking smoke and daggers, *toreros* and the divine right of kings, all that. It didn't. At no moment did she forget she was in East Welkin, Connecticut, a mile and a half from the interstate she would take back to the City.

Maury asked her if she wanted another *fino*.

"I do," she told him with instant conviction. "I absolutely do."

Maury was on the side of the hell-fire angels, or so Beth was always saying. Edna was not convinced. The man offering her black olives on a bricky ceramic plate looked like what he was, a somewhat cool wealthy guy in his sixties who carried himself with style and told good stories about the rockers who had made him rich, promoting their bands. He had recently cut off his ponytail. A mistake. If you were old and it still looked good, keep it.

"Edna says you are a person with no filters," he told her.

She nodded. "And I'm superficial, too."

His expressive eyebrows went up.

"No, listen. Superficial is not the same as shallow. It's just how I perceive the world. Colors, patterns, textures. The different ways that one thing can look against another. Backdrops, foreground. Geometry, I guess."

"You're a designer. That's how you do your job."

The moment was slipping away. Get it back. "Never mind, Maury. What I really wanted was to tell you something that's been on my mind."

"Which is?"

"I'm tired of the sexual etiquette that comes with being a single woman of forty."

"Explain."

"You're drawing me out. Did Beth coach you?"

He shook his head and signaled to the waiter, who ambled toward their table with Spanish hauteur. His arrogance of body became him. Juan Pablo whoever he was looked good in basic black and white.

"Two more *finos*," Maury told him.

Edna had a manageable little buzz going on. Going past manageable; well, that was her trademark.

"It gets old, Maury. Making sure a man is certified clean before I fuck him. Even the liberated ones lie about their sexual history, depending on what they think I want. I'm finding the process tedious. So here's the question."

She liked the poise with which he waited. Beth was right. Talking with Maury might break her mental logjam. Beth was the older sister Edna never had. They talked so much they tended to fall into a conversational groove, which sometimes they could not climb out of.

"Me being tired of the single sex scene, does that mean I'm ready for a monogamous relationship?"

"I assume there's a candidate."

"His name is Trey. He's in real estate. He has a condo in my building. I met him through the board. Divorced, two kids, nice getaway place in Vermont near some incredible skiing. And, believe it or not, all the evidence suggests my sexual history does not scare him."

"But you don't know if one man, or this one man, is what you want."

The glass of sherry – her fourth? – was pushing her over a delightful edge she knew only too well. She asked herself if she felt the slightest twitch or twinge of something sexual toward Maury. Answer: no. What a relief. She presumed that was another sign of being older. Complications used to be a good thing. They jazzed her, by definition. Now, not so much.

"I want to be fair to Trey," she said. "I'm superficial. That doesn't mean I'm a bitch."

"So what will it take to know what you want?"

"I was hoping you'd help me figure that out."

"Maybe you should take a trip."

"Is that a joke?"

"I'm thinking more along the lines of a pilgrimage."

"Where?"

"The headwaters. Where it all began."

"What is this, Zen and the art of sherry?"

"Sleep on it."

Afterward, in the parking lot, the bitter January wind was a rebuke. She had been misbehaving. Nothing new in that. She was always misbehaving. By the time she got back to Manhattan, the alcohol would be out of her system. Mostly. *Take a trip*, Maury had said.

Next morning her head was sandpaper, everything rubbing against it the wrong way. She had a ten o'clock with a new client. In the beginning, it had amazed her that people paid her to spend their money testing her design ideas on the places in which they passed the intimate hours of their lives. The amazement was gone, but it still amused her. The new person, Mildred, worked in arbitrage. Following the financial meltdown a few years back, Edna had a vague sense that maybe what Mildred did for a living was illegal. Whatever. It appeared to pay well. She had a brownstone on the Upper West Side she was turning over to Edna, telling her to make it interesting, make it look as though she had given the project big thought. Edna did interesting. She did big thought, in a superficial way. Piece of cake.

As she showered, Maury's sherry Zen came back to her. *I'm thinking more along the lines of a pilgrimage*, and what he meant came to her with an electric shiver. Back to the source. The headwaters were in Brooklyn. It was a journey to be dreaded.

"When we lived in the Village, what was my favorite toy?"

Enormous on her stool, Adrienne put her brush down on a little table covered with paint tubes and jars of oil. She frowned. In her burgundy smock, she looked more like the thing to be painted than the painter. "Toy?"

Edna tried to remember the last time she had talked with her mother when she wasn't painting. Adrienne thought better when she painted. That was her defense. In fact she begrudged any amount of time away from her canvas. Once, walking in her own neighborhood, Edna had seen, at a difficult angle, one of her mother's paintings on the wall of a brownstone living room. There was no mistaking the stubborn abstract density, the relentless merge of color into uncolor. The assertion. She could forget the painting. She would never forget the cold sweat of anger that overtook her on the sidewalk.

Adrienne brushed the hair out of her face, still frowning. At fifty nine she was remarkably blonde. You only saw the silver in a particular light, and it always struck Edna as a revelation. She was used to thinking of her mother, and her mother's power, as irreversible. Adrienne was six feet tall, with a body that had stayed statuesque longer than most. Even now, she retained a physical authority that a woman of, say, forty would envy. Edna was considered attractive. Less blonde than her mother, not as tall, but men were always looking at her, which she had long ago accepted as a cost of doing business both corporate and private.

"You had toys, Edna, I am sure you played with toys. I assume the question is meant to take me to task for my shortcomings as a mother. Didn't we go through all that twenty years ago, twenty five? I don't remember."

Adrienne worked in a Brooklyn loft, the old-fashioned way. She woke every morning of her life expecting that her significance as a painter would at long last be brought to New York light. Now and then she made money, selling her work. A series of generous infatuated men had taken care of what her mother called 'the logistics.'

Edna's frustration was already spilling over. This was the nowhere their conversations always went. Her mother seemed to take comfort from the ritual repetition of grievance; it confirmed her sense of self. It was up to Edna to make the visit count.

"Speaking of sex."

"Were we?"

"I went through long periods when all I cared about was an orgasm."

Adrienne nodded, shifting on her stool. She was painting again. "That's a normal thing, I should think."

"But there have been times, just as often, when I craved intimacy more than fireworks. The foreplay, the during play. Lying with a man afterward, telling each other our secret dreams."

"Why are you telling me this, Edna? Do you want an expression of solidarity from me? Yes, I've been there. Believe me, I have been there."

"I'm thinking about moving in with a guy. He said he'd like to marry me."

That got Adrienne's attention. She looked at Edna as though she were a stranger next to her on a bus, confessing a crime. "Think twice. That's my advice."

It was like her mother not to be curious about the man who might, in a legal sense, become her son-in-law.

Edna said, "You mean I should be more like you."

"I only mean that marriage is corrosive. One requires love. One enjoys companionship, and a bit of security is nothing to sneeze at. All quite natural. Any more than that, and the spirit dies a howling death."

"I want to find my father."

"What on earth for?"

"Because he is my father."

"I wouldn't know where to begin. We haven't spoken since you were two, or was it eighteen months?"

"Tell me what you know."

"My work threatened Gilbert. Suddenly he was tiresome, and needy, and male in all the wrong ways."

"Not that, not the part about you. Tell me what you know about *him*."

The question seemed to stimulate Adrienne. She got up from the stool and paced.

She lifted a blind and looked out the window at the neighborhood below, where kids still rode bikes and parents pushed strollers in all weathers. Edna was glad she did not perceive the same world her mother did.

"Gilbert was quite an athlete, for one thing. And he had an extraordinary head for numbers. He could memorize amazing long strings of them on a bet, even when he was drinking. Which he did more of than was good for either of us. He had family in Rhode Island, if I'm not mistaken."

That was not much, but it was more than Edna expected. She took her mother's parting shot – *think twice, and then think again before you marry this person* – with good grace. In the cab back to Manhattan, she began searching the internet. It took several hours and more patience than she was accustomed to exercising to locate a Gilbert Dewhurst in a small town outside of Providence. He was the right age, give or take. It took a day to rearrange her schedule, and to be sure she wanted to see him.

She had been ignoring Trey's texts. He was skiing in Vermont and thought she ought to be up there with him. When he called, she couldn't very well refuse to answer.

"The powder is amazing," he told her. "I feel healthy."

"I'm glad."

"I miss you, Edna."

Edna felt like her mother's daughter, failing to fill the gap of expectation by telling him how much she missed him. Nor did she tell him about her pilgrimage to the Brooklyn headwaters. Did failing to confide in him mean she did not really want a monogamous thing with Trey? What she did tell him was, "I fantasized about you last night. My finger was your dick."

"That's a good thing, I guess."

"You sound disappointed."

"Why don't you come up for the weekend?

Fly to Burlington, and we'll drive back together. Skiing is optional."

She felt the accumulation of her mistakes, her dark debilities. They stacked up around her making it hard to move, let alone maneuver. A flash caught her mind's eye – her mother's silvering hair in sunlight. What was so bad about being a superficial person?

"What if we got married and I couldn't stand being faithful to you, Trey?"

"Come up and we'll talk about it."

She extricated herself from the conversation taking more trouble than normal not to wound his feelings. She drove to Burkfeld and checked into a hotel and chickened out. What was the point? Gilbert Dewhurst was her father only in a remote biological sense. But instead of turning around, driving back to New York, she lay on the motel bed and watched a television program about hoarders. The woman they featured lived in a house full of both junk and cats and was traumatized at the prospect of losing either. Edna felt an unfamiliar sympathy for her. Crazy-hatted, cat-besotted Myrtle Bland in her sad crammed house was not a figure of fun, she was drably tragic. She knew something important she could not put into words.

Why the program caused Edna to change her mind about changing her mind was a mystery, but twenty minutes later there she stood on the threshold of an office door at the Burkfeld Country Club being ushered in by a man who looked like an English squire just back from riding to the hounds. His face was weathery red. His gray hair was a jaunty helmet. In his bespoke suit he was angular and thin and conscious of how he came across. He shook her hand heartily. She had the impression this was how he greeted all new acquaintances. How many lost children had stumbled across his threshold?

"Come sit down, my dear. Do you drink? Let me fix you a toddy."

Taking the drink from his hand, Edna blurted, "You left me with her."

He was anything but surprised. His voice was matter-of-fact telling her, "Adrienne made it clear I wasn't wanted. She wouldn't even give you the Dewhurst name. But I had my own with Edna."

"What do you mean?"

"She didn't tell you?"

"Tell me what?"

"Edna was my grandmother. The Dewhursts were Baltimore Catholics, English all day long. People who used to own counties. We've come down in the world, you and I, but we're alive and kicking."

The toddy tasted like a history lesson. Already she was denser than the person who had come through her father's door. She said, "I thought I was going to blast you for leaving me with Adrienne. You must have known she didn't want to be a mother. There's not a nurturing bone in her body."

He nodded, looking down into his glass. They were sitting across from each other on fat leather chairs. The first thing she'd do, rethinking the place, was lose the leather. The dark paneled walls would go, along with the hunting prints and the paraphernalia of golf. As shape, pure shape, the room had possibilities.

She asked him, "Did you marry again?"

"Not with any success. You have no half-brothers or sisters, sad to say. Just me, the manager of a minor club in the sticks with no claim to significance. What a letdown it must be for you."

"There's a man who wants to marry me."

He lit up, nodding furiously. "That's interesting, Edna, that's quite interesting. So, are you going to take the plunge?"

"May I have another drink?"

He was only too attentive, and the next thing Edna knew it was three in the morning and they were in a cart, tearing around the golf course in the starless Burkfeld dark. Afterward, she could not remember which of them was driving. She did remember piling out at the fifteenth hole and his handing her a club.

"You can't see it," he told her, slurring with deliberation, "but can you smell the water? That's Loch Lorna down there. More balls have gone to the bottom of the lake than Heaven has the energy to tally."

They stood on the tee and he coached her through a swing. She was so drunk she was totally relaxed, and her first address of the ball connected. Whack, and an instant later they heard it plop in Loch Lorna.

"That's terrific," Gilbert shouted. "You're a natural, kid, you were born to golf."

But she botched her second swing, and her third, and finally he put his arms around her and guided her through the next try. She smelled the liquor on his breath, and an awareness of all her life lacked swelled inside her like a sponge absorbing moisture. The ball plopped into the hungry lake.

"I don't suppose you'd give some thought to calling me dad," said Gilbert.

It was a question she was not prepared to think about, and he seemed to forget he asked it, but it was still there when she woke next morning at ten in the guest bedroom at his apartment with another sandpaper head. She found him at the kitchen table looking old, or worn down, hands around a mug of coffee. His face was chronically red, the color of overindulgence. He poured her a mugful, dosing it with a shot of rum.

"Hair of the dog that bit you," he said. "It's a family tradition."

The coffee and rum cleared her head and she told him without preamble, "I've had sex with quite a few men."

He nodded. "You come by it naturally."

"You mean you slept around?"

"Can't blame that one on Adrienne. One of those things, I suppose. What's the word? A predilection."

"So maybe I'm not cut out for monogamy any more than Adrienne was for motherhood. Are you late for work, Gilbert?"

"Screw 'em. I'm the boss."

"I'm not sure I could ever call you dad."

"Perfectly understandable. I'm hardly a shining example of the breed. You know, I tried to be in touch. When you were a kid. Adrienne made sure it didn't happen. After a while... I want to say I gave up, but the truth is I got distracted, and then I got old, and then here you come, phoning me up to say there's a good chance you're my daughter."

The tears in his eyes were hot enough to melt a murderous thick cube Edna was aware of lodged inside her. Those tears terrified her. It was time to get away. When the time came, she shook his hand, leaving him wanting what he did not perhaps deserve to get any more than she deserved to give it.

In the car, before heading back to New York, she called Beth in Connecticut. "Are you home?"

"Yes, I'm home. Why?"

"Let me talk with Maury, please."

She passed her husband the phone, and Edna told him, "I did what you said."

"What did I say?"

"I made the pilgrimage. To the headwaters."

"How did it go?"

"It changed something. I'm not sure what, yet."

"Is that a good thing?"

"I'm not sure of that, either."

"Well, then. What comes next?"

"I have to decide about Trey."

"Something tells me you've already made up your mind."

"You're wrong, Maury. This time you're dead wrong."

She wasn't sure she meant what she said, although she sensed a momentary truth in the statement; what you got from a bee sting. On the drive back to the City not a single thing that might be classed as a thought came into or passed out of her head.

February, and the snow was slushy. They rented a room downtown, above a Brazilian *churrasqueria*. Edna superintended the set up, creating something like an aisle leading to the spot where they would stand and not be married. Trey's two sons were there, mutinously uncomfortable as only an eighth grader and a sixth grader could be. Trey had obliged them to dress up, and they felt like frauds in their blazers, enslaved by antique humanoids with bizarre customs.

Beth and Maury were on hand, of course, the non-witnesses to the non-ceremony over which Mildred, the arbitrage woman, had agreed to preside. Twice divorced, Mildred got it. She really got it, and Edna was looking forward to the remarks she had composed for the non-occasion.

Adrienne had phoned Edna to say she couldn't make it; unfortunately, she had a previous commitment. But there she loomed on the edge of the invisible aisle, chicly imposing on the arm of a sleek man in a club tie who was obviously enthralled to be her date.

Trey had wanted music. Edna did not, but the occasional concession was part of the experiment she was about to undertake. She understood that. Why he chose the Ramones was beyond her, but when somebody hit the play button she took Gilbert by the arm. She smelled liquor on his breath. Gin? Didn't they say you couldn't smell gin?

"Does it bother you that Adrienne is here?"

"Hell no, Edna. I'm happy as a clam being father of the non-bride. I promise you, we'll both be civil."

They were standing outside the double doors leading into the rented room where a small group of invitees waited expectantly. She squeezed his arm. She kissed his cheek. She was happy, and surprisingly okay with the decision she had come to.

Gilbert pushed the doors open with a paternal flourish, and Edna went down the aisle on his arm soaking up the beatitude of all those watching. At the altar pseudo-space, Mildred waited in a sober suit. It was the kind of thing, Edna imagined, she wore to a meeting to convince a board of directors that the correct decisions to buy were being made, the decisions to sell. She was a decent-looking woman with boardroom authority and the voice to match. She blinked repeatedly, the only sign of nerves.

Gilbert and Edna came to a stop in front of her, whereupon Trey appeared as if by magic. He wore a sweater and casual pants, guaranteeing the ongoing resentment of his blazered sons. The men shook hands, exchanging a glance whose significance was opaque to Edna.

"Friends," announced Mildred, as someone switched off the music. "We are gathered here not to marry Edna and Trey but to celebrate their experiment. As I'm sure all of you know by now, after long thought, and much soul-searching, they have decided to give it their best shot. They're going to try living together."

Mildred had more to say. Edna sensed her warming to the moment, and her role in the moment. Fine, that was absolutely fine. Let her go on a little. She was an intelligent woman with a message to impart. Edna felt full, as though she had eaten just the right amount of a highly nutritious substance.

"They make no promises, and their expectations are fairly low," Mildred informed people in her bright, authoritative voice. "They've lived long enough to pick up some baggage. Can they carry it together? That's the question. Stay tuned, we'll find out. Because they're going to give it a try."

People were clapping. The applause sounded genuine.

Trey bent to kiss Edna. He was dignified and likable in his fever of expectation, as though everything were happening to him for the first time. It occurred to her that, whatever this was, it might be as close as she got to anything at all. As people swarmed toward them shouting noisy congratulations, she kissed him back.

The End.

About the Author:

Mark Jacobs has published more than 130 stories in magazines including The Atlantic, Playboy, The Baffler, and The Iowa Review. He has stories forthcoming in several magazines including The Hudson Review. His five books include A Handful of Kings, pub-lished by Simon and Shuster, and Stone Cowboy, by Soho Press. His website can be found at http://www.markjacobsauthor.com.

BANGKA ISLAND STORY
by Michael Paul Hogan

for Toti O'Brien

There were nine bottles of Bintang beer on the shelf behind the counter of Abdu Rama's beachfront banana shack. On the counter itself there was a watermelon, sliced, in a bowl of ice, and beside the watermelon there was a basket woven out of banana leaves containing a bunch of eight or ten or twelve bananas, all lying on their backs and basking in the sun like the gila seksi foreign ladies on Amerika Serikat TV. Below the counter there was a hand-painted advertisement for Coca-Cola, the paint faded to a pale imitation of red, the raw wood showing through the familiar looping white letters, and in front of the counter there was a three-legged wooden stool upon which Abdu Rama would sit and wait for customers, all the while smoking kretek cigarettes and gazing out at the South China Sea.

*

Weni Nelayanputri was fourteen years old and lived with her grandmother in a two-room house that her father had built before he was lost at sea. She remembered the two days and two nights of vigil at the water's edge, framed through the window of the room in which she and her grandmother slept. And then on the third day there was the truth of what the fishermen said — that disaster is an empty boat.

They hauled the boat by lamplight and torchlight to where the palm trees began beside the two-room house that her father had built before he was lost at sea. And from which, only six months later, her mother had also fled, taking the passenger ferry up the Musi River to Palembang, there to drink whiskey and smoke cigarettes and bercinta laki-laki asing to be lost, hilang, in a sea of her own drowning.

She left behind a handbag containing nearly nothing: an empty lipstick and a ***Hello Kitty*** hair-slide and a couple of one-hundred-rupiah coins. She also abandoned a red dress that Weni's grandmother had been washing at the time and which Weni now wore, very proud, very seksi, Coca-Cola red, as she walked along the beach to the Saturday market that sold rice and vegetables and chickens and fruit and birds in cages and mermaids that wept for the sea.

*

"Selamat pagi!"

"Pagi, tuan Abdu!"

"Anda ingin Coca-Cola hari ini? Es dingan!"

"Tidak, tuan. Mungkin besok."

"Okay. Selamat jalan, anak."

"Selamat tinggal, tuan Abdu. Terima kasih!"

"Kembali!"

You're welcome! Abdu Rama waved at Weni Nelayanputri and then reassembled his pose on the three-legged stool, the stool upon which he would wait for customers, all the while smoking kretek cigarettes and gazing out at the South China Sea.

*

Exactly ten years ago. The silence then the noise, the silence/noise of a keel being dragged across tide-hardened sand; the flames of the torches and the beams of the lamps reflected off the blades of the machetes and the leaves of the banana trees. They say,

"Bencana adalah perahu kosong,"

It means: "Disaster is an empty boat."

and afterwards they move like shadows between the firelight and the trees,

"Datang pergi, Weni. Come away."

and glance in through unglazed windows at where four year-old girls and their grandmothers illuminate the darkness with the fear in their eyes.

*

"Hati-hati! Be careful, child. Your feet will menjadi hitam. Turn black!"

The road to the market ran behind the beach but Weni, in defiance of her grandmother, preferred to walk along the sand, swinging her sandals by their straps, separated from motorcycles and the very occasional taksi mobil by a screen of banana trees. She almost didn't see the boy until she was past him, glancing back at a movement that caught the corner of her eye. He was sitting on the ground under the shade of the trees. He wore a faded blue T-shirt and a pair of khaki shorts. In front of him he had made a mat of banana leaves and on this mat there were nine fish, each

about a foot in length, their scales still silvery fresh from the sea, the blood around their gills undried. She looked down at the fish and then back at the boy. His hair was long and fell over his eyes and his smile when he smiled was like a coconut split with a machete. He said,

"Don't be afraid. Aku tidak hantu. I am not a ghost."

He said,

"Buy my fish if you don't believe me. Since when did hantu menjual ikan? Did ghosts sell fish?"

He smiled his smile again. He said,

"My name is Budi Haryanto. I like your red dress."

A motorcycle backfired on the road behind the banana trees and a bird, startled from within the branches, slapped its wings against the leaves. The boy and the girl looked at each other and then, for no apparent reason, merely an act of spontaneous and unaffected friendship, laughed. The girl, Weni Nelayanputri, said,

"We are fishing people. We catch. We do not buy. If my grandmother sends me to the market for rice and I come home with fish…"

She hesitated. She said,

"If you give me a fish I will let you sentuh saya baju merah. Touch my red dress."

She thought she saw a bird in the banana trees but she was mistaken. It was a trick of the sunlight on the leaves. Nothing. The leaves shook briefly. Then became still.

"I will kiss the strap of it where it crosses your shoulder," said the boy. "And I will give you three fish."

Weni had never felt the material of her dress so close to her skin. She said,

"You must close your eyes and keep your hands in the pockets of your celana pendek." And then: "If I allow you. Which I won't."

"I am sincerely sorry," said the boy, Budi Haryanto, "for offending you. But I am in love – "

"Gila! Crazy!"

" – with my fish. All night I catch them wading in the water with a spear and a lantern. Sometimes not even a lantern, just the moon. And all day I sit on the beach and – "

"Oh, oh, you are a beast! A beast and a liar! Binatong dan pembohong! I wouldn't want your fish for a thousand kisses!" And then, unsure if that was correct, she turned on her heels, her bare heels on the shaded sand, slapped her sandals together like castanets, and marched as quickly as was not *too* undignified, the banana leaves rustling with his imagined laughter, mixed up with the real laughter of children on motorcycles, jolting naik dan turun up and down along the potholed road.

*

Every evening Weni would pour a glass of arak for her grandmother and the two of them would play cards and her grandmother would say,

"Weni, child, you are dreaming. You cannot put a red three on a red nine."

Or:

"Who is this anak laki-laki who steals even the heart from the card you are holding?"

Or:

"Ah-ya! Is it love makes you put a silly jack on nenek's queen?"

But that evening, the evening of the morning Weni came home from the market silent and shy and angry and afraid, her grandmother only said,

"This arak tastes like water. Terbaker kepiting. Like bubbles from a crab's arse. Weni – "

"Nenek?"

" – Tomorrow. Besok. You will go for me along the beach and buy me fish. After *that* you will buy me arak baru. From Abdu Rama. Oh, and Weni child, – "

"Aku tidak mendengarkan. I am not listening"

" – the fish you buy need not be as beautiful as the boy who sells it."

"Nenek! Mengapa anda malu saya? Why do you shame me?"

Weni's grandmother placed a red six on a black five. She said,

"This arak is neither water nor crab's piss, but somewhere peralihan. Meaning inbetween."

*

"I have a favour to ask you, Abdu tuan."

"I listen."

"Can you tell me if you ever buy fish from a boy who sells beneath the banana trees?"

"That is not a favour, child, that is a question. But the answer is no. Who is so crazy to sell beneath a banana tree? Who is so crazy to buy?"

"It was a foolish question. But a favour I have…"

Abdu Rama laughed a short dry laugh. He said,

"Yes, child, I know. Your tightfisted nenek has been buying arak from Dedi Surya who, as everybody in the universe knows, makes it from his own piss then waters it down with the piss of crabs. *Now* she wants Uncle Abdu's five star gold label satisfaction guaranteed in Amerika Serikat rinsed-out Coca-Cola bottle. True or not true?"

"True, Abdu tuan," said Weni Nelayanputri. She tried not to openly disrespect her grandmother by smiling, although the joke had been a familiar one these many years and she was on the edge of knowing that not smiling made the joke better, not the disrespect less. She said,

"If I meet a boy under a banana tree, what shall I do?"

Abdu Rama took a draw on his cigarette. He said, and his voice had the joke erased from it, as a Coca-Cola sign may be erased by wind and sea, he said,

"If he sits under a banana tree, he is not a boy. You shall walk away, anak sayang, stay fortunate, get not eaten, tidak dimakan, by some ghost who steals an empty boat and sells imaginary fish." He flattened his eyes against the horizon, staying silent for the space of a minute. He said,

"They say disaster is an empty boat. A worse disaster is an empty heart. That is what it truly means to be a ghost."

He seemed about to say more and Weni, her chest filled with something she could not describe, neither fear nor disappointment nor love, but something more than and containing each, felt as though she were underwater, looking up through the surface of the sea. The sky shimmered. The sunlight was shattered like a yellow vase. The keels of the boats were visible, their paintwork rippling blue and red and green. She opened her mouth not to speak but to breath. She said, "Abdu Rama!" and Abdu Rama said,

"Ah, sudahlah! Never mind! Hujan membersihkan daun. The rain cleans the leaves. Daun minum hujan. The leaves drink the rain. Disaster? Tidak ada jenis perahu. Disaster for your nenek is an empty bottle! Tell her I shall bring it personally when the sun is behind the trees. More time for marking the cards she will cheat me with. Weni – "

"Paman? Tuan?"

" – is he handsome, the boy who pretends to be a ghost, who wishes to make you believe he is more than a man?"

"He is a *real* ghost and that is why he sits under banana trees and pretends to think he can cheat me. He is a fool!"

"Even a ghost can be a fool. They are human in that. Tingkat tertentu kredit. True. Benar. And who is a wise man under a banana tree?"

"I will burn my red dress," said Weni Nelayanputri, ignoring the question, and stamping her heel into the sand, "and sew a new one made of all the black pieces." She said,

"The Coca-Cola can is red and the Coca-Cola inside is black. That is *exactly* the color of my new dress. Gila seksi Amerika. Who can tell me this is not my beach? Abdu Rama tuan – "

"Weni. Putri."

" – I am to meet a boy with a motorcycle. Who will drive me to the market. Very proud with absence of walking. That is my decision. Who will not care if my feet are black like Coca-Cola, only my heart like a Coca-Cola tin. Oh, and tuan – "

"I listen because the sea is silent. Carry on."

" – Are you happy? Sometimes my nenek asks me. Because I see you every day in the to-and-froing of rice and minyak goreng. Always alone. Always gazing. It seems to me – "

"It seems?"

" – It seems." She hesitated. She said,

"Forgive me, tuan. Tampaknya tidak ada. It seems nothing. In the meantime, I am newly decided! Semua sampah! I shall wear my red dress every day and care nothing for boys. Boys or ghosts or motorcycles. It is not for me to care. But I often wonder – "

"Wonder?"

" – how a boy can be a ghost and still have eyes the color of the sea..."

There was a silence the width of a wave and Abdu Rama said,

"I do not know." He examined the tip of his

cigarette and flicked the ash with his fingernail. He said: "And am too old to become wiser than a child."

*

She woke up screaming and the windows were fire. Her nenek said "Calm, calm, child," and the silhouette of her was black against red. The gray of her hair a swish of a brush. She said,

"Stay sleeping, child."

and there were voices, urgent voices, and then shouting somewhere distant, and then the profile of her nenek against the flames outside. She said (Weni said),

"Is my father home now?"

and there was the sound of her mother and the *thwack-sh* of bare heels against impacted sand. And a voice saying,

"Bahkan perahu beruntung!"

and then the silence concentrated in her mother's shoulders. And afterwards nothing merely to remember. Just a different silence. And shapes and shadows and nothing clearly. Like a village in the morning when the storm has been.

*

"Selamat pagi, tuan Abdu!"

"Selemat jalan!"

Weni Nelayanputri swung her sandals so the heels *slap-clicked* like Spanyol kastanyet. Like Spanish castanets. She said,

"Nenek says: Buy bananas if they are green, not ripe. Oh, and she says also: If Abdu tuan is feeling stupid, meaning bodoh, he can come and lose all his Coca-Cola seksi lazy money playing hati yang mengalahkan." She hesitated. She said, "Abdu tuan – "

"Uh-huh?"

"It is nothing. Oh, but something – "

" ? '

" – I am instructed to tell you that my father's boat is to be painted blue and red and green and made fit with caulk to sail again. Berlayar lagi. Tuan...?"

"I listen."

"Was my mother beautiful?"

Abdu Rama removed the kretek cigarette from his mouth between the two fingers of his hand and held it the way a broken mast is balanced above the sea. He said,

"I have no recollection."

He said,

"Benar-benar. Truly. Aku punya tidak ingat sama sekali."

He used his thumb and his middle finger to snuff the cigarette. He flicked it away. He said,

"In fact I am lying to you, child. Anak-anak. She was more beautiful. Even than everybody. Even than the sea."

There was a silence. Weni said,

"There is a boy on a motorcycle, tuan, who says I am in my red dress seksi merah cantik wanita."

"He speaks tidak semestinya. Without manners. But not untrue."

"But if he should ask me to let him touch my dress, I will tell him exactly what pipe he should smoke with! Like Nenek says: Ratu pintar; jack konyol. For good measure. Smoke *that!*"

She went down the beach eighty-ninety yards until she was a red triangle between the banana trees and the sea. She turned around. She put one hand either side of her mouth. She said (she shouted),

"And even not a motorcycle unless it's seksi

merah Amerika Serikat. Harley Davidson. Johnny Depp ya. Noise like aeroplane! Benar-benar!"

Then she laughed and waved her sandals and disappeared behind an outcrop of the banana trees.

FIN

About the Author:

Born in London, Michael Paul Hogan is a poet, literary journalist and fiction writer. A former columnist for Island Life in Key West, Florida, he is the author of six volumes of poetry and has published extensively in the USA, UK, India and China. His short fiction has most recently appeared in Big Bridge, Peacock Journal and Scryptic Magazine.

SUMMER STORMS
by Omar Essa

The geese are unkind. They stand militant along the border of the pond like NYPD officers during parades in Manhattan, as if the pine trees were the skyscrapers they're meant to defend. They were absent during the lightning and torrential rain that had only just ended. They had clearly known when the violence was about to bring judgement unto the water; they'd vanished just in time and returned once a light drizzle was all that remained. They often fight with each other. I am convinced one of them- distinguishable for his unique gray feathers which are a darker shade than the others- must be sleeping with all the other geese' wives, as they always try to fight him and they yell back and forth at each other, in a suspiciously organized half circle with Darker-Goose in the center, throwing insults at him in their revolting honk-language. Darker-Goose always stands his ground and usually triumphs in any engagements of physical aggression.

A heron lives on the pond as well and usually observes these conflicts from the shallow parts of the water, standing tall but hunched like a disapproving bard. I often wonder what the heron's name is. Surely in any children's book like those my mother was fond of reading to me- the subgenre that curses animals with the ability of speech- the author would have given it the name of one of the ancient Greco-Roman philosophers, but I like to think its name is Vernon.

Often I sit out here with marble knuckles barely keeping connected shaking and unfaithful hands that spill my coffee and drop my cigarettes into my lap when I try to raise them to my lips. I come out on the balcony to meditate in my personal, outre fashion but these non-narcotic stimulants make me tense and don't help with the frequent, subtle shaking. In the past thirty-six days I've marked my outfits with more burn holes and coffee stains than the previous six years.

I sit out here to forget. My mother forgets a lot of things, but only in certain moments. She will not remember memories I was sure we shared in one conversation, but after some time has passed and I bring that same memory to her again she will smile and relive it with me. This is the type of forgetting I try to mimic when I breath in the scent of the trees and absorb the sounds of the cardinals and water falling into water and even the shitty wails of the geese.

Forget the money, you don't need it anyway. Forget the failures and the girls and forget your emotions. Forget the aesthetics and your purpose because it's meaningless and these thoughts are going to ruin everything WE are working for. Forget the money even though it's all that matters.

The geese are getting hostile again, and in the moment I was trying to forget everything my cigarette had burned down to the filter between my fingertips, dripping ash onto my bare right foot. *Forget the ash. Forget the* geese. *Forget the silence when you pray and the noise you hear when everyone else hears silence. The noise is me telling you who you are and you should forget me too. For a moment you are nothing. Forget your job and your mother who forgets- and the untouchable money forget your money and their money and all the damn money- and forget about the world and the hyperbolic disaster of America and all the beautiful music in the world and every-*

A gorgeous bolt of lightning struck me into consciousness to which, seconds later, a roll of thunder replied. The geese flew out in a disorganized frenzy, shrieking and shameful. The heron was already gone, of course, because it knew dimensions more than any goose about the way things are and what they will be. That is why it had to find a pond to live on with no other herons.

About the Author:

Omar Essa is an aspiring writer and poet from New York. The son of an Egyptian and and an American, His work focuses mainly on emotional and social conflicts explored through accounts of personal experiences.

DO US PART

by Jack Coey

There was an old woman and a nurse in a room. The old woman sat in a chair holding a cane. There was a tray in front of her with a partially full plate. The nurse bent over and wiped her face with a napkin. The nurse believed when old women talked about their lives it's a sign they're about to die. Miss Macintosh started doing that, and it was making the nurse anxious.

"How about you eat some of your peas?" coaxed the nurse.

"I had a dream about my brother, and I remember when he died. We were living on Spruce Street, and it was just before my thirteenth birthday. He was three years older than me, and golly, did he like fast cars! My father was an engineer for a medical parts company, and he was sad, I remember, and I didn't know why until I got older. My mother was anxious; she was trying to decide whether to go back to school because she was afraid my brother and I would outgrow her. She volunteered at the library, and Josh and I were honor roll students. Josh was an end on the football team, and only a senior had more catches. My father enjoyed working in his garden, and strangers would compliment how lovely it was. He wasn't around much, and when he was, he was quiet. When I got older, I figured out he had a friendship with a lady a couple of houses down."

She sadly smiled.

"It was on a Sunday morning at two o'clock, I saw the blue lights flashing in our driveway."

The nurse handed her a glass and a pill. She swallowed the pill and smiled. The nurse took the glass back.

"I always felt warm going into my brother's room. He had posters of sports cars, and team banners, hanging from his ceiling and on his walls. There was a model of the three - masted ship on his dresser, and baseball bats against the wall, and oh yes, a guitar too. His bed cover had a New York Jets logo on it. He had a couple of model planes hanging from the ceiling and good gracious – that empty fish tank. I remember the open dictionary on his desk; my father forbade him to have a computer in his room. After the cruiser in our driveway, the room became forbidding to me. My father would avoid it, my mother would stand in the doorway like in some kind of prayer, and I would close the door."

"Miss Macintosh, the sun is out. Would you like me to raise the shade?"

"Thank-you, Evelyn. I would enjoy the warmth."

The nurse pulled the shade, and sunlight filled the room. Miss Macintosh raised her face to the sunlight. She closed her eyes, and let the sun warm her face. The nurse stood and watched her. She opened her eyes; she was momentarily confused.

"You were remembering your brother," prompted the nurse.

"Oh yes. Where was I? That's right. After his death the house became still. We spoke to each other only to meet a need. Josh's friends came by to pay their respects, and they sat lined up on the couch, silent, until they left silent. After a week, no one came anymore. I turned thirteen, I remember, and my mom talked about hearing Josh from the yard. Father Patterson came to the house to offer succor. My father was absent, and I could hear my mother's voice from Josh's room. She spent a lot of time in there, and I would close the door only to have her open it again. I heard a vacuum sometimes. The funny part was when my father was at home she wouldn't go in there. I said to my friend Curtis one day walking home from school,"

'My mom is weird since my brother died. She like goes into his room, and talks to him, but she doesn't do it when my dad is around.'

'Crazy,' was Curtis's comment, *'Maybe there's something in there that makes her feel better.'*

"I thought Curtis was onto something. I waited until mom was in the basement doing laundry and I snuck into the room. There were the team banners, and the photographs, and the empty fish tank, and I remembered how excited we were when we got fish."

Miss Macintosh laughed as she talked.

"There were two of them – the first died two days later, and the second lived till four. Father gave Josh and me a lecture on responsibility, and we felt guilty. "

'What are you doing?'

"It was my mother and there was a funny look in her eyes."

'Josh is in this room and you are not to violate him by being in here. Please leave.' "I ran from the room in terror to my room, and cried hard."

The nurse removed the tray.

"In the days that followed, I was distracted at school bad enough so Miss Phillips noticed it, and sent me to see Mrs. Prescott, the school nurse, who was about a million years old."

"Oh sure, Abigail Prescott I knew her. Wonderful nurse."

"I was scared to death, I can tell you. Mrs. Prescott closed the door, and I sat on an exam table, and she sat behind her desk. I remember she looked at me for a long moment before she asked,"

'Would you like to hear a story about your brother?'

"She caught me off guard, and I didn't know what to say. I nodded my head not knowing what else to do, and she asked,"

'You sure?'

"I nodded again."

'There was a dance last spring, and the Lewis girl was there – you know Madeline Lewis?'

'Yeah.'

'None of the boys would go near her, and I'll never forget how your brother walked across that empty dance floor in front of everybody, and asked her to dance. I watched the reaction of the other kids, and I know your brother was teased unmercifully. That kind of courage is impossible to forget.'

"I didn't know what to say to her, and we sat in silence, and I remember I could hear talking from the hall. Finally I whispered,"

'My mom.'

'Say again, honey? My hearing is not so good.'

'My mom.'

'I know, Betsy, I know.'

"I felt like she understood without me having to say anymore, and I wondered how she was able to do that."

'*I want you to go back to class and finish out your day. I'm going to visit your mother, but that's a secret between you and me, okay?*'

"I don't know exactly what she did, but I know I felt better."

"I need to take your blood pressure," said the nurse.

Miss Macintosh was silent until the nurse was done.

"It was sometime later Mrs. Prescott told me how she sat in the teacher's lounge, one day, reading, and inadvertently overheard the home ec teacher and the industrial arts teacher, sitting on a couch on the other side of the room, talking. She heard the name Mrs. Cheever, who everybody knew was separated from her husband, and then, she heard my father's name, and couldn't help paying closer attention. The home ec teacher was telling the industrial arts teacher she saw them at a restaurant around midnight, and thought it odd for my father to be out at that time of night with a woman who was not his wife."

Miss Macintosh thought for a moment, and leaned on her cane; stood upright, walked to the lavatory, and closed the door behind her. She came back out again, blinked her eyes, and sat in her chair.

"There was a time I saw candlelight coming from the doorway, and I looked in, and saw my mother on her knees with her head bowed. I tiptoed to my room, and lay down on my bed, and thought about Mrs. Prescott, and how she knew more than she said. I must have fallen asleep, for the next I knew, I was awakened by something hovering over me."

'*Josh sends his love,*' said a voice.

'*Mom, is that you?*'

'*I saw Josh; he sends his love.*'

'*Mom you're scaring me.*'

'*No, honey, it's all right.*'

'*Go to bed, Mom.*'

'*Josh needs a haircut.*'

'*Is Dad home?*'

'*Your father is a very important man. I hope you know that, Betsy.*'

'*Yeah?*'

'*You see how much he works?*'

'*Yeah?*'

"We heard the front door open."

'*Good night, honey.*'

"I felt a kiss on my forehead, and lay in the dark until the dark of sleep."

"Then one day, Mrs. Prescott sent home a note with me. My mom sighed, '*Oh God,*' when she read it, and answered, '*Tell her, I guess so.*' The next morning, I stopped at Mrs. Prescott's doorway, and said, '*yes*' to a smiling Mrs. Prescott looking over the rims of her glasses. I got home from school that day, and my mom had the tea ready at three –thirty when Mrs. Prescott drove into the driveway. I stood by the doorway and said hello before going into my room. Mrs. Prescott told me what happened. She said she sat in a straight – backed chair, and my mom sat on the couch, and she talked about the golf tournament that weekend.

'*I didn't think Phil Sheridan was that good of a golfer,*' she commented.

'*Oh Gracious, I always thought he was a duffer,*' my mom said in a loud voice, '*Sugar?*'

'*No thank-you.*'

'*These are Irish biscuits; quite good.*'

'*Does Mr. Macintosh still play?*'

'*Oh Mercy, no, he's much too busy.*'

'*Does Josh play?*'

"My mom gasped."

'*He dabbled in it before giving it up.*'

'*That's right, football?*'

'Yes, that's right. Several colleges are look-ing at him.'

'Didn't I read his obituary?'

"My mom looked at the floor. Then, she explained,"

'My son Josh is away for a visit; I expect him back next week.'

"Mrs. Prescott told me she felt sad. She bowed her head, and began to speak,"

'It was the summer of 1965 that my son, Benjamin, went with his roommate to Alabama to help with voter registration. The boys had two weeks because his roommate, whose name was Hanson, had to come back north for foot-ball practice; he was a big boy who wasn't afraid of much. They lived with Negro families. They were walking a girl down a country road one night when a pickup truck drove slowly by them and stopped. Four boys got out stinking of whisky and approached them. They had grins on their faces as they said the most lewd things to the girl. One of the boys reached out to grab her, and Benjamin's roommate grabbed him by the throat and squeezed until he took back his hand. The other boys backed slowly away, and they got into the pick-up and drove slowly away. Two nights later Benjamin disappeared. The sheriff said he thought Benja-min must have gotten homesick. My husband and I along with the Hanson family appealed to The Department of Justice to investigate what happened. They found Benjamin in a shallow grave with his throat slashed. A couple of weeks later, they arrested two brothers named Gowrie who were acquitted by an all – white grand jury a month later. The two brothers lived out their natural lives in peace and quiet. I had experienced an evil more powerful than a mother's love for her son; I was humbled and helpless. I was left with a knowledge most peo-ple don't have, and everyday I dedicate myself to the healing of my fellow man.' Mrs. Prescott painfully smiled. The only sound was the wind in the leaves.

'Would you care for a biscuit?' asked my mom.

'No, no, thank-you,' answered the nurse, 'I want you to know I know what you're going through.'

'Josh is visiting his uncle in Minnesota, and will be back next week.'

'Perhaps I'll come by to say hello.'

'Oh, I don't know if that's a good idea. Josh will be tired from his travels so I don't want to plan any activities for him, maybe later on. Are you sure you wouldn't want to try a biscuit?'

'No, no thank-you,' answered Mrs. Prescott as she got up to leave."

Miss Macintosh stopped talking and looked at her nurse.

"Do you want to lie down and rest for awhile? There's no need to go back to these memories, is there?"

"Yes, yes, I must tell the story."

The nurse knew then.

"I guess Mrs. Prescott was being told by a number of people that my father and Mrs. Cheever were being seen together at times and places when and where they shouldn't have been. She told me how she saw Mrs. Cheever across the aisle in church one Sunday morning. Mrs. Cheever had her head tilted back, and her eyes closed like she was in some kind of rever-ie. Mrs. Prescott told me she felt disapproval. She said she thought, 'Poor Mrs. Macintosh can't distinguish between what's real, and what's not, and this one is pretending to be something she's certainly not.' Father Patter-son came to the pulpit and invoked a prayer. Mrs. Prescott said she tried minding her own business, but couldn't resist the temptation to observe Mrs. Cheever who was praying very devoutly. 'I don't believe her,' thought Mrs. Prescott. Next came a hymn which Mrs. Cheev-er sang with gusto while looking to her left and right. 'Oh, she's looking to see if others notice,' thought Mrs. Prescott. Father Patterson began his sermon. His theme was being faithful. 'Humph!' spouted Mrs. Prescott. After the ser-mon was a prayer and final hymn executed by

Mrs. Cheever with fervor. After the service, there was a social in the basement, and the congregants gathered for coffee and doughnuts. After a few minutes, Father Patterson came into the room, and Mrs. Cheever, urgently, came to stand by his side. *'My Gracious, the woman is shameless,'* thought Mrs. Prescott. She watched as Mrs. Cheever wrote a check for the church's restoration fund, and when she handed it to Father Patterson, he beamed.

'I wonder if he knows how she carries on,' thought Mrs. Prescott. She sighed, put down her coffee, and headed for the door."

They listened to a siren in the distance.

"Could you get me my sweater, dear?" The nurse went to the closet and took out a sweater, and put it over Miss Macintosh's shoulder.

"Thank – you, dear. I saw Mrs. Prescott again when Sabrina Sterling wrote a bad word on my paper and Miss Phillips saw it, and pointed,

'You write that?'

'No,' I answered.

'That is your paper.'

'Yes.'

'I want to start this project so I want you to go see Mrs. Prescott, and sort it out with her.'

I was embarrassed, and looked down at the floor. She went to her desk, and gave me a pass. I left the room, not looking up, and Mrs. Prescott was surprised to see me. She left me to go talk to Miss Phillips. She came back in and closed the door.

'So what happened Betsy?'

'Sabrina wrote a bad word on my paper.'

'Yes?'

'She's mad at me because I'm friends with Curtis.'

'Oh, Sabrina Coates or Sterling?'

'Sterling.'

'You didn't write it?'

'No.'

'All right, Betsy. I'm going to send you back to class, and I will talk with Miss Phillips.'

'I don't want to go back.'

'Why not?'

'Nobody likes me.'

'That's not true. I like you.'

'I mean kids don't like me.'

'Oh, I don't think that's true.'

'Sabrina was trying to get me into trouble.'

'Have I told you you are in trouble? So I guess it didn't work, did it?'

"I didn't know what to say to that. Then, she said,"

'Sometimes Betsy when people are mean to us the best thing to do is to let them know they don't bother us.'

'Is it true a man killed your son?'

"I remember poor Mrs. Prescott jerked her head back liked I'd slapped her in the face."

'Yes Betsy, a man killed my son,' she whispered.

"I remembered hearing voices passing in the hallway."

'That's what Curtis told me.'

The nurse folded a blanket from the bed, and went to the closet.

'The world can be a cruel place, Betsy. My job as an adult is to teach you in the face of cruelty you have to be brave. You have to believe life can be better than it sometimes is, and when you get to be old like I am, you will know, it's the only way to live that makes any sense. Do understand that, Betsy?'

'I think so.'

'I hope you will think about it in the days to come.'

'Your son was brave and it didn't make any sense.'

"I remembered Mrs. Prescott smiled sadly, and she said,"

'You're right, Betsy. Benjamin is with me always and the courage with which he lived inspires me to make the world better than it is. He's not here in body but in spirit.'

'That's like mom and Josh. Mom talks to Josh all the time.'

"I remember she looked at me not knowing what to say, and I couldn't figure out why. It was only when I was older I realized being in denial, and dying helping others isn't exactly the same."

"Isn't it more about how they lived...?" asked the nurse over her shoulder.

She spun around when she heard the cane hit the floor.

DEMOCRACY AT WORK
by Thomas Kearnes

Den Mother, of course, was not her real name. While she spoke, Jameson swished the name *Greta* around his mind. Greta, Mother Greta, the Den Mother. She was speaking so eloquently, about how the Sunset tribe had fallen into harmony after the last vote, about the shattering calm on the beach at dusk, speaking so eloquently that Jameson let the shot fall out of focus. Panicked, he nudged a lever, and Greta's image sharpened. After glancing over his shoulder at Mona, one of the producers, he sighed audibly. Maybe she hadn't noticed him fumbling with the camera.

"Cut!"

Shit, now Mona was angry. Greta stopped talking but didn't budge from the boulder. Unlike the other contestants, Greta didn't seem to possess an on/off switch, an inherent phoniness that snapped into place whenever the camera rolled. She was Jameson's favorite to film, so natural and elegant, so at ease. She reminded him of mist descending over a hilltop, enveloping it completely like unexpected peace.

"The mic can pick up every sound." Mona grimaced. "Every damn sound."

"Can we edit me out?" Jameson suggested.

"Never mind. I think we have enough."

Greta stood, her mouth puckered with concern. As Mona started back to camp, she mouthed *are you okay?* Jameson smiled broad-

ly and for a moment forgot the lashing Mona was no doubt saving for production camp. The producers didn't wish to rattle the players with staff strife. Monty Whitman, the show's creator, felt it disrupted the game's authenticity.

Greta called out to Jameson as he and Mona walked away. Mona rolled her eyes but he spun around, the camera perched on his shoulder, blocking his view. "Don't stay in the sun too long," Greta said. "You'll burn up like the rest of us."

He tried to thank her, but Mona interrupted. "Good luck, Greta. We'll see you tonight." She always wished the contestants good luck. Eighteen days into the game, the words sounded so mechanical.

Greta departed, back to the Sunset tribe, but Jameson couldn't hear her retreat over the pinging gravel and broken brush beneath his and Mona's feet. The producer shook her head and muttered, "I thought I'd enjoy this more."

"What's that?" Jameson had to kill time. Maybe she'd forget his clumsiness.

"Some sad shit is going on at the Moonrise. When both tribes merge, it'll be a bloodbath."

"What? Have they gone cannibal?"

"No, they've…" Mona paused, gazing over the shrubbery at the desolate beach. Her wistful expression was something only a lover should see. He didn't wish to know her that intimately. "I'm shocked none of us saw it coming. They've *organized*." She explained that five on the Moonrise tribe had vowed to stick together and vote as a bloc at every elimination ceremony. They'd already kicked off Biker Blonde followed by Miss Black America, and now only Kid Christ remained. "The Sunset tribe is fucked," she said. "We'll see how tonight's vote goes."

"Isn't that cheating?"

"You know Whitman. He's making it up as he goes along." She forced her way past a cluster of bamboo branches. They smacked Jameson's chest. "The players can vote out anyone, even the decent people."

"Like Greta?"

"What have I told you about using real names?" They walked in silence a few moments. "Yeah, don't get attached to Den Mother." Her pitying tone rankled him. The Moonrise bloc had figured out in the first week that Den Mother was the Sunsets' de facto, well, den mother. Several cameramen had filmed the Moonrise bloc speculating about the scope of her influence.

"And we have to sit back and let it happen?" Jameson's upper lip curled in disgust.

She cut her gaze to him. "You bet your ass. Unless it's a one-on-one, you don't exist."

The game Whitman had developed, *Savages*, was unlike any ever produced for television—perfect to air, he said, just as the Nineties ended and a new millennium began. Sixteen Americans, divided into two tribes of eight, competed on a remote island for survival, the last player winning a cool million. Every three days, the losing tribe voted out one of its own. When ten players remained, the tribes merged, resulting—Whitman had assured the network—in free-for-all, social Darwinism. This merge happened tomorrow, the combined tribe's first vote taking place two nights later.

Jameson's face fell. The camera felt like an albatross on his shoulder. "This is crap." He knew he sounded like a child. "It isn't fair."

"Of course it's not fair. It's television."

The crew called production camp Inferno. The island was located near the equator, only one-fourth the size of Delaware. The game took place on the western end while the Inferno was on the eastern half. The camp was a snake pit of dampness, underbrush and wires of varying thickness plugged into over a dozen generators. The crew occasionally had to yell over the machines' incessant drone. An editing bay stood at the far edge of camp. Whitman claimed the network's deadline for the first episode was tight, so editors would have to start cutting footage before the game itself had ended.

Jameson was surprised Mona abruptly parted ways with him after arriving. He'd been ready for another tongue-lashing. He would've been fired the first week had there been enough to crew to fill the void. While Whitman had invited two alternates in case one of the players backed out at the last minute, he'd failed to bring along any backup crew.

He knew he should nap before his evening shift with the Sunset tribe. Scenarios of varying heinousness polluted his mind, all of them involving a dumbfounded Den Mother, Greta, stumbling from the elimination ceremony. All losers were whisked away by motorboat to a neighboring island the crew had named Purgatory. Whitman refused to say what amenities, if any, awaited those who couldn't survive the vote. He had to warn her, warn the whole Sunset tribe. He'd grown fond of them, the five that remained. They were silly and desperate and totally unprepared for America's scorn.

The cameraman who was sometimes Jameson's friend cooked sausage links over a modest campfire. Jameson kept calling him Cooper but knew that wasn't his name. He didn't complain, however, whenever Jameson said it. Not-Cooper glanced up from his food and asked how the shoot went. Jameson knew he didn't care. After the first two or three days, the crew had drafted nicknames for every player. For example, the Moonrise bloc was run by

Gentleman Jackass and She-Beast. Jameson had nursed a slight crush on Frat Rat, from the Sunset tribe, his acres of teeth and feathered blond locks, but wisely hid his attraction when among his macho coworkers. At any rate, Frat Rat was voted out on Day Nine. Not-Cooper nodded glumly as Jameson described his latest fuck-up. The sunlight bore down through the palm trees' broad leaves. No matter where you stood, the heat seeped through your skin.

"The merge is gonna be a shit-storm," Not-Cooper smirked and rotated the links in the pan.

Jameson swallowed. Was he the only one who gave a damn? "I wish there was something we could do."

"Just let the bastards go down with the ship. No life jackets."

In his tent, Jameson set his travel alarm clock for seven that evening. His doze was dreamless and fitful. Several times, he ascended to semi-consciousness, smothering beneath the oppressive heat. Despite this, he never rose from the floor. If he mimicked the position associated with rest, his mind and body would be fooled. Thinking about Den Mother, the way she dropped her voice to a murmur when interviewed at night, made the heat tolerable. When his alarm chimed, he rolled around under the sheets, as if wondering what noise had stirred him.

"You were off your game with Den Mother," Mona said. Jameson had just changed into his last clean T-shirt. "Kevin can fill in. Get some more beauty sleep, kid."

Jameson stood at the edge of Inferno as Mona led Kevin, a doe-eyed and scrawny Latino, into the jungle. It was stupid. He didn't always shoot Den Mother, not even typically. But Mona had promised! His arms and back grew slack as he stared at the dirt. Why waste time bitching at him after the botched interview? A simple snub was less fuss. She'd thrive if deported to the other side of the island and given a chance at the million.

The sun finished its descent, and most of the crew not shooting had gathered around the campfire. Not-Cooper strummed an old George Strait melody on his boxy black guitar. The others watched him because he was the only one doing anything. The crew's bodies were limp, like fresh roadkill, stretched upon the stumps and boulders and fallen trees around the campfire.

When they landed on shore a week before the players, the jungle had seemed lush and forbidden, the perfect setting for a game designed to reduce players to their most primal selves. It revealed itself, however, to be a mere repository for every insect, reptile and critter that no one could name and no one could avoid. Whitman had offered a weekend vacation in Palm Springs to whomever had amassed the most mosquito bites by game's end.

Landing a multi-month stint filming a hot new show that would revolutionize television had been a windfall. Jameson had spent the previous year submitting his paltry resume and acquainting himself with his friends' spare rooms and sofas. With the money he was making now, he could afford a studio apartment. If he got hired for a second season—Whitman was confident the network would demand one—maybe he could afford a neighborhood without crack dealers or constant police patrol. His mother had been so proud, calling from across the continent in Virginia. She reminded her son that this was his dream...enjoy it! Jameson no longer knew the substance of his dreams. He was too spent to muster even modest perspective.

The editing bay was inside a claustrophobic makeshift suite, walled off by army green canvases. The equipment—the VCRs and switches and screens and spools—was two days away from the trash heap; Whitman hadn't seen the point in exposing top-shelf machinery to these punishing conditions. Surprisingly, no one was working at the console. It was the first time he'd surveyed the whole editing bay. It impressed him in the way pachyderms impressed him—distantly and disconcertingly.

To the side was a file cabinet containing every last tape filled with average Americans scheming and starving on a remote island. Whitman hoped to recycle the tapes as the early episodes were assembled. If your heart broke while the camera rolled but some douche erased the footage, maybe it didn't break after all. Ecstatic, James found the top drawer unlocked.

After riffling through the cassettes, he found one marked *Greta*. No one informed whoever labeled these that the crew agreed nicknames would discourage inappropriate bonds between the players and themselves. A whole cassette of Den Mother's warmth and wisdom, her greatest hits. Jameson recalled enough about the machines from his junior-college courses to bring Den Mother's image up on a monitor.

It was obvious she wasn't from L.A. or New York or Florida or anywhere one would find middle-aged women of fighting age, never realizing they were fighting death. Jameson could remember her mentioning it, but he decided she was from Minnesota, maybe Wisconsin. She'd allowed crow's feet, laugh lines and worry lines to invade her rosy-cheeked face. Her hazel eyes softened whenever she spoke of others who needed her affection or counsel.

Jameson watched raptly, zipping through a minute or two then allowing the tape to play. He didn't have enough time to watch it all. Maybe he'd catch the best parts, like channel surfing. More than once, she insisted that she knew this was a game and she would have to vote out the very tribesmen she claimed to adore. Still, Jameson couldn't dismiss her as craven and insincere like the other players, even the ones he liked. How must it feel to call her *Mom*? The head editor, a burly woman who ate nothing but granola bars, crashed his reverie.

"Your ignorant ass just shoots these losers," she huffed. "You leave the watching to me."

He gulped and pushed himself away from the monitor, almost flipping over his chair. "Sorry, Brenda. I thought I could help." Hearing those words leave his mouth dehumanized him.

She smirked and chomped her granola bar, rolled her eyes and ordered him to scat. He rushed out, too embarrassed to get a last glance, Den Mother perched on a boulder or a tree trunk or the beach, assuring him, assuring everyone at home, that these players could inspire more than derision. Inside the tent, Jameson didn't bother with sleep. He stripped off his clean shirt—he'd need it for his next date with Den Mother.

The crew kept up with the game's progress thanks to a constant flow of producers and cameramen in and out of Inferno. The Moonrise tribe, dominion of Gentleman Jackass and She-Best, had lost the immunity challenge, the last before the merge. At the elimination ceremony, their voting bloc jettisoned Kid Christ. The pudgy cameraman didn't stifle his glee recounting how the contestant burst into tears and threw back his head, arms raised, demanding that God avenge his betrayal. Reportedly, She-Beast muttered that God had nothing to do with it.

The Moonrise bloc had evicted every tribesman not in its alliance. Nothing left to do but target Sunset's players starting tomorrow. Jameson's gut twisted, perspiration coating his face. He had to warn Den Mother. Neither Mona nor any other producer knew of his special connection with Den Mother. They wouldn't know to keep Jameson far away.

He didn't dream about the game. Instead, he trudged along a Venice sidewalk, terrified those interviewing him for jobs would notice his massive erection. After that, he dreamed of a long-ago afternoon at Chuck E. Cheese. It had been his first visit. The playroom had been grimy with bad lighting, not shiny like the commercials promised.

Not long after sunrise, a booming voice instructed the crew to circle the campfire.

Monty Whitman hadn't rallied the troops since the first day of shooting. Jameson stumbled out of his tent, his last clean shirt on his back, albeit no longer clean. Whitman wore his typical uniform: dark khaki slacks and shirt, huge pith helmet, wraparound shades. One might mistake him for a tourist determined to "experience" the wilderness. He gestured incessantly while he spoke. The crew attempted enthusiasm, but it was too hot and they were too bored with the players hatching their schemes of mundane malignance.

"This shoot has surpassed my wildest expectations," he called. The tide fell against the beach as he paused. Jameson found the sound soothing. "My players, your players, have come to win! They're lying, they're scheming, they're bringing every kind of excitement John Doe American could want. Best of all, they're doing this wearing only swimsuits." A few crewmen laughed, but the others weren't sure if Whitman wanted that. "I have better news. Your schedules will ease up a bit. With us losing another player every three days, that leaves fewer to shoot. Enjoy the break. You've earned it!"

"Fuck that," someone in back cried. "We want our bonus!"

Whitman crowed with laughter. The crew followed, this time certain it was the proper response. "One last thing," he added. "I know none of you would dream of violating our most important rule, but it's imperative that nothing we say or do influence the players." His fingers made a V and flicked back and forth underneath his eyes. "Let's keep each other honest..."

After that inspirational interlude concluded, Mona informed Jameson they'd be one of the teams shooting the merged tribe's first interactions, in addition to quick one-on-ones. The young man's voice cracked, he was so desperate to hide his enthusiasm. Ten players, even more producers and crew—surely he'd have a chance to warn Den Mother. Alas, he had no idea how to do it. If caught, he'd be sent to Purgatory along with whatever player got the business end of the votes.

Two hours later, on the opposite end of the island, half a dozen cameras aimed their lenses at an expanse of beach. Soon, the crew heard the hollers and merriment of both Sunset and Moonrise players converging. Their joy jumped tenfold to find a large feast of wine, bread, meats and cheeses awaiting them. Until today, all they'd eaten was rice provided by the producers and whatever wildlife they caught. Jameson wondered how this food wasn't "interference" with the game. The thought left his head, however, when Mona began calling instructions.

A half-hour later, while the players gorged like Vikings before a voyage, the producers began subtly extracting from the feast first one player and then another for interviews. Jameson worried when Den Mother wasn't selected first, or the time after that, or the time after that. Maybe the producers didn't need sound bites from *all* the players.

"Since you're Den Mother's favorite," Mona said quietly, "I'll go fetch her. She spills her guts when you're filming."

Jameson nearly dropped the camera, he was so excited. He retreated a few yards into the jungle and began experimenting with angles. Den Mother greeted him warmly and sat on a fallen palm tree as instructed by Mona. Jameson grinned. She'd instinctively selected just the right position for his shot. He was amazed at how perfectly Den Mother segued from playing the game to confessing, the interview almost over before he realized his only chance to warn her about the Moonrise danger would soon expire.

"How does it feel," Mona asked, "playing the game with five strangers you've known only from challenges?"

"Maybe the Moonrise tribe is just like us." Den Mother winked at the lens. What made her do that? Did she know Jameson had a message for her? "They had to make some hard decisions at their elimination ceremonies, but I'm sure those were based on merit, not personal feelings."

Mona's contempt seemed to elude Den Mother, but Jameson read her face as easily as a billboard. "Could the Moonrise be playing the game differently than you?'

Den Mother shrugged and smiled. "Anything's possible in this game." She laughed. "I learned that real damn fast."

"Has your tribe decided which Moonrise member will get your votes?"

"Oh, there's been talk that a couple of us might still vote for each other."

Mona, so contained during interviews, paused. Jameson assumed that she, like him, was stunned. She asked if the Sunset tribe might still be too focused on eliminating each other to think about Moonrise.

"Sure," Den Mother said. "Besides, maybe no one on Moonrise deserves to go home just now." She swatted at a horsefly. "It pains me to say this, but we have a few personal conflicts among us five. You'd think after nearly three weeks, we'd be past that." She smiled but it didn't stick. "You look surprised, Mona." The situation was more critical than Jameson had speculated. "Young man, close your mouth," Den Mother laughed. "There are flies everywhere." His eyes widened to learn Den Mother watched him like he watched her.

Mona recovered her composure. It was like watching a receiver bobble a Hail Mary only to seize it at the last moment. She said, "It's heartwarming how much affection you have for strangers, Greta." Jameson's mind was so busy calculating how to warn Den Mother that he didn't notice Mona ease back from her boulder. He knew from experience that when she straightened her back, withdrawing physically from the conversation, it meant she wished to conclude the one-on-one. It surprised him to hear Mona wish Den Mother luck.

The contestant told Jameson to be careful—his cheeks and nose were bright red. "That damn sun," she said. "My kingdom for some cloud cover!"

He jerked the camera from his face. With no lens between them, it took him a moment to calibrate his perspective. "Moonrise is voting as one," he stuttered. "They think you're the leader. If they get rid of you first, the other four will be easy." He didn't need to look beside him to imagine Mona's jaw dropped in shock, quickly followed by white rage. He focused on Den Mother, whose features kept realigning while decoding his outburst.

"Jameson, what are you talking about?" she managed. "How do you know—?"

Mona leapt between Jameson and the contestant. She literally pushed Den Mother back toward the feast. The contestant stumbled, arms flailing, and Jameson feared she'd topple, her skull smacking against a stone. If he kept imagining Den Mother in danger, he could keep imagining himself as her savior. Mona insisted all sorts of rumors circulate among the crew. She encouraged Den Mother to ignore Jameson and please never repeat this rumor to any other player. Mona smiled wildly. "I think you might take it all, Greta. I really do." Ignoring her, Den Mother looked over her shoulder a last time before joining the tribe. She mouthed *are you okay?* Jameson's gaze was fixed on a tree trunk. Had he already finished his mission? He stood dumbly as Mona demanded that he return to Inferno immediately. Whitman would be told about this, she promised. Circling the perimeter of the feast, Jameson willed himself not to glance at her. He'd done what was necessary, and now Whitman would do what he felt necessary.

After returning to Inferno, the disgraced cameraman told no one, not even Not-Cooper, what he'd done. When Mona stormed into camp, however, he watched helplessly as the gossip leapt from person to person, like malaria. Brenda, in particular, shot him a dirty look. He crawled into his stifling tent, stripped naked, and tried to recall the breathing exercises his last therapist taught him. The crew didn't announce dinner. Were they avoiding him as ordered, or were they appalled like Mona?

Drifting to sleep, he knew it made no difference.

Three hours later, he woke to a commotion outside. At his tent's opening, he watched the crew scramble, a trio of cameras rushing toward the island's other side. He didn't know what to think. The first post-merge vote was still two nights away. The immunity challenge wasn't scheduled till hours before the vote. He was about to rise from his tent when Not-Cooper blocked his way and slowly shook his head.

"What the hell's happening?"

"Damage control, dumbass. Whitman moved the elimination ceremony to tonight. Can't undo what you did, stupid shit, but once Den Mother's gone, no one left in the game will know. Apparently, she didn't share that info with the others."

The heat, he never got used to the heat. Enormous mosquitoes, bugs the size of butterflies, swarmed the two men. He'd made things worse. Not only did Den Mother fail to act on his warning, Whitman had pushed her execution date two days forward. His head swam with confusion and denial. He imagined this terrible isolation and dread closely resembled what a real island castaway might experience. The whole game seemed to him a claptrap devoted to instigate mistrust and melodrama. Not knowing why, he quickly looked around Inferno to make sure no one was filming his humiliation.

Not-Cooper shoved Jameson back into his tent. He ordered the young man to wait for him. Jameson did as instructed. He wasn't among friends.

After an interminable half-hour, Not-Cooper ordered the young man to come outside. There, Jameson found the entire crew—every cameraman, every editor, every producer—circled around the campfire. The ring of indignation was menacing like he'd been told the elimination ceremonies were.

Whitman strode forward, halted inches from Jameson's nose. He wondered if the show's creator would throttle him while everyone watched. After all, he'd named his game *Savages*.

"I wanted to fire you hours ago," he said, "but I realized it was more appropriate, more in keeping with the integrity of this game, if I let your fellow crew members decide. They've all cast their votes and placed them in a jar." A vote? Insanity! Whitman was the undisputed boss. Why should he care what the peons thought? Jameson's face flushed with humiliation, and he realized that was precisely Whitman's intent.

Mona, cheeks scarlet and eyes aflame, read the slips of paper one by one. Each had *yes* written upon it. No one had informed him, but Jameson assumed that meant *yes, fire his traitorous ass*. Each vote felt like a punch in the throat. Kevin mouthed an obscenity when he caught Jameson's eye. The former cameraman halfway hoped the crew, those just as miserable and bug-ridden as him, would spring to his defense.

After the last *yes* was read, Whitman directed the young man to make his way down a narrow, twisting path that ended at the beach. There, a motorboat would whisk him away to Purgatory. He hadn't thought to pack and was too humiliated to mention it. Jameson didn't know where he'd stay once banished, or who'd be with him. Part of him expected the boat's captain to toss him overboard before reaching exile. The path took over twenty minutes to traverse. More mosquitoes, more bamboo branches slamming into his chest. He made the beach just as dusk faded. He expected a boat to be waiting, but there was none. Exhausted, he flopped on his back atop the sand.

Jameson didn't remember falling asleep, but he recognized the voice calling his name, waking him. He couldn't believe it. She was here! Better yet, there was no camera intruding, no Mona plainly not giving a shit what happened to anyone. Den Mother wouldn't be standing beside him, however, if she hadn't been eliminated.

Whitman liked to contend that *Savages* was more a "reality" show than a traditional game show. Game shows, he said, had a troublesome reputation, all their tackiness and sugar-high enthusiasm. Jameson suspected, however, that audiences would connect most quickly with the elements of *Savages* that were frank manipulations: the elimination ceremonies, the immunity challenges, the gradual shedding of garments until indecency knocked.

Den Mother laughed, brushed his shoulder. "You were right, young man. It was brutal."

"Why didn't you do something? Tell someone?"

"I knew at the start I wouldn't win. The odds weren't good." Mentioning them by their real names, she praised She-Beast's aggression and Gentleman Jackass' charisma. "I made a promise before the game: I wouldn't disgrace myself just for a little money."

"Greta, a million dollars is a *lot* of money." *Greta*. He thought of her as *Greta* now.

"One day it'd be gone, though, and I'd have to look in the mirror."

He shrugged her hand from his shoulder, pouted and glared out at the ocean. A small but increasingly loud roar signaled the motorboat coming to collect them. Why had he fought so hard to save her if she would've never saved herself? "This is crap," he said. "It's totally not fair."

Greta laughed and, silently, Jameson forgave her. At Purgatory, maybe she could bake cookies. He'd wash the insect eggs and grit from her hair. He would clear her dishes after each meal. She'd tell him about her real kids and he could pretend to be one of them. His last clean shirt was drenched with sweat. "Admit it, though," he mumbled. "It wasn't fair."

She draped her arm over his shoulders. Her touch felt familiar and friendly, like a bathrobe. "Only children believe life is fair."

"I was talking about the game." Jameson smiled, thankful no one was filming.

"So was I." Greta shrugged and smiled. "Television is just like life, in a way..."

A chill trickled down his spine. That wasn't what he'd needed to hear. It sounded absolutely true, so it must be forever ignored. He wished the motorboat would hurry up.

Still, he hoped Greta might bake treats for him in Purgatory. He recalled, as a child, sinking his teeth into an oatmeal cookie one Christmas. At least, he thought he was that boy. Maybe he was remembering a commercial. The motorboat slowed, its engine sputtering, Jameson took Greta's hand, guiding her aboard. The woman squeezed his fingers and mouthed *thank you*.

About the Author:

Thomas Kearnes graduated from the University of Texas at Austin with an MA in film writing. His fiction has appeared in Hobart, Gertrude, A cappella Zoo, Split Lip Magazine, Cutthroat, Litro, Berkeley Fiction Review, PANK, BULL: Men's Fiction, Gulf Stream Magazine, Wraparound South, Night Train, 3:AM Magazine, Word Riot, Storyglossia, Driftwood Press, Adroit Journal, The Matador Review, Mary: A Journal of New Writing, wigleaf, SmokeLong Quarterly, Pidgeonholes, Sundog Lit, The Citron Review, The James Franco Review and elsewhere. He is a three-time Pushcart Prize nominee. Originally from East Texas, he now lives near Houston and works as a cashier. His debut collection of short fiction, "Steers and Queers" will print at Lethe Press in 2019.

A MOMENT OF CALM
by Kobina Wright Limitless

October 7th. Bali anchored herself in the leather-like spa chair soaking her feet in hot, robin-blue, soapy water. The funds that would cover the day's pampering had been previously reserved for other things and she would fight guilt over this spa level treatment later. From her tablet, on the Press Enterprise website, she read about a judge in Montana who was blocking the use of the drug Pentobarbital in state executions, thereby halting executions in Montana until the law requiring an "ultra-fast acting barbiturate" was changed, or a substitute drug was found. She read about a ten-year-old who shot his best friend over five dollars. She put the tablet down.

It was 85 degrees outside and somewhere around 60 degrees in the nail salon. The hot, robin-blue water enveloping her feet saved her from shivering and wishing the experience forward. Despite the over-conditioned air, Bali felt golden, down to the balls of her feet. This morning, even before she opened her eyes, she, again, felt the absence of the nasty gray-cling. She opened the glass doors to her gallery, then shortly after, left Elias to manage it while she scuttled out to the Riverside Museum of Art with her teenage sidekick, Jane, who was out of school for reasons only teachers knew. At the museum, Bali purchased a mixed media wall sculpture by the Thai artist, Chutima Kerdpitak, which incorporated a rubber chicken and a window panel. It was March's birthday gift Bali had agonized over from the gift shop. Afterwards, she dropped Jane off. She had rehearsed discussing framing options for the assemblage art with Elias in her head, until she arrived at Happy Hand Nail Salon.

In recent days, there hadn't been any ominous phone hang-ups at the gallery. No leaping shadows. No broken car windows. And as far as she could tell, Jane hadn't even gotten her sick. When Bali had picked her up before heading to Riverside, Bali had noticed, with annoyance, the wadded up tissue in Jane's hand... her watery eyes... She would have never invited the girl out had she known and was even tempted to kick her out of the car once Bali saw her – but didn't have the heart. She'd have to remember to call Jane's grandfather, Mike, to check on her later.

Bali sat, staring out into a portion of the parking lot over her pedicurist's shoulder. The sunlight bounced off many of the windshields in the parking lot, creating a alternate light source for the interior of the spa at high noon. She watched the foot traffic in front as people ran their errands and lived their congested lives. She caught her breath. A man walked by the salon window. Short hair. Clean shaven. Attractive. Like a supermodel. But it was no one she knew.

She suppressed the urge to hurl bottles of nail polish through the plate glass window, like glass paint bombs. This looking-over-her-shoulder, one-woman act was getting old. Up until a few moments ago, she thought she had packed her fear away in recycled paper and padded felt. She thought she had lined up all her concerns, each organized by weight, cut and wrapped to be manageable. Fear was not her thing and she was now resenting the man she knew was responsible for the feeling that kept tying her up.

While her pedicurist painted her toes in a color called "Pretty Little Peanut," was forced to admit the truth to herself, even if she wouldn't say it out loud. She meditated on this, rolling the thought around in her mind like a pebble as her toenails were expertly covered in glossy tan polish. As she further examined the idea, she realized suddenly that there two truths, not one. She was a one-legged chicken in a den of foxes and the new revelation nudged the pebble from her mind to her throat.

Truth #1: Bali had a real-life stalker. Truth #2: She would not be able to handle this alone.

WHAT IF
by Erin Bank

"Can't I have your seat?" The young woman fails to notice any pertinent details of the world around her, besides the five large shopping bags she's hauling onto the bus, not least of all the age of the man she is addressing and the cane propped by his side. All she knows is that he's in the closest seat to where she's awkwardly standing. That, and she knows that she's angry that the Uber app isn't working on her phone, leaving her stranded, except for the bus. She is already composing the email and tweet in her head. Why wouldn't the app leave her logged in and her information saved just because she got a new phone? Of all days for her family's driver to call in sick. This day is not off to a good start.

"I can't stand with all this stuff." She waves her right hand in the general direction of her problem, as if he hasn't noticed the massive loot she was carrying. In her waving, she nearly whacked the phone she was holding, ensconced in a furry green case, into a young man who was boarding behind her, trying to get around her, a blue hooded sweatshirt pulled up over his head. He bobs out of the way and proceeds into a gap between the configuration of seats that is just wide enough for his small frame.

The old man looks at the young woman, then around the bus, which is still stopped as people board. It is on the late side of morning rush hour, and the bus is crowded with a mix of commuters and tourists getting a jump start on the holiday weekend. Among those sitting are elderly and deserve the seats or have their headphones in and heads down, pretending not to notice. He'd forgive the blonde family speaking a guttural European language—he couldn't tell if it was Dutch or German—hunched over a paper map, trying to determine their whereabouts, each pointing to a different quadrant of the city. The other on-boarders squeeze past the young woman, shooting dirty looks at the person refusing to move to the rear of the bus, a few mumbling choice words under the breath that she either ignores or doesn't hear.

"Perhaps you'd like to use my cane." He nods towards it and notices that she isn't looking or even paying attention to his gentle snark. She instead is glaring at the woman pushing a shopping basket who is trying to get around her, knocking into her bags and causing them to swing on her arms. He tries to remember if she's asking him or telling him to move.

"I don't expect someone like you to understand, but it's considered good manners for a gentleman to offer his seat to a lady." She hasn't made eye contact, but she has seen what she needs to see: even though she is riding the bus, she is someone who knows (or, at least, her daddy knows) important people, and he is a black man who does not. He probably doesn't even know what Uber is.

The man barely notices the implication: it has happened his entire life and he is tired. And he also knows how to pick his battles. He is on his way to the homeless shelter at which he volunteers every week: that is his current battle. Anyway, what if he stood and helped the still confused Dutch/German family find their way?

"All passengers please move to the rear of the bus," the driver's exasperated voice comes on the intercom. He can't see directly behind him at what is happening, exactly, only that people are crowding into the front of the bus and can't move back. He can hear mumbles about someone blocking the aisle. The only person not reacting has his headphones turned to a volume so loud the man can hear the beat of the bass leaking through. Him, and the young woman of course, who either ignores or doesn't hear.

Without a word, he slowly pulls himself off his seat using his cane in one hand and the center pole with the other for balance. The young woman shoves through and slides into the seat next to a hunched Chinese woman muttering to herself before he's fully standing. In lieu of a thank you, she immediately starts tapping away at her phone.

The old man now searches around for a handhold, and he finds one next to the man in the blue hoodie and near the German—he can now hear them clearly—family. He is dusting off the corner of his brain that knows how to ask them where they're trying to go, when the bus lurches to a sudden start. He stumbles bumps into several people, most of whom give him sympathetic glances and try to stabilize him. All except one.

"Hey, man, what the fuck!" The bearded man with his headphones on sonic mode speaks too loud as the old man stumbles onto his foot. The old man's apology goes unheard, his voice unable to penetrate the music, which he supposed was the point. How convenient. The bearded man must have at least seen the man's lips move, because he gave an indignant huff and a masterful eye roll in response. He slid the massive earphones down around his neck and opened his mouth to retort, but was interrupted.

"He didn't mean it—can't you see he's old and it was an accident?" The young man in the blue hooded sweatshirt comes to the old man's aid, offering a hand under his elbow for support and his real estate next to both a pole and a seat back to hold on to.

"Whatever, man, mind your own business! He stomped on my foot!" He shakes his black steel-toed boot to emphasize the point.

"I'm just trying to help him so he doesn't fall on anyone else." The young man isn't looking at the bearded guy, but instead tries to focus on steadying the old man as the bus picks up speed.

"Well what a fucking hero. Can't imagine what you'll do for him next." He rubbed his tongue against the inside of his cheek. The bearded man sees a few smirks on other passengers, which is just the fuel he needs, even though he misinterpreted their uncomfortable reaction as approval. "Hey, I could use your help, too—getting out of my way." He shoves the young man hard, sending him back into the old man, who becomes pinned against the pole. Alarmed, the young man's instincts tell him to raise his fists in front of his face. The driver looks into his rearview mirror at the sounds of commotion; seeing fists, he comes to an abrupt stop.

"Absolutely not! No fighting! Get off before I call the police! I see you in the blue sweatshirt!" The driver shakes under the confrontation—he has no authority to take any action besides stopping the bus and hoping for the best. Every day he prays for a smooth day, one that will get him the money he needs to feed the mouths at home and send back to his parents. Every day he has to kick at least one jerk off his coach, seems to be more and more all the time, he doesn't understand why people can't just ride the bus in peace without bothering anyone.

The young man lowers his hands and realizes the entire bus is staring at him. The young girl snaps a photo with her fuzzy green phone.

The old man pats him on the shoulder in solidarity. Their shared skin color connects them in an understanding that the best thing, but not necessarily the right thing, is for the young man to quietly get off the bus.

The crowd parts for him as he makes his way to the back door, not entirely sure what just happened. However, even in that moment, the young man knows this is going onto his list of things he's seen, one of many things that will make up everything.

The bus pulls away, and the young man finds himself stranded on the street, miles from where he needs to be and on the edge of anywhere he wants to be. He isn't too sure of where he is, exactly—close to downtown but not in a good neighborhood and so doesn't want to be here for long, nor does he want to risk walking even though the day is bright and warm, the first sunny day after a stretch of rain. The air is fresh, what he can smell of it, anyway, over the soapy sidewalks cleaned daily to hide the traces of human deposited overnight. He can't afford a taxi, and besides can't imagine that one would stop for him especially in this neighborhood, so he looks in the direction his bus had been heading. The bus is stopped a block down, and he sees the old man with the cane get off and look down the street in his direction. Is he seeing things, or did he salute him? Maybe he was just pulling his hat down. He waits a minute, long enough for the old man to cross the street, before making his way to the shelter, where he knows he'll be able to check when the next bus is coming and get his wits about him.

As he approaches the shelter, he sees a jean-clad ankle. He peeks around the large advertisement for the local community college serving as one of the three walls, and sees what he deduces is a homeless man taken up temporary residence in the structure. He is propped up at an awkward angle, leaning against the corner with one leg stretched in front of him across all four seats, the other on the ground next to a large garbage bag nearly bursting at the seams. His eyes are closed and mouth wide open, the only sign of life a snort upon realizing he is no longer alone. His stench is particularly pungent on this unseasonably warm day.

The man peeks out of one eye long enough to realize the young man isn't a city official sent to force him to move. He readjusts his position slightly, crossing his arms in front of his chest, muttering, "Bus just went by. You missed it." Followed by some muttering the young man couldn't understand.

The next bus prediction is blinking an error message. "Thanks, man. Guess I'll be joining you for a bit." Instead of trying to sit, he leans one shoulder against the opposite wall. The man grunts, his eye already closed.

The young man digs out his phone from his pocket, verifying what he already knew: his battery died overnight. He had in fact spent three awkward minutes silently digging around the cramped apartment that wasn't his, in the corner where there had been a lineup of cords extruding from a power strip, hoping to identify a charger. He had—it was the wrong kind. Too embarrassed to wake her from where she had filled in the space he had left when he rose, belly down splayed across her bed, he sat for a moment in the sliver of purple sheet she hadn't covered with a limb or her beautiful mountain of hair. In that moment, he had to leave. He would have been prepared to stay another hour while his phone charged, maybe investigate the possibility of them still liking each other in the morning; now, he could think of nothing worse. With the stealth of experience, he dressed and slipped out of the apartment, leaving nothing but a faint whisper of the smell of his body and a sad kiss he had blown by way of farewell.

In the shelter, he closes his eyes, it had only been an hour since he had left her apartment and already he can feel the heat of the shame of it rise up his cheeks and down his legs, culminating in a punch to the gut. It's not the evening he's ashamed of, he has had enough such evenings to be numb to them. Rather, it's the image of skulking around for a charger, afraid to wake this person he didn't even know, seeing himself from above as a complete mess. It's the image of him leaving her and wandering around her neighborhood in concentric circles until he found a bus stop, putting his hood up despite the temperature to ensure he wouldn't be seen in an awkward confrontation had she decided to arise and look for him. This is a new feeling, this morning shame, and it is making the young man restless and confused. He chalks it up to getting old, and then quickly changes his mind and decides he must be coming down with something. He's in a new city, after all, away from the skeletons of his past, why should he be ashamed at having a good time last night? His indigestion is three parts hangover, one part unconscious awareness that he's no longer having a good time on these nights.

Glancing out of the shelter, he sees a newspaper dispenser with last week's free newspaper. He saunters over to grab one, desperate for something to occupy his time. After the incident on the bus, he doesn't feel like trying to talk to anyone, let alone a bum, not that he seems to be that interested anyway. And he doesn't want to stand there and think about last night or this morning. Better to just distract himself with the list of the top twenty restaurants he'd never be able to afford and wonder over its placement in the free mailer.

He heads back to the shelter and sees the man twitching and swatting invisible flies. Periodically, he scratches at a scab on his left forearm. The young man tries to ignore him. He flips between articles lamenting the rising cost of living and gentrification peppered with advertisements for marijuana dispensaries and gay night clubs. Minutes pass, and soon the young man can no longer ignore the suffering in front of him. He sighs. "Hey, man, are you okay?"

The man looks everywhere but at his face. "Whaddya mean? Are you saying there must be something wrong with me?"

"No I... just... do you have anywhere do go? Do you need anything" He stammers, realizing he no longer has the words to indicate that he wants to help because he realizes he doesn't have what the man needs. He has no money, no phone—not that he knows who to call, anyway—and only the vague knowledge of someone who's only lived a few months in a place. He absolutely doesn't know how to help this man, and too late he realizes that perhaps ignoring him and not offering anything would be better than offering him platitudes that could only be interpreted as condescending.

"Never mind, forget it."

The man could now focus long enough to stare him straight in the eye, which was enough for the young man to process the red eyes, the dilated pupils, the missing teeth. There is more to his story than being homeless. Without a home but also without sanity, without sobriety, without society. But with a sense of righteousness and indignation, a potent cocktail aged by years of injustice and addiction.

"Forget it, boy? You're a damn kid. Do you think handing me ten bucks is help? That's a damn bandaid." The scratching has increased in intensity, a new trail of blood appearing beneath his fingernails. His lucidity shocks the young man, who has been expecting slurring and nonsense. Apart from an uneven cadence to his words and breathlessness, he is making perfect sense.

"I know... I'm sorry. I didn't mean..."

"No one ever means anything. You just wanna buy your ability to sleep at night, knowing you helped some drugged out bum on the street turn around his life for ten lousy dollars."

All the young man can do is blink. Blink at this man in response to his truth. Blink because he finds himself in a place he's only ever circled around and doesn't know the etiquette or what he's supposed to do next. Blink because now he wishes he could give him ten dollars and simultaneously feels guilty over wanting to buy his way out of this.

His mind flashes to an image of him sitting beside this man, breaking down under the weight of his truth. What if he listened to the man's story, heard his voice, brought him hope?

Instead, he blinks. He blinks because he is scared.

The homeless man, tired of waiting for a response, leans back and recrosses his arms, muttering something to himself about a damn entitled kid.

The young man stands still blinking. A bus arrives. He looks at the driver, then back to the man, before climbing aboard through the open door.

The young man makes his way to the rear of the bus, and sees an open seat next to a window. A large woman wearing sunglasses and a wide-brimmed church hat is sitting in the aisle seat, the folds of her dress (and maybe her body) extending onto the window seat. The young man considers his morning before carefully asking if he can take the seat. With a sigh, the woman doesn't stand but instead adjusts her legs so they extend into the aisle, assuming he had enough room to slip through. With some awkward gymnastics to avoid the people in the row ahead and the woman's lap, the young man manages to slide into the vacant seat. He knows he'll be on the bus for a while, so he puts his hoodie up to lean against the window. He soon finds it too bumpy, so he slides forward and lets his head hang forward down to his chest. He cross his arms and squeezes his eyes shut, wishing the world away. He fidgets again, trying to find a comfortable position in the plastic seat.

"Rough night?"

The young man angles his head in the direction of the woman, surprised to see her turned towards him. His fidgeting has drawn her attention. Her expression was neutral, he couldn't tell if she was angry at his intrusion or amused at his state or maybe both but she doesn't really look friendly even though she doesn't look hostile.

"Something like that, yeah." He thinks he sounds unduly gruff, although it's how he feels. "And this morning hasn't been much better." He finds himself trying to smile, even though he really doesn't owe this stranger a smile and certainly doesn't have much to smile about.

"Well, honey, it's not my place to say, but here you are on a beautiful day, so things can't be all bad."

For the second time that day, the young man finds himself blinking, this time at her brash kindness. Her face still hasn't changed—not the hint of a smile or a frown, but just nothing. It slowly dawns on him: she's blind. This both shocks and comforts him, as if it allows him to be just slightly more than anonymous, able to have the best parts of human connection without the risk of judgement.

"I can't argue with you there," he says, now grinning and shaking his head from side to side.

At the sound of sirens and the flash of lights, the bus slows down to let an ambulance by. A block later, the bus is forced to a complete stop. The road is closed, with emergency vehicles blocking traffic, and no way for the bus to bypass.

"Looks like we're going to be here a while. I'd suggest getting off and walking two blocks south to catch the 31." The garbled message from the intercom causes the entire bus to collectively sigh and murmur their frustration. A slight old man that the young man hasn't noticed appears to help the woman from her seat, guiding her carefully and expertly into the aisle.

"Have a good day," the young man calls after her. But she is swallowed into the crowd and disappears down the stairs.

Standing once more on the street, now close enough to home to continue by foot but far enough away from anything familiar to feel isolated, the young man looks around to get his bearings. He can't help but be curious as to the nature of the accident that is blocking the busy street and caused the bus to stop. It must have just happened, moments before the bus arrived, since the ambulance is just now arriving and early stages of confusion cause horns to blare and drivers to attempt to sneak by in the left-turn lane only to be stopped by a cop. The young man approaches the intersection, where in the midst of the squad of police cars, ambulance, and fire truck (he wonders, why a fire truck when there is no fire), a silver sedan is caught mid-U turn, its tail sticking awkwardly into the intersection. The young man doesn't see another car, sees no damage, but sees a distraught man on his cell phone, hunched over onto the roof of the car, hiding his face and shaking his head. A police officer stands vigil nearby, taking notes on her clipboard and watching the man. The young man proceeds into the cross-street, now the crosswalk in front of the sedan is visible along with the back of the ambulance awaiting the stretcher that is down on the ground and over which a flock of uniformed responders huddle.

The young man stops short. In the street, away from the point of action, a shopping bag. Next to the shopping bag, a fuzzy green phone.

For the first time that day, tears rise into the young man's eyes. His life seems to flash before his eyes, and he is dizzy. He had been part of the seconds gained and lost in her life that had led her to be in that place at that time.

Next to the green phone, in the middle of the street, he suddenly sees the missing phone charger, the newspaper from the bus stop, the blind woman's hat.

He shakes his head, bouncing the image from his brain, and turns toward home.

About the Author:

Erin M. Bank lives, works, runs, and writes in San Francisco, CA. She writes personal essays, short stories, the occasional poem, and is working on her first novel. Her work is about finding her own voice and about characters finding theirs.
She blogs at latentlollygagger.wordpress.com.

OTHER PEOPLE

by Pavel Sokolov

Birds took turns singing. As one paused, another would immediately come in. Each of them spoke its own language, not at all concerned about being understood. Then, suddenly, a sharp screeching noise broke in and concealed the birdsongs. Mom started the coffee grinder in the kitchen. The hazy residue of the night's sleep evaporated. The coffee grinder broke off and bird singing resumed. The window in Julia's bedroom was open. All she could see through it was birch foliage. The trees swayed in the wind. The leaves quivered in panic, flashing their pale underside. Julia flung the blanket aside and stretched. Got up decisively and headed for the bathroom to take a shower.

A brief stop in the hallway. The dim slough of the mirror reflected her sleepy face and messy hair. The bathroom door was wide open, blocking the passage to the kitchen and thus shielding Julia from mom. After the shower, Julia showed up in the kitchen brisk, and undazed.

Conversations with mom were irritating. So, in her presence, Julia would always subdue the superfluous feeling of joy one gets from simply being young.

"Good morning!", she said.

"Is it good?" mom replied in a bitter tone. Her face had no make-up, her hair was wet, and the corners of her mouth were dropping down. A look of condemnation in her eyes.

A burdensome silence ensued. After breakfast, washing her coffee cup in the sink, mom asked:

"How many lessons do you have today?"

"Four."

"What time will you be home?"

"About ten. After the studio."

Mom went to work.

......

Late in the afternoon Julia was having dinner in the buzzing beehive that was Tea Spoon Café. Her meal, befitting the name of the place, was a meager pancake and a cup of tea. The scarcity of it helped stay alert for the acting class later in the evening.

Outside a whirlwind of people picked her up and carried her around Sennaya Square and over to Griboyedov Channel Embankment. Cars were slowly moving single file like ants. Tousled branches of cottonwood trees were hanging over the water of the channel. Leisure boat passengers were looking up at the bustling crowd of pedestrians with subtle disdain.

It was end of May, but the radiant sunlight declared that summer had begun. The street was overflowing with traffic noise and weary hustle of people on the sidewalks. Then there was a shaded dreamy side street, a glass door of a front entrance with a white marble staircase inside. The building seemed to be deserted. Julia went up to the second floor and pushed a tall white door with a brass handle.

The former Port Nightclub was empty and dim. Daylight came in sideways from an adjacent space. Vinyl records, suspended from the high ceiling, were turning slowly in the draught. The scruffy walls, once variegated, were now faded. The bar seemed oddly out of place. Chairs stacked up in the dark auditorium were collecting dust. Walls in the stuffy dressing rooms were covered with old concert posters.

About ten minutes later, the door leading form the stairway was opened again, and, one by one, a whole gang of foreigners trickled in. The space was immediately filled with the ruckus of their voices. They were shaking of their backpacks and bags, exchanging excited remarks, curiously eying Julia on the sly. She remembered that Predanov mentioned Zavolotsky bringing in a group of American students for the summer. A tall blond guy caught her attention. He had a wide friendly smile and was looking straight at her.

"Hello!" he was speaking Russian with an accent. "Is this where Zavolotsky theatre studio is located?"

"Yes, it's here", she replied. "By the way, I speak English guys."

There were exclamations of boisterous joy and relief: "Wow, she is the first person we meet here, and she speaks English! Isn't that amazing?!", "How awesome is that?!"

Everyone introduced themselves. The guy who spoke Russian was Alexander.

"I am Russian. Born in America, but my parents are from Russia," he said.

The Americans were getting acclimated, sharing new experiences with one another and taking in the eerie space of Port Club, which had seen better days.

Gradually, Predanov's students were dribbling in. The class traditionally started with the hardest routine of all – a struggle with one's own sloth. The gears of the soul refused to turn, submerged in tenacious cold oil of vulgar mundane life. Time seeped away in otiose conversations. Predanov – the acting teacher – walked in at about half past six. He was tall and lean, had a sinew neck and a large bold head, a sharp pointed chin, a roman nose and an es-

tranged look in his eyes. Without saying a word, he walked into the large classroom with his bouncy gait. Here he sat at a small props table and fostered young talent.

After a warmup, they showed their observation sketches. Pavel did a fisherman on an embankment fascinated by his float. Igor, wearing a pink fur hat, did a foreign tourist. He walked around slowly with a silly smile, taking a picture a second. Predanov's face would light up like a bulb every time he liked something.

"Let's get our American friends involved. Does any one of you speak Russian?" Predanov asked the newcomers.

"I do," Alexander replied.

"Very well," said Predanov. "Just you?"

"Yes"

"Then you translate," Predanov suddenly looked at Julia.

"Julia, you speak English, correct?" he asked, remembering.

"You could say that," she confirmed.

"Great! So you can translate English to Russian."

"No problem!"

"Here is what we'll be doing: one of you come out here and face the audience. Julia, stand here," he gestured to a spot in front of the group. "Introduce yourself. Just say your name, that's all. Got it?"

"Hi, my name is Julia," Julia said in English. Everyone smiled.

"Hi Julia," someone said.

"You like to hit the ground running, don't you?" Predanov said. "Wait a minute. So, the rest of you, in the audience, look at Julia. She is beautiful, isn't she? Imagine that you are seeing her for the first time. You need to picture her entire personality. Come up with as many details as you can. Where she works or goes to school. What she likes and dislikes. Her hobbies, interest, etc. Don't guess and don't say things you actually know. Use your imagination. Got it? If your imagination doesn't work, you are wasting your time here. Then Julia will sit down and someone else will come up here."

Timid at first, and then getting bolder and bolder, assorted details of Julia's phantom personality emerged: "She plays basketball", "Julia is a photographer", "She likes big transparent umbrellas", "She has a rich husband", "Julia plays the harp", "She is a model".

"Julia is an English teacher," Alexander said.

Julia looked at him. He was looking straight at her again. His eyes were sparkling with laughter. His smile was confident and catching. A smile like that is sure to lift your spirits. Because of this and because Alexader guessed her occupation correctly, she returned a happy and candid smile.

...

After the class, the group decided to go out for drinks. One girl couldn't make it, she had an early flight to Italy the next day. Igor was advising: "You must try the pizza over there!" "Right, and in Russia you have to buy a fur hat," Julia thought.

In a huddle they headed down Morskaya towards Nevsky Prospect. The air was cool. The sun was behind them just above the rooftops. It flooded the right side of the street with thick evening light, blinding the store windows.

When the head of the procession reached Nevsky, they stopped to wait for the others. The group gathered again, but the zeal was gone and the enthusiasm had faded. A few faces betrayed a desire to part ways with the rest of the group.

"We are going for a walk around the city," Alexander said. "You guys are welcome to come with us."

Some people went to the bus stop, others headed down Nevsky for the Metro station.

"Let's go to Palace Square," Julia said, and the group of foreigners headed down Morskaya Street with Julia and Pavel.

The expanse of Palace Square opened up in front of them like a chess board with a giant Queen of the Alexander Column in the middle. The sun was blasting in their faces from the roof of the Admiralty building.

Miniature chess pieces from a travel set were spread around the Queen. They were riding bikes, skateboarding, posing as make-believe kings for pictures with tourists. A pair of miniature horses was harnessed to a vintage carriage.

Half an hour later Julia, Pavel and their new friends were sitting at a table in The Dark Side Café on Konushennaya Street. It was dusk outside, and through the window they could see a pale gray stripe of sky above the buildings across the street. Above them orange lampshades were glowing, muffled in scarves of cigarette smoke.

They were sited in a corner around three tables joined together. Pavel was sitting next to Julia. He was a rather gloomy and quiet guy. Medium height and stocky. His crooked nose swelled into a pockmarked potato. Under thick dark brows, his small eyes were set deep and really close to the nose. The straits of high temples met above the forehead, edging an island covered with reed of stiff hairs.

Alexander was sitting opposite Julia and sharing his story, "My parents immigrated to the United States in nineteen seventy-five. My dad is in artist. He wasn't allowed to work in the Soviet Union. Now some of his works are in the Guggenheim museum."

"I think I've heard something about that," Pavel said.

"Are you an acting student?" Julia asked.

"No. I am studying production design at NYU"

"Is Zavolotsky your teacher?" Pavel asked.

"Yes, Zavolotsky is our scenic design professor."

"How did you like Igor's sketch of the foreigner?" Pavel asked feverishly.

"It was pretty funny," Alexander smiled. "I noticed, you can often tell a foreigner by a silly smile. And in cities as beautiful as St. Petersburg tourist are walking around astounded and taking pictures every step of the way."

"As long as you don't lose any valuables in astonishment," Julia said jokingly.

"Still, he shouldn't have done that sketch in front of you guys," Pavel insisted. "It wasn't nice."

"Actually, Americans do smile more than the Europeans do," Alexander tried to calm him down. "When you exit the arrivals gate at an American airport, there is always this huge smile looking at you from all sides. Russians would call it a 'duty smile', I think. They say, Russians are like coconuts, hard skin on the outside, but soft inside. The Americans are like peaches, soft on the outside with a hard seed inside."

"Natural science 101," Pavel grinned. "I liked how Igor advised Nadya to try Pizza in Italy. It's like coming to Russia to buy a fur hat."

"All right. Stop picking on him," Julia said.

Pavel finished his beer and left.

They sat in the café just a little longer and then decided to go walk around the city some more. They crossed the Konushennaya Square and went along the Moika River.

"Your English is really good. How did you learn to speak it?"

"Our school had a special focus on teaching English. Then I majored in English in university. I've been teaching English for three years now."

"Aha, so I guessed your occupation correctly!" Alexander smiled with joy. "Do you like teaching."

"I liked it at first. We had teachers in the family for several generations. It's like a family tradi-

tion, I guess. But, to be honest, I'm sick of it. It's an honorable profession, but I won't do it all my life. It's a bore! I'm going to be an actress!"

"I see, your intentions are serious," Alexander smiled. "But it's hard. Success is not guaranteed."

"Success is never guaranteed to anyone. But some people achieve it and others give up. Theatre is my passion. I'm so obsessed by it, I think theatre is life. Everything else exists for the benefit of theatre."

"That's brash! What's your plan? Are you going to get a theatre arts degree?"

"I don't know, it's complicated. I might apply to the Theatre Academy. What prompted you to major in production design?"

"My dad for sure. I'm interested in all genres of art. Theatre, music… Theatre especially. I think all people are intrinsically actors."

Julia liked Alexander from the minute they met. At first, she ignored the feeling. This was a routine way to filter out objectionable or frivolous seekers of her benevolence. However, as they talked, she felt the effect of his charm stronger and stronger. Alexander was a tall, handsome guy with genteel looks. He was well mannered and educated and could sustain a conversation on nearly any topic. They found a lot of interests they had in common. He loved Saint Petersburg and was planning to spend his free time in theaters and museums. They exchanged phone numbers. Even though Julia was attracted to Alexander, she tried to remain aloof so as not to betray her emotions.

On Sadovaya Street she looked at her watch. It was past midnight. The Americans were staying in some student hotel on Kazanskaya Street. It didn't make any sense to walk any further with them. Moreover, Julia suddenly remembered that she never let her mother know she'd be returning home late.

"I need to get across the bridges before they are drawn. You can't get lost here. Just keep walking straight until you get to Nevsky. Then you'll be fine," she said.

They waived down a gypsy cab. The driver seemed upset that the foreigners didn't need a ride and Julia was the only passenger. He kept silent the entire way.

She realized that she hadn't called home because of a subconscious apprehension about an unpleasant talk with her mother. She just didn't want to think about it. The stroll and conversation occupied all her thoughts and emotions. But now she was expecting to be drenched in her mother's anger. Suddenly, she felt desperate to break out of the ignominious and venomous atmosphere of her home. Her life had been poisoned by constant fear of yet another altercation.

Alexander's life was clearly very different – dazzling and full of marvelous stories and enviable friendships. He was breathing a different kind of air. The fugacious touch of his strange life invigorated Julia. It suggested the possibility to escape the suffocating care and reproach of her mother.

When Julia came home, she found the apartment quiet and all the lights turned off. She realized that the discharge of her mother's exasperation had been postponed and would probably be attenuated by the delay. However, in the morning, her mother hardly said a word and sat at breakfast with a resentful look on her face. Julia also tried to keep conversation to a minimum. Her late return of the previous night was never mentioned.

...

Two days went by in ordinary routine chores and concerns. Then Alexander called her. He wanted to go see *Long Day's Journey into Night* at the Maly Drama Theatre and asked if she wanted to come along. Of course, she did.

After the show, Julia left the theatre feeling that life was an easy slant of deep steps, and she had just climbed one step higher. The show was riveting. Alexander raved about it: "The

scene design is very authentic! I always notice this stuff. This means they really did a lot of research." Julia laughed: "I saw an American film version of 'Crime and Punishment' recently. There must have been a thousand samovars on the set of that film for authenticity."

"The characters are really believable," Alexander continued. "It must be the 'psychological realism' tradition that continues since the time of Stanislavsky."

"The show was outstanding!" Julia agreed. "As far as tradition goes, I think Dodin is much better at staging modern plays. He has no luck with Chekhov, for example. Most actors don't know what to do with a pause. They just stare into the distance and look sentimental. I guess life has become a lot faster, than it was a hundred years ago."

"Well, O'Neal is not a modern playwright," Alexander said. "He is just a little younger than Chekhov. Contemporary to the Futurists. Coincidentally, he was also at war with the public taste and started a revolution in the theatre. Made ordinary man his protagonist."

"This play is autobiographical, right?"

"Yes. His childhood was not fun. He was never able to have a normal family life as an adult either. He was married three times. Both his sons committed suicide. He renounced his daughter after she married Charlie Chaplin. My father actually knew her personally when she lived in New York after Chaplin's death."

"Wow! That's really interesting! Have you met her?"

"Yes, I have. But I was too young to remember it."

The quiet Rubinshteina Street with its bright glowing restaurant signs led them to the ever streaming and seething Nevsky Prospekt. They walked down Nevsky to Dumskaya Street. It was reeking and ringing with anticipation of the night's bash. A melody, dreary as the smell of a drunk's breath, emanated from a bar. "Oh, what a woman..., what a woman," a hoarse, low-pitched voice was drawling. Next to the bar a topless, scrawny man with his hands resting high on a solid, wooden gate was leaning forward and vomiting. The song in the next bar was perky: "Woman, I don't want to dance. I don't want to dance!" Across the street, under a neon sign reading 'Feather Row', was a crowd of glamorously dressed young people wishing to squeeze into a night club. A little further – under frayed, yellow arches – the smug, sassy, decadent aesthetes of The Dacha Café were drinking beer and smoking. Alexander and Julia turned into Lomonosova Street and went into Hell's Bells. The place was smoky and loud. All the seats at the bar and most of the tables were taken. They stayed here a little bit. Julia didn't want to come home late, and said she had to make the last train. Shortly before midnight Alexander walked her to Gostiny Dvor station and then went to The Dacha.

Two moonfaced bouncers were at the door. The place was packed. Alexander had to make his way to the bar through a dense mass of elbows, shoulders and backs. He would say: "Excuse me." Faces turned to him – joyous, indifferent, intrigued or haughty. Every once in a while, he met people moving in the opposite direction, holding in their hands plastic cups of beer full to the brim, not spilling a drop. He mostly heard English with various accents. The crowd got thicker in front of the bar. Alexander found a gap and first put his hand on the bar, then moved in sideways and turned to make some room for himself with his shoulders. The barman noticed him and gave an affable smile.

Alexander took a sip of cold beer and looked around. There wasn't any reason to move away from the bar. He chatted with the bar man. With his background it was simple to start a conversation with virtually anyone. When asked about his accent, he had a ready answer: "I was born in America, but my parents are from here." This guaranteed some interest and curiosity.

The tall, blaring bully that was leaning on Alexander from the right soon disappeared. His seat was now taken by a smiling, dark-haired young girl. She was a few inches shorter than Alexander. The luring, bare skin of her knees and thighs glared down below. The girl was engaged in a lively conversation with a friend sitting to the right of her, though she was palpably aware of Alexander's presence. A few times, as if by accident, her elbow brushed against his arm. A few minutes later she turned to him.

"Could you throw something at the barman? He is pretending not to notice us," she said.

A conversation between them sparked up instantly – his background was of service again. The girl's name was Marina. She told Alexander about her studies at the Culture Institute, where she was the class elder, and about donating blood and using the money to party.

They sat at the bar drinking beer for a while. Marina's girlfriend was visible somewhere on the periphery of his perception at first and soon disappeared. They moved into the adjacent room and tried playing foosball. The balls flew in all directions, except where they wanted them to go. The game caused more laughs than excitement and they soon grew bored with it. Then they made friends with a fun group of three British guys, one Russian guy and four Russian girls. They left The Dacha tipsy and high-spirited when the sky was a clear light blue and the air was filled with scents of early morning – a mixture of hackberry and the vapors of beer spilt on the sidewalks.

They stopped a gypsy cab and got in the back seat. In the cab Marina started unbuckling his belt and unzipping his fly. That felt adventurous, as if it bonded them in a mischievous and naughty conspiracy. The unwitting driver was making politically incorrect jokes with a silly smile on his face.

Marina lived close by – near The New Holland Island. The tall bay windows of her room faced the Moyka River. Wildly overgrown shrubs flooded with the early morning sunlight and hanging low over the water concealed the gloomy brick loaf of the former prison. The furnishing of the room consisted exclusively of a mattress laid directly on the floor, stacks of books along the wall and a pink CD player.

Alexander had vague recollections of acrobatics in bed as well as a conversation about BDSM and about a mysterious boyfriend who should be coming to town in a couple of days. Then a dark silent void. He woke up in early afternoon and looked around the room, bewildered for a few seconds. Then remembered where he was. A painless hangover seemed appropriate for the peculiar circumstances he was in. He was alone in the room. There was blissful hollowness in his soul and a sensation of unusual freedom in his numb limbs, as if he'd shed a heavy shell. He took a deep breath of city air streaming into an open window, put on his rumpled clothes reeking of cigarette smoke, and went looking for the bathroom.

He rubbed his face with ice cold water until it felt as if lots of tiny needles were pinching his cheekbones. The procedure made him feel invigorated. The communal apartment seemed oddly deserted. Quiet voices reverberated through its empty spaces. The ceilings were so high, they were hardly visible. Alexander entered the kitchen and found Marina and her girlfriend he saw in the bar yesterday. The kitchen was the size of a school gym. The walls were painted green up to about two meters, and then continued as dirty white to indefinite height. Gas stoves were lined up along one wall with pipes thrown up in a synchronous salutation. The two girls turned out to be roommates. They were sitting on the window sill, smoking cigarettes and discussing their mutual friends. Alexander bumped a cigarette from them.

A jet stream of smoke came out of his mouth, swirled and clouded the dusty rays of sun light, then floated up and disappeared. Soon the conversation of two strangers, which Alexander had nothing to add to bored him and he left. He came out of the building to the Moyka River Embankment and headed towards St. Isaak Cathedral.

...

The latest rift between Julia and her mother started about a year ago. Mom believed that Julia should continue her education and get a graduate degree. Everyone on the mother's side of the family was a teacher, and Julia was supposed to continue the tradition. After about a year of teaching at a school Julia realized that teaching could only be a temporary occupation for her and would be followed by brighter and greater things. What specifically they would be was not quite clear, but a graduate degree was definitely not one of them.

After joining the theatre studio Julia became obsessed with theatre. She thought about applying to the Theatre Academy and realized that another degree would need to be paid for. She didn't know how to come up with the money for school. Meanwhile, her theatre 'hobby' seemed dangerous and was a source of constant irritation to her mother. Now, on top of that, Julia often stayed out late.

They were going out with Alexander. Scrutinizing paintings by Filonov in The Russian Museum. Sunbathing on the lawns of The Mars Field. Drinking grappa at the sidewalk café on Italianskaya Street. Strolling through the deserted parks of Oranienbaum. Walking on the cottonwood fuzz covered sidewalks of Petrogradskaya. They watched a magical production of *Exit the King*. Got drunk and deafened by music in Achtung Baby with Alexander's friends. Once, at four in the morning, they were walking through Dvortsovaya Square. A drizzle started and stopped and started again. There wasn't a single other person in the square, and, hiding in the arch of the General Staff building, an unseen musician was playing a trumpet. They took shelter from the rain on the covered porch of The New Hermitage, by the feet of the Atlantes entwined with the swollen blood vessels. Then they stopped a gypsy cab and a half hour later were in Julia's apartment. Mom was spending the weekend at the summer house.

The next day they woke up late. The sun was

high and hot, melting the dark green birch leaves. There was no wind. Along with the summer air, noise of the sprightly Sunday bustle was coming into the room. Kids were screaming with joy. Cars were zipping by in the street. A traffic cop sounded his air horn and yelled something in his megaphone. Suddenly the lock on the apartment door snapped. The door opened, and somebody came in. Alexander looked at Julia as his eyes grew larger with amazement. A mischievous smile lit up on his face.

"Game over. Mom is back," Julia said. "That's a bummer. Mom knows how to mess things up."

"What do we do?" Alexander asked.

"Get dressed, obviously," Julia smiled. "Let's go in the kitchen and have breakfast."

At breakfast they felt a bit constrained. They spoke in soft, quiet voices. Mom peeked into the kitchen for second, muttered a cold 'Hello', and disappeared into her room. Alexander's mood turned sour. He quickly finished his breakfast and left, pleading some urgent chores he had to run. Julia locked the door behind him and returned to the kitchen to finish her coffee. A Sunday that could have been hot, leisurely and imbued with sea air, was shot down just as it was taking off, faded and became steeped in the bleak tranquility of the apartment.

A few minutes later mom came into the kitchen looking like a cat returning to its favorite spot after an intruder had left. Without uttering a word and not looking at Julia, she made herself a cup of tea and got some cookies out of a cupboard. She wiped some breadcrumbs off the table, sat in her seat by the window with a grimace of annoyed reproof. Still not looking at Julia, she asked:

"How are your graduate school applications coming along?"

"They are not."

Julia felt there was a storm coming, but she was unable to get up and walk away. It was as if avoiding the fight today she would only postpone it. Mom's regular fits of exasperation were a source of constant fear, always present in Julia's mind, usually hibernating, and rising at first signs of another altercation. The fear felt like a lump in her throat and something sour on her tongue. She could only make it go away by accepting the challenge. She had to stand tall and face the surge of her mother's rage, and stump it out and chase it away.

"Do you plan to apply?"

"No, I do not!"

"You have no heart! I worry about you every day. Do you plan to be a bum for the rest of your life?! You are running around giving lessons. Is that a job?!"

"Mom, what do you mean 'be a bum'?! I am doing theatre. You know that!"

"I see what you are doing! What's this theatre studio good for? Finding a sugar daddy? You need to stand firm on your feet, do you understand?"

"For god's sake, mom! What are you talking about? Have some decency!"

"You need to have some decency! If you are looking to get married, guess what, he'll play you and dump you. Mark my word!"

"You should be the one to know! Dad left you because you were a bitch. I won't live with you for much longer, don't worry. You mark my word!"

...

A couple weeks later Julia and Pavel were at their friend Lena's birthday party. The three of them had been classmates at school. Lena lived with her parents in a new apartment building on Parnas. Mom and dad have magnanimously relocated to their summer house for a few days.

The party was winding down. Some guests have already left. Some were sleeping on the couch in the living room. Julia, Pavel and Lena were in the kitchen finishing off the wine.

"Lena, we haven't talked since forever," Pavel said. "Where are you working these days?"

"In a glossy magazine," Lena said.

"What magazine?"

"Well… A glossy one."

"That's money!" Pavel said. "When was the last time we saw each other? We should meet more often."

"By the way, Lena is getting married," Julia said. "So, we are not going to see her at all."

"Wow! Didn't see that coming!" Pavel said. "So why won't we see you. Are you going to follow your husband to Siberia, like the Decembrist wives?"

"No, nothing like that!"

"He is a DA, or something, right?" Julia said.

"Yep. Works at the Attorney General's office in Moscow."

"That's money!" Pavel said. "Where did you guys meet?"

"In a night club."

"He owns the club too, doesn't he?" Julia asked.

"Yep. Him and his friend."

"He can't own a night club, he is a state official," Pavel said.

"Nothing is impossible if you try hard enough," Julia said smiling.

"Well, I don't think we'll see much of Julia either," Lena said. "She is moving to the States with the American guy."

"You mean Alexander?" Pavel looked surprised. "I had no idea it was that serious."

"Oh, come on! I haven't been invited to the states," Julia said.

"He'll get a visa for you, I am sure," Lena said. "That's where you'll get your theatre degree. That's real money!"

When Julia and Pavel left Lena's party, the subway had been long closed. A rowdy bunch of young people were trying to hail down a ride. Some madcap driver showed up and picked up a few people. Julia and Pavel waited for about ten minutes. No other cars were in site. They walked out to Engelsa Avenue.

An old, beat up Lada with dim headlights came rattling towards them. The driver stopped on the opposite side of the street and rolled down his window. "Where to?" he asked. "First to Grazhdanka," Pavel said, "and then to Vasilievsky Island." The driver rolled up his window and sped away leaving a cloud of stinky smoke. "It's impossible to leave this place," Pavel yelled, looking upward, as if appealing to God for help.

They started walking up Engelsa towards Prosvescheniya Avenue.

"One of my friends lives in America," Pavel said.

"Who is that?"

"My parents' friends Zaslavkys. Their son Sergey. We were friends when we were kids. He came to St. Petersburg and got married recently. I think they met on the internet and went out for a while."

"How did they go out, if he lives in the States?"

"Sometimes they met in France, sometimes in Spain. They travelled all over Europe together. Now they live in New York."

On Prosvescheniya they finally hailed down a gypsy cab.

…

Warm summer days were running out fast like sand in an hour glass. The temperamental St. Pete summer ripened, got covered with giant burdock leaves and was relentlessly dragging the sunset south-west.

Alexanders stay in St. Petersburg was nearing its end. Julia expected to have a conversation with him that would bring clarity to their future relationship. She didn't know how to start the conversation and waited for Alexander to take the initiative.

One day in late July Julia and Alexander agreed to meet by the fountain in front of the Admiralty at six in the afternoon. Her last class got cancelled and she had some free time. She was strolling down Fontanka Embankment past St. Michael's Castle. A crowd of loafing spectators was congregated over the Little Finch statue. A bare-chested man's figure protruded out of the water. The young man, unfazed by the onlookers, would dip in the water, pick up the coins tossed in the river by tourists, and put them in a bag. Lost in thought, Julia walked over the bridge and started crossing the street. She heard an engine revving and looked to the left. Behind the windshield with the sky reflected in it she saw the driver's chubby face, buzz cut, indifferent expression. Before she felt any fright, she leaped forward and painfully sprained her ankle. She threw her arm with the purse awkwardly to the side to keep balance, limped onto the sidewalk and turned around. A large white Mercedes with the traffic police markings sped away. "Jackass!" she thought.

Julia went into the Summer Garden and sat on a bench. For roughly twenty minutes she watched the swans and ducks swimming in the pond and the pigeons soliciting for food scraps by the ice cream cart. The pain receded. Julia got up. Stepping on the sprained foot was almost painless. She started walking down the central alley and then turned right. This part of the garden was practically deserted. She came to the Fontanka bank and walked down the granite steps to the water. Waves, impassive and indifferent to everything, ran over the surface of the water and shattered against the granite. Julia watched them for a while, thinking that, in the exact same way, waves were slapping this embankment ten, twenty, a hundred years ago.

She came out of the Garden onto the Neva embankment, walked to Suvorov Square and crossed over to Millionnaya Street. A petite girl in police uniform was closing the heavy gate of the Marble Palace. Behind the wrought iron fence, in the damp shade of the trees, a stout Alexander III sat on his corpulent horse. Millionnaya street was deserted and calm. The sun roasted the asphalt. On the bridge over the Winter Channel she saw an unusual couple. The man, about fifty years old, conspicuously a foreigner, was standing with his back against the bridge railing. A woman of about thirty-five was standing in front of him. She was saying something to him in a serious tone, then turned and started walking away. Stopped for a second, turned around impetuously, then kept walking away without looking back. The man just stood there, crushed and desolate.

Julia walked into Palace Square. Little figures of people were crossing the square in all possible directions, silent in the muffled hum of the city. Julia crossed the square, dreadfully walked through several lanes of a traffic jam, and entered the Alexander Garden. Benches were arranged in a circle around the fountain. Julia sat on one of them. Blissful, quiet life was rocking gently in the sunlight, like a boat anchored in a cove. The city was buzzing in its eternal commotion outside the garden. Alexander showed up soon. They walked deeper into the park away from tourists and moms with strollers and sat on a bench. A dilapidated replica of Farnese Hercules towered over them.

Alexander looked reserved and contemplative, as if he wanted to have a conversation about something but didn't know how to begin. Suddenly, his voice sounded impassive: "You know, after I leave, we won't be able to stay in touch."

"Why not?" Julia was astounded.

"Well, because... How do I say this... I am engaged."

Alexander looked at her, waiting for her reaction. For a split-second Julia was puzzled. Then she felt a sensation, as if a vein got bloated in her throat. Her lips tightened, and her face froze, concealing resentment. But resentment glared in her eyes. Alexander turned his head and stared at children playing in the distance.

"So, you had a vacation fling," Julia said.

Alexander turned to her again: "I am sorry."

Julia got up and started walking towards Palace Square. Alexander caught up with her.

"Go away," she said.

He stopped and watched her leaving for a second, then turned around and walked in the opposite direction.

...

Julia's first reaction was rather light, as if she hadn't quite realized what had happened at first. On the first day she simply resented having been dumped. That had never happened to her before. All her previous break ups were initiated by her.

Then, a day later, she was overwhelmed by a surge of cold, heavy depression that would recede and roll in again in the following days. Work diverted her, and when she was teaching, she would almost forget that Alexander existed. But as soon as she was left alone with her feelings, dejection would set in again. She was aggravated with herself for making such a mistake, and the heavier her gloom became, the more she scolded herself for having such high expectations. She would curse Alexander and then suddenly hope that he would call and everything would be fine again. Then she hated her own weakness, and Alexander seemed repugnant again. One of her worst emotions during these days was disappointment with people in general. She felt she could never trust anyone now.

Mom was out of town, and Julia was living in the apartment by herself. She had been enjoying this, but now solitude accentuated the dejection that descended on her. She felt conflicting emotions. "I wish mom was here. That would probably make me feel better," she thought at times. Then, suddenly shuddered, remembering that mom would be back in town soon. Somehow, she would feel guilty and embarrassed in front of mom.

On Sunday they were supposed to have their last class with the American students at the theatre studio. That morning Julia felt she wouldn't be able to bring herself to go to the studio. She spent almost the entire day lying on the couch, having nothing to occupy herself with. When darkness fell, she didn't turn the lights on, didn't move at all, just watched the windows in the building opposite the street light up in different colors. The window was opened a crack and she could hear the wind howling outside.

Julia closed her eyes and soon felt as though she was tiny as an ant lying in a corner of a giant empty room. When she opened her eyes, this feeling disappeared, but as soon as she closed them again, it came back. She turned over to lie on her stomach and hid her face in the pillow. Then she felt a sensation as if something heavy was weighing down on her entire body, as if she was covered by a blanket of rock. She could clearly see herself lying on the couch in a big empty and dark apartment. Everything around her seemed dismal. She felt an unbearable fear of the future. Suddenly, she felt there was nothing cheerful ahead. Dreams of the theatre seemed futile. Julia could see no prospects for herself in any other profession. The thought of seeing her mother depressed her.

Julia's throat was dry. She got up and, a little unsteady, walked to the kitchen. In the darkness, she could see a bottle on the counter. It was half empty, with a plastic cap and a greasy yellow label. "What if I drink that?" she thought. She felt a sudden rush of daring excitement. As if someone was taunting her: "You can't do it, can you?" At the same time, Julia felt that with this single act she could solve all her problems. She grabbed the bottle, tore the cap off, and swallowed two gulps of the liquid. Sharp knives slashed the inside of her throat. She felt an impulse to vomit, but the hot lava was already flowing down her throat. She felt short of breath and was gulping for air. Not seeing anything in the darkness she rushed through the hallway and ran out of the apartment. The stairway was dimly lit. In a fit of panic she started ringing the neighbor's doorbell.

The neighbor, an elderly woman named Olga Pavlovna, first opened the door just a crack and peeked out. When she saw Julia, she opened the door wide. Julia tried to say something, but her throat could only produce a croak. "What's wrong Julie?!" Olga Pavlovna let her in.

Stabbing pain pierced her stomach. Her head was spinning. The old lady was saying something, but Julia couldn't hear. She leaned against the wall, then sat down on something soft. She felt nauseous. Then she couldn't see anything. A sort of white noise consumed everything.

About the Author:

Pavel Sokolov was born in Russia and to date lived about half of his life in Russia and half in the United States. This gave him a good understanding of both cultures, and he sees that people in the two countries have more in common than many are willing to admit. As Pavel says, "It seems that people around the world are learning more and more about each other, and there is a great interflow of cultures."

THE BIG MOVE
by Maria Frangakis

After nine years in San Jacinto, without electricity and indoor plumbing, we were finally leaving. We were moving to *la casita hermosa,* the beautiful little house, as we called our future dwelling in nearby Río Hondo, the neighboring "big city." The house had been under construction for eight years, even surviving the great flood of 1958 when the water rose above the windows. After the house was roofed, my father asked the mason he'd hired for the construction to move in with his family to prevent theft of building materials. The understanding between them was that he might have to vacate on short notice when the time came for us to move there ourselves.

I'd heard about this impending move ever since I could remember, but it was one of those magical things that would happen "after the next harvest," although it never seemed to materialize. The harvest hadn't been good that year, either, but we were leaving anyway. For the last couple of days my parents had been talking about it more than usual. I heard them talk about it as I went to bed the night before, and were still talking when I got up. That morning they were not only talking, but were getting our worldly belongings crammed into the back of Papá's truck. He was saying something about possession being three-quarters of the law, adding "If we don't move right away, we'll lose *la casita hermosa* for certain!"

I hated not knowing what was going on, but knew not to bother my parents for an explanation. At seventeen and sixteen, Conchita and David, my older brother and sister, understood perfectly what was going on and seemed to mirror my parents with their talking, giving me ample opportunity to eavesdrop.

"The mason wants to keep the house!" said Conchita. "Someone overheard him bragging in the pub about his plans to finish the house himself since my father didn't seem to be in a hurry to do it anytime soon."

"Apparently," David added, "the mason figured that since the contract for water and electricity was on his name, it would be enough proof that he was the rightful owner. He thinks that a judge might rule in his favor because he's been living there for over five years, and is prepared to fight Papá in court to keep the property."

No wonder we were leaving so suddenly. Papá and David left San Jacinto carrying the great cedar wardrobe, the wrought-iron bed and the cots. David said that the mason and his wife were having breakfast and almost choked on their *chorizo* when they heard Papá announcing that we were moving in. With David's help, Papá began unloading the heavy pieces, placing the wardrobe and the wrought-iron bed in the master bedroom and the cots in the other two rooms. The mason's few belongings were there but Papá didn't seem to mind. As Papá went back to San Jacinto to get the rest of our belongings, David remained in the house to watch over our belongings.

Quickly, Papá filled the truck with the wobbly table and its matching wobbly chairs, two straw hampers, the big tin tub filled with pots and pans, a few buckets and Papá's chair, the one with the owl stenciled on its back. Mamá put every sheet, blanket and quilt we owned on top of the pile so that we could sit safely and comfortably.

At eight, I got to travel on the back of the truck, along with the rest of my siblings except for Mariana, who was only three and had to sit in the front with Mamá. We were so happy not only because of the move, but also because Mamá had packed us lunch for the road, as she always did whenever we were going on long trips. She made us *burritos de frijoles* and hard-boiled eggs just in case we got really hungry in the thirty minutes that it would take us to get to *la casita hermosa* in Río Hondo.

It was the middle of August and Mamá was six months pregnant, almost replicating the previous move to San Jacinto nine years before in July, when she was pregnant with me. Our new house didn't have actual windows or doors yet, just the cutouts on the brick, but it had two bathrooms complete with toilets and spouts where the showerheads would one day be installed. Papá had been right all along: who needed an outhouse when we could have toilets?

Our new house had beautiful tile floors; each room with a different color and pattern that my father had chosen himself without consulting my mother since he was the one traveling to the city on business all the time. I had never seen such extravagance in any other house. But the most amazing thing was that it had running water and electricity. There was one faucet in the kitchen and another one in the patio. Mamá was thrilled that she would no longer have to carry water. We couldn't stop turning the water on and off and flushing the toilets.

Despite the novelty, I knew I was going to miss *el monte*. There was a huge *guamuchil* tree in the property that produced pods, like green beans, but curly, which we called "*roscas.*" They were tasty, but gave us terrible bad breath and the tree couldn't be climbed

like the old mesquites in *tierra de nadie,* back in San Jacinto. Over the brick fence that separated the neighbor's property, hung the branches of a mango tree and a real lemon tree. We could eat the mangoes that fell over our side of the property, but were forbidden from climbing the fence to cut any from the branches over it. As for the real lemons, nobody would ever consider eating that awfully sour citrus and so it remained rotting on the ground. There was also a peach tree, but its fruit was tainted since it grew right next to our very own, albeit condemned, outhouse. Papá had actually built an outhouse on that property for the mason and other workers to use before running water and toilets had been installed. By the time we moved in, it had been treated with large amounts of lime and filled with dirt.

The house was also fitted with one light bulb, which hung low from the ceiling in the dining room. It had a little chain on its side that one pulled to turn the bulb on and off. It was marvelous to think that I'd never again have to clean the glass shades for the oil lamps the way I had to do each afternoon in San Jacinto. In this house I'd just pull that little chain and we'd have light as if by magic.

We took over the house like a swarm of bees. That night, and for the next couple of days, the mason, his wife and their grown son slept on the back porch in their cots. Mamá must have been really happy with the move because for the first time she didn't seem to mind our yelling and screaming—she actually seemed to enjoy it. The mason's wife kept shaking her head and every once in a while, she would cover her ears, making sure we could see her do so. City people were too sensitive, I thought.

After three days, she could bear our screams no longer and the three of them moved back to their own house, a shack on the other side of the canal where the poor people lived.

About the Author:

Maria Valenzuela Frangakis was born in a dusty village along the International Highway in Mexico's Northwest. After earning a B.S degree in chemistry, she attended the University of Arizona's Graduate School, earning her M.S. in Microbiology. She spent twenty-five years as a scientist in academic and pharmaceutical labs. After earning her M.B.A., she went on to found Enarxis Research, a biotech consulting company. Her works have been published in Typehouse Literary Magazine and Adelaide. She currently lives in Chapel Hill, NC.

WHERE THE SPIRALS LEAD

by Jenny Hayes

We were drinking iced coffee and watching a cheesy talk show with some model whose life had gone from fabulous to tragic and back again. I was nested in a nubbly purple loveseat, surprisingly comfortable despite the patches where its fabric was flaking off. Allie sprawled on an orange velvet couch, which made a loose border between the living and dining part of the room, with the tiny kitchen right behind. It was the first time Allie had invited me over, and I liked how cozy the apartment felt with everything together in one space.

The door clicked open. "Alysandra?" a low voice trilled. Her mom walked in, one paper grocery bag nestled in her arm, another starting to shimmy down her hip.

"Give me a hand, would you?" she called out.

"Fine," Allie groaned, jumping off the couch and grabbing one of the bags. "Mom, this is Tasha."

"Hi," I said, hoping it wasn't obvious I'd been staring. She was beautiful—which I suppose shouldn't have been surprising: she was Allie's mom, after all, and they had the same bronze skin, the same piercing eyes, the same thick mane of dark hair, though her mom's was shorter and tinted with a burgundy sheen. Everything about her seemed deliberately curated: green jumpsuit, golden scarf, red lipstick, things that you wouldn't have thought would go together but somehow made a striking effect. She seemed to come from a completely different world than my mom, with her stringy hair and thick mascara and beaded halter tops and old suede jackets. Her slew of awful boyfriends. Her huge drafty house with dirt-cheap rent because she used to party with the landlord back in the day.

"It's nice to meet you, Tasha," Allie's mom said. "I'm Rhonda. Are you staying for dinner?"

"Uh—"

"Yeah, Tash, stay!" Allie chimed in.

I didn't need convincing. Anything Allie's mom was making would be better than the TV dinners I had at home. Even the Salisbury Steak that I'd stashed in the back of the freezer for a special occasion.

Rhonda clattered around in the kitchen. "So, did you do your homework already?"

"Yes, mom," Allie groaned. Neither of us had even opened our backpacks, but I wasn't about to say anything. I'd do mine later, at home. Not that anyone would notice or care.

I can't remember what Rhonda cooked that night, though I'm sure it was something colorful and spicy and delicious. She poured herself a glass of wine and gave us a couple of root beers and we sat around the little wood table, talking and laughing and helping ourselves to more. Before I was halfway home, I was thinking about what to say to make sure I got invited back again. But it turned out I didn't have to do anything.

"That was fun last night," Allie said the next day at lunch. "We should do it again."

"Totally," I said. "Your mom's really cool."

Allie rolled her eyes. "She's kind of a pain," she said. "But I guess she's all right."

#

I guess I'd say Allie and I were best friends already, even though we'd only met six months ago, back at the start of the school year. It seemed goofy when our tenth grade history teacher made everyone sit in alphabetical order, but it turned out that my last name, Keller, fell next to Khatcherian, and the girl with that name had purple boots, and black hair with a blonde streak, and a backpack covered with hand-drawn swirls and lightning bolts and skulls. The next day we pulled out our textbooks and found we'd each made some additions to the regulation paper cover. "That's rad," she said, pointing at my annotation of the Berkeley High School initials: *Take away the High and all you have is B.S.* I was hardly the first person to come up with that, but I accepted the compliment while admiring the shades and devil horns she'd added to George Washington's head. Within a few weeks we discovered we could crack each other up with just a well-timed look, and we had plenty of opportunities as our teacher droned on about treaties or elections or whatever he'd picked to torture us with that day.

After that first night, I went home with Allie after school a couple of times a week. We'd watch TV, do the occasional bit of homework, Rhonda would come home and cook some-thing amazing, and then I'd walk back to my house. On the weekends, Allie usually crashed with me. Rhonda had no objections to Allie staying at my house as often as she liked. We conveniently forgot to mention that we basically had the place to ourselves.

I guess I should explain about my mom. Even when she was home, it would be a stretch to say there was anything resembling parental supervision. She was impulsive, forgetful, incapable of making plans—more like a teenager than I was. And allergic to steady employment, though she always managed to jumble together enough odd jobs to get by: canning preserves and drying herbs on a friend's farm, selling dreamcatchers and feathered roach clips at craft fairs and rock festivals, working for an organic catering company making whole-grain salads and sugarless pies or serving hors d'oeuvres at fancy hippie weddings in the hills.

Her personal life was just as chaotic. She was always getting hung up on one dude or another, only to have him toss her aside, just like my dad apparently had way back when. It was bad enough watching her get all lovestruck when it was so obvious how it would go—I would've started a pool on how soon things would crap out if I had anyone to lay odds with, and I would've made bank—but on top of that they were always the grossest guys you could imagine. Grizzled acid casualties, pathetic drum-circle troubadours, beer-bellied losers who tried to act tough. All of them old enough that you'd figure they'd have more of a life by now. Which I suppose makes sense, considering I could say the same about my mom.

Lately she'd been spending more time away from the house than in it. She made sure I had a little cash and the freezer was full of packaged meals, and I was lucky if I saw her every other week. So when Allie stayed with me, we could do what we wanted. Usually this meant going to parties, where Allie hit the keg or indulged in whatever was being passed around. I usually had one beer and that was it. I liked the taste okay, but I figured someone should stay clear-headed enough to make sure we got home safe, and I never liked how getting drunk made me feel so uncontrolled. Weed didn't have the same destabilizing effect, so sometimes I'd take a few hits. It always gave me a funny nostalgia about parties I got dragged to when I was little. The first time someone handed me a pipe at a dance in eighth grade, I laughed. I'd known that smell forever, but never realized what it was.

Sometimes there were boys we were chasing, or the other way around, though to be honest this was more of Allie's thing too. She flitted from one crush to the next—making out in corners, holding hands at school—and right when I'd think she might start hanging out with the guy more often, wondering where that would leave me, they'd have some blow-up and she'd move on to the next one without even taking time to mope. She talked a lot about what it might be like when she finally did it with one of them, wanting it to be someone worthwhile but also anxious to get it over with. I wasn't in a hurry for that at all. I'd had a few gropes and kisses, but nothing that had gone far. It seemed like the guys who liked me were never the same ones that I liked back. I figured sooner or later someone good would come along—someone who was cute, and nice, and fun to spend time with, and took me seriously—though since I hadn't met any guys like that yet, the thought had crossed my mind that this might be an unrealistic fantasy, and maybe I'd have to take what I could get. But if that was the case, I decided I'd pass for now. If I'd learned anything from my mom, it was that there was no shortage of questionable guys out there ready to cruise into your life.

At the end of the night, or the beginning of the morning, we'd come back to my house and crash. We slept in a new place whenever we felt like it, working through every comfortable spot in the house: the mattress on the creaky floor in my attic bedroom, the lumpy couch downstairs, the musty futon in an otherwise empty room I'd practically forgotten was there, and occasionally my mom's king-size, under the red batik bedspread, with the window open and a light breeze drifting in. I liked having Allie in the house with me, and I tried to avoid thinking about what it would be like at the end of June when she left for New York to spend the summer with her dad.

Once in a while, if there were no parties to go to, we'd spend a Saturday night at Allie's. I always tried to wake up early to drink coffee and read the Sunday Chronicle with Rhonda while Allie slept in. We'd read interesting bits aloud to each other, or debate which movies might be worth seeing, or laugh over a cartoon. And then before I knew it I'd be telling her about how I wanted to go to college on the East Coast, and that I sort of wanted to major in English but I wasn't sure it was practical enough, and how one day I hoped to travel around the world. Or maybe I'd just talk about the new lipstick I wanted to get, or bitch about some teacher. It didn't matter what we talked about. It just felt good to have her listen.

Other times we'd hardly talk at all, and I liked that too. Just sitting there, close to her, reading the paper or staring at the painting by the door, the big blue one with a forest of white swirls. Allie's father had painted it. She said it was the only one her mom had wanted to keep after the divorce. There were a couple of his other paintings in Allie's room, but I liked the blue one best. I'd follow the swooping lines of all the circles and spirals, tracing their paths, trying to map out every shape and structure. No matter how hard I concentrated, I always reached a point where I couldn't keep track of which one went where, and I'd have to start over. I knew I'd never be able to finish, but I never got tired of trying.

#

One Sunday, Allie and I woke up at my house around noon. It was hot out, even though it was only May, and we decided to go swimming up at Strawberry Canyon. We walked over to Allie's house to get her bathing suit, and as we approached we heard laughter out the window. Not just Rhonda, but a man's laugh too.

"Who's that?" I asked.

Allie's eyes narrowed. "I have no idea." She unlocked the door, jangling her keys a little louder than necessary. Rhonda was sprawled across the couch in a luxurious pink silk robe. Sitting at the other end, rubbing her feet, was the guy: kind of chubby, with curly dark hair and a weird beard that sort of disappeared into the hair on his neck and chest. Which was bare. The way he was sitting I wasn't sure what he had on for bottoms, but at least I could tell there was something there.

Rhonda smiled at us. "Hi, Alysandra," she purred. "Hi, Tash. This is Keith." He gave us an odd little mock salute.

"I just came to get my swimsuit," Allie said. She ran into her room, leaving a silence that clogged the air. I was still trying to think of something to say when she rushed back in. "Okay. Bye." She bolted out the door, and I followed quickly.

Halfway down the block she hissed into my ear. "Did you see that guy? He was *gross*." She shook her head. "I can't believe it. My mom has a guy over for the first time in ages, and it's some creep like that!"

"Yeah, he was kinda weird," I said. "But you never know. He could be nice."

"No way," Allie said. "I got a terrible vibe off him."

I didn't press it. He did seem a little strange. But I figured if Rhonda liked him, he was probably okay.

#

A couple of weeks later, I was startled awake at three a.m. by a knock on the door.

Probably just my mom forgetting her key again, I told myself, though I was a little nervous as I tiptoed downstairs. I peeked through the crack in the curtain and saw Allie on the porch. As soon as I opened the door, she pushed past me into the room.

"Jeez, you scared me!" I said. "What's going on?"

Her eyes jumped around the room. "Keith came over and spent the night," Allie said.

"Really?" I'd been at her house for dinner. Rhonda had made Indian chickpea stew and green salad. When I left it seemed like the two of them were settling in.

"Yeah. He showed up around ten. And I could hear them giggling in my mom's room for like, hours."

"Gross," I said. I almost laughed, but I could tell Allie was really upset. "Well, I guess you just have to deal with it, right? I mean, your mom's seeing him, and—"

"Tash," she said. "That's not all. I woke up in the middle of the night to go pee. I forgot he was over so I left the door open." She shuddered. "And when I looked up, he was there."

"Where?"

"In the doorway. Watching me."

"What? Are you sure?"

"Of course I'm sure! He was *staring*."

"Ew!" I sort of couldn't believe it. He did look kind of creepy, but I didn't think he was *really* creepy. "What did you do?"

"I left, obviously!" She shook her head. "He didn't even say anything. Fucking perverted asshole!"

"Yeah," I said, rubbing my eyes, feeling sleep wanting back in now that my panic had subsided. "Well, let's go to sleep. C'mon."

Allie kept staring across the room. "I'm just gonna stay down here," she said. I shrugged and went back upstairs to my room.

#

Allie's voice woke me the next morning. When I heard her slam the phone down, I wrapped a blanket around myself and walked downstairs. She was on the couch, staring at the floor with her arms wrapped around her knees.

"What's going on?" I asked.

"She doesn't even believe me," Allie said. She grabbed a pillow and clutched it to her chest, then launched it across the room, barely missing one of my mom's macramé hanging planters. "I'm so sick of her!"

"I'm sorry, Allie," I said. "That really sucks."

She shook her head. "That guy's a pig. I knew it the second I met him."

I wanted to believe her. But it seemed possible that it could have been an accident. Maybe he'd been getting up to use the bathroom and just had terrible timing. And it didn't seem like Rhonda would take his side over Allie's, unless she knew he was telling the truth. But how could she know?

I didn't say any of that to Allie. I knew she didn't want to think about any alternate explanations. Instead, I told her she could always stay at my house more often, if she felt like she needed to get away.

So for the last few weeks of the school year, Allie basically lived with me. She'd go home every now and then to get a change of clothes, but she slept at my house every night. Sometimes I heard her arguing with her mom on the phone. I kept hoping they'd work it out, and every so often I tried to ask how things were going. But she never wanted to talk about it.

And then it was July, and I was alone again. Allie was in New York with her dad, probably doing all kinds of fun big-city things. My mom was visiting some friends out in the sticks. It had stretched from a long weekend into the

rest of the week, and then the next, and who knew how much longer. I didn't really count on seeing her anytime soon.

I found myself walking past Allie's house, wishing I had an excuse to knock on the door and see Rhonda. On Sunday mornings I would buy the Chronicle so I could read the same stories as her. I wondered if she was still seeing Keith. And whether he really was a perv or if he just got up at the worst possible moment that night.

Some days I'd walk a few blocks over to Willard Park, where there were usually people hanging around that I knew, at least a little. One hot afternoon it was just me and Gina, a girl who lived nearby and went to the alternative school and always had weed she'd snagged from her dad's sock drawer. She lit up a joint, and I didn't really feel anything, but she kept giggling like crazy. Gina decided we needed to get some snacks, and I said sure. I was a little hungry, even if it wasn't the full on munchies she was making it out to be.

We walked to Andronico's and headed for the chips and crackers. Gina started trying to show me how it said SEX on the Ritz Cracker box if you stared at the right spot. I held the box up, looking for the secret writing, but all I saw was crackers. Then I looked down the aisle.

I spotted Keith first. He looked straight at me, though it didn't seem like he remembered who I was. Then I heard Rhonda's voice, coming closer, talking about some kind of cheese she wanted to buy. I froze, still holding the Ritz box in the air. All summer I'd been hoping to run into her, but I didn't expect such a physical punch when I did. I felt it burrowing up my chest, bursting into my throat.

Gina was oblivious, languidly trailing her fingers across a row of Saltines.

Rhonda stepped into the aisle, still chattering at Keith. Then she glanced over and caught my eye. I grinned and stepped forward. Her face moved, but it wasn't the smile I expected.

She put her hand on Keith's shoulder and moved away. As if she hadn't just been about to walk in my direction.

I threw the Ritz box into my tote bag and dragged Gina out of the store. She thought I was bad-ass for stealing the crackers, but she didn't realize I just needed to get out of there. I handed her the box and told her I wasn't feeling good. I needed to go home.

#

Sitting on the porch steps, I replayed the grocery store scene in my mind. I figured Rhonda probably resented me for giving Allie a place to run away to, and I could understand that a little. It was sinking in that things would never be like before, even if the two of them made up. I didn't matter to Rhonda, not the way I'd thought, not the way she'd mattered to me. All the magic of her spicy noodles and her silky robes and her beat-up beautiful couches might as well be on some other planet from me now.

I sat there for a long time. The sun was getting low and I told myself maybe I'd stay on the porch all night. But eventually I had to pee, so I unlocked the door and went into the bathroom. I washed my hands, splashed water on my face, and looked in the mirror. I thought maybe I'd look different, feeling so distraught. But it was my same familiar face. Brown hair, thin lips, six freckles across my nose. Just a regular boring girl.

I went into the kitchen and got a glass of water, then realized I was pretty hungry. I opened the freezer, trying to remember if I still had push-up pops in there, but it was just musty ice trays and the pile of TV dinners. My hand reached into the crevice in the back, past the Fried Chicken and the Beans n' Franks and the dreaded Veal Parmagiana, until I found it. Salisbury Steak. I knew it was basically just meatloaf, but there was always something I loved about that little oval patty with the name that

sounded royal. It was just about all I had left that had ever felt special.

I turned on the oven and tore open the cardboard box. The aluminum tray felt cold and heavy as I slid it onto the rack. I listened to the oven pop and click while I sat on the floor, looking at the empty package. I didn't really believe Gina about the words on the Ritz Crackers, but I thought if I stared really hard, like it was one of those Magic Eye puzzles, I might see a message. Some secret wisdom hidden in the gravied meat, potatoes, peas, and cobbler. It didn't seem like all that much to ask.

My concentration broke when someone knocked on the door. I got up and saw a guy in a faded tie-dye t-shirt with a hole near the neck. He had dark eyes, thick stubble, and scraggly black hair streaked with gray. At first I didn't recognize him, but then I had a vague memory that he was one of my mom's flings from a long time ago. One of the decent ones, I was pretty sure. I opened the door.

"Hey ..." he said, sizing me up. Then he pointed his finger. "Tasha, right?"

"Right," I said.

"Man, you're all grown up now!" I didn't say anything, and he gave me a pouty face. "You don't remember me?"

"Kind of," I said. I thought maybe I remembered all of us being on a boat together, but I wasn't sure. I didn't want to say anything in case that was somebody else.

"I guess that was a long time ago. You were like this big." His hand bounced around the general height of my torso. "Me and your mom had some good times," he said. "I'm Alvo."

I recognized the name. It was one of many lodged into my brain. All jumbled up together, like a drawer full of keys you didn't think you'd ever need again but hadn't ever bothered to throw out.

"Well, she's not here," I said. "She's out of town for a while."

"Damn," he said. "I was just passing through. Been a while since I've seen her and I thought I'd say hello." He reached up and wiped some sweat off his face. "Man, it's hot out here. You mind if I come in and have something to drink?"

I nodded and stepped out of his way. "Do you want a glass of water?" I asked. "Or I think we might still have some orange juice."

"Brought my own," he said, giving me a wink. He sat down on the couch and pulled a six-pack of Olympia beer out of his backpack. "You want one? I mean, I know you can't be twenty-one yet, but I won't tell." Like there's anyone to tell, I thought. Like she'd even care. I sat next to him and popped open a can.

"So what's your mom up to these days? The last time I seen her ..." I half-listened while he told the story, some festival where they'd crossed paths and rekindled old times in some manner. I didn't really want to know the details. The beer tasted sweet and cool and it felt good to talk to someone who knew my mom, even if it was just for a month here and a week there, whatever it had been, all those years ago. I traced little spirals with my finger in the drops that frosted the can, and then it was empty and he gave me another one, and I listened to him talk some more, and then I traced new spirally shapes on the can I had after that, and then my finger was tracing shapes on Alvo. And then there was no more beer but it didn't matter, I didn't need one, I didn't need anything, or so I wanted to think, not even the Salisbury Steak that I smelled burning as I slipped my shirt over my head. The next day I would reach into the oven for the blackened tray, the meat charred into a lump of coal, my thighs and chest so scratched from stubble that it would take all summer for the little pinprick scabs to fade away.

About the Author:

Jenny Hayes grew up in Berkeley, California, and now lives in Seattle. She is a graduate of the low-residency MFA program at U.C. Riverside - Palm Desert, and her writing has appeared in Geometry, Litro NY, Jenny Magazine, and elsewhere.

End

FATHER OF AL LIES

by Jenny Butler

Deep within dark premonitory dreams, the White Canon is juddering in his sleep. In his dream, the headstone looms large, its name defaced, chiselled and chipped away. He had helped pour the concrete over that grave, as if the one in it was a vampire about to rise up and suck the blood of the nearest sleeping innocent. The people knew he would do, and has done, much worse than that if he were to rise again, like a stinking, loathsome Lazarus. They poured concrete so nobody could desecrate the grave or dig up the body, defile the defiler.

Maggie held her baby close as she neared the church wall. The steeple was intimidating, oppressive, to her. "Just keep the wee child safe", she thinks, heart racing. She is holding the baby close, her baby, keeping her safe. The child cries and she realises she has been holding the baby too tight. Beyond St Matthews, she breathes a sigh of relief as she approaches the door of her sister's house. She will never set foot in that church, or any church, never give one of them an opportunity to lay a finger on a sweet angel like her Róisín, tiny rose that she is. She regretted parking the car so far from the street. She wouldn't have had to pass the church on foot if she had driven in but she could never be sure if there would be space on the street.

East Belfast looked grey and dreary as it always had. She wondered how her sister could bear to live here still. She walked past the O' Donnell's house and smiled to herself as she saw the same ornament in the window as was

there twenty years back. Mrs O'Donnell used to go crazy when the dog, a wee snappy thing, would get excited and jump up on the window, knocking it over. Old Mr O' Donnell, their grandfather, had been murdered by loyalist paramilitaries, "Orangies" they used to call them as kids. She hadn't been back in Short Strand for sixteen years, an enclave stranded indeed like a stretch of Catholic beach in a sea of Unionist hatred. The troubles have died down but the tensions were still here, she could feel it in the air.

Her sister Mary's son Ruairi would mind the kids as the two went out to the pub, "only for a few, mind", her sister said, "so we won't be long". They decided to walk to the pub as it was close by and her sister linked arms as they walked along. Maggie had missed this. The way to the pub was down the lower Newtownards road and then Mountpottinger Road. Throughout the Troubles there was a Royal Ulster Constabulary base in Short Strand, heavily fortified due to IRA bomb attacks. It was gone now, demolished in February 2011, and Maggie was glad to see the back of those bastards! She remembered reporting the abuse, blurting out what that monster did to her. She was fifteen and frightened, not just of the RUC station ominous and imposing before her, but petrified of not being believed, of how she would tell a stranger – what if the words didn't come out when she tried to speak? What if they laughed at her? Her father had warned her not to go to the police but she plucked up the courage to go in the double doors, the inside one she had to press against to open when the buzzer went. The Policeman sneeringly said, "Hey sarge - we've got a fuckin bead mumbler here sayin' she's been molested by a *priest*! A raping papist!" The sergeant laughs, "a wee popeblower now is it? Go home and say your prayers you stupid girl". Maggie had heard this slur before, but she knew the copper was trying to make an innuendo out of it. Her heart sank but in a way she had expected this. She'd had eight years of incredulity, stares, shame, not being believed. She knew, too, that the RUC men used to think that the station call-ins, and especially call-outs, were set-ups, attempts to lure them into nationalist strongholds to be ambushed in retaliation for what was going on down the stations.

She was relieved to reach the pub that looked warm and inviting. They sat in the snug and Maggie was happy with that. She didn't like being observed, watched by strangers. She looked at the shapes through the frosted glass and swirly colours like an abstract painting. Patrick watched the two women as they brushed past him, laughing together. He recognised Mary but couldn't place the other one though she looked familiar. He turned back to look at the TV and the shock of what he saw on the screen actually made him sit bolt upright. His mouth might have been open and he hoped nobody had noticed as he sipped his pint and tried to remain calm and normal-looking. The brunette newsreader was enunciating about the papal nuncio. The headline in sliding text along the bottom of the screen: A former papal nuncio will be tried in Vatican city state for sexual abuse of children and possession of child pornography. He felt cold sweat down his back and tried to regain his composure. The woman whose name he couldn't remember was at the bar and he hoped she wouldn't look in his direction. He felt faint. How mortifying for a grown man to faint! He gripped his pint and tried not to remember. It didn't stop the flashbacks coming in quick succession. Desperately trying to

remember to forget didn't stop the nightmares either, night terrors, waking up in cold sweats.

Patrick had never told a sinner, not even his wife Aisling who he had been married to for nineteen years! He knew she wouldn't love him less, but feared she would think him weak. How could she view him sexually if she knew what happened him? How would she feel cooking dinner for a rape victim? No, he'd never tell. His memories were recurrent and vivid. The priest, in his memory fat-faced with grotesque misshapen features, used to hook the altar boys around the neck with the cincture from his habit and drag them backwards into the sacristy. The altar boys would try to dodge it, frantic, but some were new to the role and not so deft at evading the loop, like colts at their first rodeo. Patrick had been eight when it first happened and the priest, a large imposing man, asked him to carry the vestments into the sacristy. Patrick felt elated at being singled out, important even. He placed the garments, which seemed heavy to him, in the vestry cabinet. When he turned around, the priest had no clothes on! He felt confused and unsure whether this was part of altar service. It was the first time he served as altar boy and he wanted to do it well and to be like the other boys who were ten and eleven. The priest was glaring at him malevolently and said, spitting through his yellow teeth, "don't look at me, boy. Face the wall".

Aisling lifted out the tray slowly from the oven, trying not to drip any oil from the roast potatoes. The news was on, something about a high up cleric being a pervert. She turned to look at the TV and the tray dipped, spattering her hand. She wasn't burnt but it had spilled on the floor. She reached for a paper towel and bent down to wipe it. She felt an overwhelming sense of dread that almost pushed her into the ground, like a weight on her back. Hyperventilating, heart racing, the images flooding back, things she'd forced herself to forget. Her Communion Day, supposed to he a happy day, when the priest took her by the hand and led her around the back of the church. He said he had "a wee something" to give her. This man she trusted, "such a nice man of God", that's what her mother called him. She spied in his hand a white silky bag like she had seen some girls had for their Holy Communion money. She felt very special that she was going to get a bag too, and from the *priest himself*! She beamed up at him and he smiled back, though it seemed more like a grimace and she felt uneasy. Around the corner now and he throws her small frame against the wall. "Don't you look at me" he growled. Her lovely white dress bloodstained, her innocence forever destroyed. Her mother was angry about her bloodied knees in the photographs, "I told you not to get your dress dirty", as she picked the gravel roughly out of her soft creamy-white skin. On their wedding day, Paddy thought she didn't want to marry him. Imagine that! But how could she tell him she just didn't want to wear the wedding dress? White dresses made her feel dirty, sullied.

Niamh bends down to place flowers on her parents' grave in the lovely little church in Cavan and remembers the day they died. Straight after the funeral, which wasn't long after the car crash, the nun took her by the hand and told her that nobody wanted her so she had to live with them and "no more crying, now". In the orphanage, she looked forward to when the nice man, the "Father", would come with sweets in a bag just for her. They would draw pictures in crayon together and he seemed happy when she sat on his lap and told him secrets. She told him that the nuns would beat her with a belt or punch her in the back of the head with a big ring on and he made a shocked face and said it was "terrible". He made her feel safe and wanted and when the Father came to speak to her "in private", she was ready with all her new secrets and tribulations. In the room, he locked the door, surely, she thought, to ensure the secrets would not be overheard. His demeanour changed when he ordered her to face the wall. Her stomach lurches to think of it. Every time

she hears her neighbour's dog barking, as a grown woman she feels panic because it reminds her of him wheezing, grunting, jowls wobbling as he said threateningly "don't look at me, you little bitch". She didn't understand the things he had done, not knowing yet was sex was, and she told a Sister Assumpta. She was startled when the nun started screaming "you're the Devil's child!" and hitting her across the face with the bunch of keys she carried on her habit. She was made kneel outside in the cold and rain all night in just her nightdress and pray for her sins. She prayed so hard! It must have been her fault for keeping secrets. Remembering now this memory that will never fade, she sobbed as she looks in the mirror to see her key-scarred face staring blankly back.

Wayne looks out across the bay to the lighthouse. On the radio he heard that Rhode Island is sinking slowly as sea levels continue to rise. He ponders what it will be like here in the future, whether he would be able to stand where he's standing, and he gets to thinking about his childhood growing up in Providence. Life was good until First Grade when his dad walked out on them leaving his mother to raise four kids with no income. He had to go to school and he hated it! He wanted to stay home with his mom but she had to work two jobs. She was delighted when the nice priest came with money and sweets for all four of the kids! He would even play with them when she was at work. Through stutters and stammers, Wayne had told her about being made to face the wall. He told her how, while it was happening, he focused on the statue of Our Lady in the living room and cried out to her for help. He had tried to grasp the statue, even, in the hopes that Our Lady of Mercy would bring an end to the pain. His mother had said nothing but the other priests who came to the house asked him lots of things. They told him he should never tell anyone about the "misconduct" and the Father would be sent away for "counselling", though he didn't know what these words meant. He didn't much care about the meaning if it meant the scary man would be gone away. He couldn't look at the Blessed Virgin without getting a feeling like a kick in the gut. The sorrowful man looks at his arms patterned with cigarette burns and razor-slices and back level with the plastic statue eyes of the Mother of Sorrows: "can you help me now?"

Little children who told trusted adults became dumb after repeated admonishments not to "make up lies", "a priest would never do that, don't be ridiculous!" Others never told, thinking it was them alone the monster preyed upon. Dumb mouths made shapes to blind eyes that looked upon deaf ears. The people stood with their feet in the blood and the filth and stared toward heaven. Angels wings fell into the accumulating filth and white feathers stuck to bleeding hearts that littered the ground. Hundreds of children scream in unison but the false-virtuous pretend they fail to hear as they kick a broken wing around the dirt. Children's tears collected until they eventually rushed out to form the waters that baptised more babes, held up by the soiled hands of the predator priest.

Eventually the children's tears formed cleansing rivers and washed away the façade to show the people that this was *not God's Will*. Waters fell from heaven and the pure droplets went into the mouths of the people caught in the purifying downpour. The droplets found their way into the hearts and East Belfast voices started to shout out, followed by Dublin cries of indignation, Welsh calls of "it happened to me", Italians who thought it was "just them", and the wave of voices crashed onto American shores to meet hollers of "me too". The tide continues to turn, gaining traction to wash away the predators from the face of the earth.

And so, they poured concrete over the grave with only the light of a hearse to work by. In the dark and in secret, their most familiar time, they poured concrete. This effort was to avoid daylight protests, demonstrations at the Church itself actively, deliberately, covering up this horror for over forty years. If only they could cement this in, keep it down, but the waves are stronger than any concrete they can mix. The White Canon shed a tear as the cement was poured over the grave of his foul friend. In his dark dreams, his tears turn to blood and black stinking brimstone for he is crying for the Father of Lies. In early evening he heard the furious shout from within the font and when he tried to bless himself it was hot blood marked on his forehead! This is the Mark of the Beast. He knows the vociferous waves are coming, rising high above the steeples, reaching up so God can hear them. Soon the deluge will come to wash away their concrete faster than they can produce it, wash away all of their revolting reliquaries containing cups of children's tears, the unholy grail they sup from. With it, the sea of righteousness will sweep away the white habit that covers the disgusting creature within. The White Canon will be exposed. The concrete sets against the backdrop of a beautiful sunrise. This is a new dawn.

END

About the Author:

Dr Jenny Butler has had short stories published most recently in The Same Literary Journal and The Raven's Perch Literary Magazine and previously in Fictive Dream Magazine, Literary Orphans Literary Magazine, Corvus Review, The Flexible Persona Literary Journal, Tales from the Forest Magazine, The Roaring Muse, Mulberry Fork Review, Killjoy Literary Magazine, Firefly, The Ginger Collect, Foliate Oak Literary Magazine, Flash Fiction Magazine, and 81Word Story Challenge. Her piece titled 'Apophenia' was nominated for the Best Small Fictions Anthology 2018. You can read more about her on her website www.drjennybutler.com. You can also find her on Twitter @jenny_butler_ and on Instagram @spiral_eyed_grrl

ASK ME AGAIN
by Andy Spisak

Leah finished her call with the client and reached into the drawer for her handbag. She had agreed to meet Doug for lunch at twelve-thirty, and it was already ten minutes to noon. She would never make it through the mid-day traffic to reach the restaurant on time.

All morning she had been on the phone. The market had dropped again yesterday, and the calls began as soon as she arrived at her office. Leah was the newest investment advisor at the firm, so Wyatt assigned her the accounts that no one else cared to deal with—small affairs with little prospect for growth. Most of her clients had never thought about investments until they had to—because their spouses had died or their partners had fled.

As Leah checked the restaurant's address on her phone, Alicia walked into her office. Alicia had recruited Leah from business school, and they became friends soon after Leah joined the firm. On most days she would stop by Leah's office close to noon, and the two would head out to lunch.

Yesterday, as they were walking back to the office, Alicia confided that Wyatt had invited her to go with him next month to a three-day conference at a resort on the Eastern Shore. Leah knew that Alicia, with her Armani dresses and Amy Adams-red hair, had no need to exaggerate her appeal.

"Was he serious?" Leah asked.

Alicia looked at her and shrugged. "You know

Wyatt. If bullshit were an Olympic sport, he'd be draped in gold. I'm surprised he even asked. He knows my father works at the Foreign Office and could scuttle his London deals with a few phone calls. Anyway, I was probably the third woman he asked."

"Thanks for the heads-up, but I think I'm way down on his list," Leah said.

"I wouldn't be so sure. He wants to meet with us this afternoon. Something about a new investment product. He made a point of asking me to bring you along."

Leah considered Wyatt's meetings a burden of the job. He would begin with a joke that, although not overtly sexist or racist, often approached offense. Next, he would describe his weekend plans, which during the summer revolved around his boat, the *Short Sail*, which he docked in Annapolis. He would then turn to the purpose of the gathering, which more often than not involved trying to convince people to invest their money and their trust in products with questionable prospects.

Leah tossed the phone into her handbag. "I can't go out with you today. I'm supposed to have lunch with this guy in Bethesda."

Alicia stepped toward Leah and smiled. "So... who is he?"

"We were in some classes in grad school. I haven't seen him since. He called me the other day and wants to get together."

Alicia gave Leah a mischievous look. "For lunch?"

"Yeah. He said he wanted to catch up, that he had an idea he wanted to talk about."

Alicia smiled. "As long as it doesn't involve a trip to the Eastern Shore."

Leah stifled a laugh. "Thanks. Hey, if I'm late for the meeting, can you cover for me with Wyatt?"

"Sure. I'll tell him you're at a job interview."

Leah rushed past Alicia on her way out of the office. "He'd probably be glad to hear it."

Leah had always thought of herself as a creative person and planned to go into advertising after finishing her MBA. Although she had an offer from a small ad agency in Atlanta, she also had a husband in the Army. Mitch was stationed in Virginia and could not accompany her to Georgia. So, a few weeks before graduation she attended a career fair sponsored by her school at the Four Seasons. A tall woman in a purple print blouse and black blazer offered Leah one of her business cards.

"Hello, I'm Alicia Stampe, McFadden Investments," she said, as she handed Leah a folder of brochures.

"Leah Blythe." She stuffed the material into her handbag and began surveying the room for her friend, Maddie, whom she was supposed to meet at the hotel.

"We're young for an investment company, started twenty years ago. But we survived the recession. In fact, we've added several large accounts during the past year."

"Thanks, but I don't think I'd be a good fit," Leah said.

"Why not?"

"Well, I just think finance is too by-the-book. I was hoping for something with more possibilities."

Leah scanned the room again for Maddie to no

avail, but spotted a *tapas* bar tucked between displays on microfinancing and urban farming. Alicia sensed in Leah's impatience an ambition driven more by restlessness than by ego.

"Tell me, Leah, what's one of your proudest accomplishments?"

Leah shifted her weight to her back foot as she considered Alicia's intent. "Well, when I was in high school I won the Oklahoma Geography Bee."

"Really. So what was the deciding question?"

"What is the longest river in Canada?" Leah replied.

"The Saint Lawrence?"

"No, everyone thinks that. It's the Mackenzie."

Alicia laughed. "I should have known that. In the UK I could never take Commonwealth studies seriously. All of those far-flung countries. What does it mean, other than they have the Queen on their coins?"

Nonplussed by Alicia's flippant comment, Leah handed Alicia her resumé and headed toward the *empanadillas*.

A few weeks later Alicia called and invited Leah to come to the office to meet Wyatt, who spent most of the interview prattling about his accomplishments. Leah found Wyatt glib, but harmless, and accepted his offer to join the firm, where she now spent most days assuring divorcées that their children's education funds were secure and cautioning retirees about depleting their savings. And on this day, she was going to have lunch with a man she hadn't seen in over a year.

* * *

Leah had met Doug in a marketing class in business school. She had stepped into the classroom and had taken a seat near the back of the room, just as the professor began asking the usual "why are you here" filler.

"I'm here because 'Psychology and the Media' is closed," she said.

Doug turned around from a few rows in front of her. *Another refugee*, she thought. She was wearing a navy blue tee shirt with the inscription "I am not an Evil Weevil" in silver letters across her chest. After class Doug walked up to her and squinted at the design below the lettering on the tee.

"Is that an insect kissing a flower?" he asked.

"It's a boll weevil—from the school I taught at in Oklahoma—it's their mascot. He's eying a cotton plant," she said.

"Ah, so you're not a bio major here by mistake."

Leah weighed whether he was being sarcastic or just flirting. But he had noticed. And so did she.

The professor had paired them to work on a marketing study, and they agreed to get to the following week's class early to discuss the project. Doug arrived first. He threw his backpack onto a small metal table and pushed it close to a corner in the back of the room, then dragged over a couple of folding chairs. He set the backpack on the floor and took out his iPad and a bottle of water. Leah walked in around ten minutes later. She was carrying a small canvas tote with a red and orange koi fish design.

"Sorry I'm late," she said. "I don't think I'll ever get used to the traffic around here."

Doug found her frustration a curious departure from her usual self-assurance. "No, it's not Oklahoma. So, how *did* you wind up in Washington?" Doug asked.

She pulled over another chair and tossed the tote onto it. "My husband's in the Army. I knew when I got married I'd be moving around, but when he told me about coming here, I didn't want to go. He wants to start a business after he gets out. He thinks my MBA will come in handy. What about you?"

"My wife's at Georgetown for her Ph.D. Jessica and I met at NYU. We got married after finishing school and came down here about a month later." Doug reached for his bottle of water and almost tipped it over. "So besides the traffic is living here as bad as you thought?" he asked.

Leah looked into her tote and pulled out two tangerines. She rolled one across the table toward Doug, who began squeezing it like a stress ball. "I miss my mom, but otherwise it's OK," she said. "Mitch travels a lot, so school fills up the time. I'd only been out of Oklahoma once. My dad was a salesman—oil drilling equipment. The summer before my senior year in high school he won a trip to Padre Island—some kind of sales bonus. I remember going out to the beach in the middle of the night to watch the Perseids. It was the last good time we had as a family."

"What happened?" Doug asked.

Leah leaned forward and began inching toward the edge of the chair. She looked at Doug and wondered if he was meddlesome or just curious. "He met a woman on one of his trips, at one of the gas sites in McAlester."

"Are you still in contact?"

Leah disliked talking about her father, but she did not find Doug's questions intrusive. Rather, she welcomed the invitation to vent. "Not much. A couple of months before I graduated high school he told my mom he was leaving. Just like that, as if we didn't matter. He came to my graduation. I saw him a few times after I went off to college. I can't stand seeing him with his new wife—he's an asshole."

Leah and Doug continued arriving at class early, sometimes to discuss an assignment, but often just to talk. One night Leah mentioned that she needed to speak to the professor after class. There had been some incidents on campus—a couple of students had been robbed—so Doug asked Leah if he could wait for her and walk her to her car.

"Sure," she said, "I won't be long."

Doug walked outside, sat on a concrete step, and checked his phone for messages. Leah came out a few minutes later, and they began walking to the parking lot.

"Did you get things straightened out?" Doug asked.

"Yeah, I'm going to miss next week's class. I asked for more time to turn in my research proposal."

"Work conflict?" he asked.

"No, I'll be in Oklahoma. Mitch's brother and his wife just had a kid. We're going for the christening."

As they walked Doug reached for her hand and was surprised that she didn't pull back. "Guess you're looking forward to going home," he said.

Leah looked down for an instant, then looked at Doug. "Yeah…though in some ways it seems like a dress rehearsal."

When they got to her car she looked at him and smiled. He drew her closer and kissed her. Leah was startled but not offended. "What are you doing, Doug?" she asked.

"Where do you *want* to be, Leah?"

Leah pulled back and considered her various, precarious responses. "I don't know. But I think you should be with Jessica." She was no longer smiling.

* * *

Doug arrived at Café Paolo about ten minutes early. The noon hour sunlight reflected off the travertine tables, and for a moment he considered keeping his sunglasses on. The host brought him to a table that was adorned with a clear slender vase holding an orange bird of paradise. Leah walked in a few minutes later. She wore a cream-colored suit and a lavender blouse. She was wearing her hair longer than she had in school. It framed her face perfectly. Doug thought she looked magnificent, *Leah and her Klein blue eyes*. A waiter came to the table, handed them menus, and asked for a drink order. Doug ordered a gin and tonic.

"I'll have a mojito," Leah said.

Leah glanced around the room and focused on a poster of the Cinque Terre. She looked back at Doug and noticed that his tie matched the color of the sienna buildings in the poster. It was the first time Leah had seen him in a business suit, which she thought gave him a more serious bearing than she remembered from school.

"I was surprised to hear from you. It's been a year since school. Did you go with that consulting firm?" she asked.

"Yeah, I was in Pittsburgh when I called. We have this client looking for new ideas for state lotteries. So far, we've come up with 'Big Dog'—scratch off three fierce Dobermans, win ten thousand dollars. Maybe three Chihuahuas should be worth five bucks."

Leah began to laugh. "Not exactly what we talked about in grad school."

"Yeah, it's ridiculous, but it's what passes for business these days. We had a focus group and this fortyish housewife said we should have a game that offered a prize to attend celebrity awards shows. 'You could call it Paparazzi!' she said. The group loved it, of course."

"And that drove you to call me?" Leah asked.

"I've missed talking with you."

"We haven't—since graduation," she said.

"I wanted to call, but I thought you'd be busy with work. I imagined you taking dance lessons during lunch time."

"Dance lessons?"

Leah had never thought about dance lessons, but they now appealed to her as an excuse to escape from the office. Doug's aside reminded her of how he had a way of anticipating her.

The waiter brought them their drinks and asked for their order. Doug looked down at the faux-leather menus and asked the waiter for a few more minutes. Doug moved his gin to the side to clear some space between him and Leah.

"How's your mother?" Doug asked.

"She's doing great. I talked her into going back to school, so she took some classes at the community college in medical records administration. She's working for a pediatrician and loves it. What about you?"

"Well, I'm planning to go to New York this weekend," Doug said.

"A special occasion?"

"I'm going to see a singer, Melinda Giles. When I was at NYU I'd go to her shows at a small club in Brooklyn. I was listening to a jazz station the other day and heard one of her songs. She's just starting to get some notice."

"I guess Jessica's looking forward to getting back to New York, even if it's just for a weekend."

"Jessica's in Africa. She's interning at the World Bank as part of her doctoral program. They sent her to Tanzania to work on a development project."

"So you're going by yourself?" Leah asked.

Doug paused for an instant and then just said it. "Actually, I'd like you to come with me."

Leah, now both enticed and entangled, picked up her glass and fixed on the glossy flower on the table. "And here I thought you were looking for a good *risotto*."

Doug didn't respond immediately, a pause that gave Leah an opening.

"Tell me, Doug. What is it that you want?"

He looked across the table at Leah as she batted a swirl of hair that had fallen across her forehead. "I want to look back years from now and know I did everything I could," Doug said.

Leah smiled and tilted her head to move the curl away from her eye. "I'm here now. Why not leave it at that? Sometimes it's better not to want more," she said.

"I can handle the disappointment."

"I'm not talking about disappointment." Leah leaned back in the chair; her shoulders dropped in a sigh. "A few weeks before I turned ten my mom took me shopping. We went to one of those big department stores, and I saw this jewelry box. It was dark red with a black and gold arabesque design. I asked for it for my birthday. My mom said it was too expensive, but I kept hoping—thought about it every day. On my birthday, she handed me my present. I tore off the wrapping as fast as I could. It was the box. I was so happy at first. But that night I was lying in bed, and I looked at it on the night stand. I felt this strange sadness coming over me. I no longer had the anticipation. I only had … it."

"So, I should just keep the idea?" Doug asked.

Leah reached across the table and touched Doug on the hand. "See, it's not that hard."

Doug saw the waiter leaving a nearby table and gestured him over. "We should probably order."

They finished lunch and headed back to their jobs. Doug got into his car and began checking his messages while driving back to the office. A couple of clients had questions that could wait until tomorrow. The last message was from his boss, who said he took the "Paparazzi!" idea to the senior managers. They were going to have the lawyers look into getting clearances, and he wanted to meet tomorrow morning to start a marketing plan. The thought of working on the silly game brought on a wave of dread, threatening the exhilaration of seeing Leah.

Doug called the office and told his boss's assistant that he was going to see a client who needed to meet him right away. He exited the interstate onto a state highway that headed west, toward the mountains. He called up a playlist from his phone. Ella Fitzgerald began singing "Come Rain or Come Shine." It was one of the songs he had listened to at the jazz club in Brooklyn. He turned the music louder until it filled the car as he drove past the trees and the road signs, over their long, jagged shadows across the highway.

On her way back to the office, Leah got a text from Alicia that she'd be leaving early to take her Springer Spaniel to the vet, but that she would fill Leah in on the meeting with Wyatt in the morning. Leah got back to the office around two-thirty, returned some phone calls, and worked on her monthly sales report before leaving a little before six. She stopped at the market on her way home to pick up a few things for dinner. She had just started slicing an avocado for a salad when Mitch got home. She walked out of the kitchen, put her arms around him, and kissed him.

"You're home early tonight," she said.

"They moved the briefing to tomorrow. Remember that field test I told you about? Well, I'm leaving for Fort Sill on Thursday. I'll be there ten days," Mitch said.

"Thursday? I didn't think you'd have to leave until next week."

"Yeah, they're pushing it. At least I'll have time to visit Jeff over the weekend."

Leah smiled. "Tell him and Linda I said hello."

Jeff was Mitch's older brother—and template. He owned a construction supply business near Oklahoma City. He and Linda had been married eight years and had a couple of kids.

They walked back to the kitchen, and Mitch straddled the stool across the island from Leah, who resumed preparing dinner.

"Jeff said he wants me to take a look at some land. One of his customers is selling off parcels from a farm he inherited. He said there's a ten-acre piece that would be perfect for building, after I finish up with the Army next year," Mitch said.

Leah placed the paring knife on the counter and looked at Mitch. "And then what—you'll join Jeff's business?"

"I might. At least for a while, until I can start something of my own. I was thinking maybe comm support—cell towers, fiber optics, that sort of thing. It's close to what I'm doing now," Mitch said.

Mitch had often talked about life after the military, about returning to Oklahoma. But Leah found his new sense of purpose unsettling. She stepped away from the counter to check on the chicken she had put in the oven. She looked back at Mitch.

"That'll take some money to get started. I won't be earning what I'm making now back in Oklahoma," she said.

"Don't worry. I can work on that with Jeff. Maybe a loan to get me started. He's flush," Mitch said. "You'll be close to your mom again. Maybe we can finally start our family."

Leah placed the baking dish on a trivet. She put her hands on the edge of the island and leaned forward, mantis-like. "Sounds like you have it all worked out."

Mitch grinned. "How about your day? Did Wyatt come up with any new scams?"

Leah shook her head and asked Mitch to help her carry the dinner to the table. She didn't say much about her day, and she didn't say anything at all about her lunch at Café Paolo.

The next day Leah got to her office just after eight. She noticed the light on in Alicia's office and walked over. She placed her hand on the door frame and leaned in.

"Hi, Alicia. Sorry I got back after you left."

"That must have been quite a lunch," Alicia said.

"Not really. We were just catching up on things since school. Complaining about our jobs, wondering where we'd be in ten years."

"Uh-huh."

"How's your dog?"

"Oh, she's fine. It was just a check-up. She enjoys going there. The vet has a Yorkie she likes to play with."

"So, what was the big meeting all about?" Leah asked.

Alicia stood up, pointed to some folders on her desk, and dismissed them with a flip of her hand. "Typical Wyatt—always a new scheme. He has some investments he wants us to push. He tried explaining them, but he didn't make much sense. Something about diversified risk pools. He wants us to review these reports, then call some of our clients and get them to invest. I don't think I can. I have to go back to London."

"Why?" Leah asked, as she began walking toward Alicia's desk to look at the folders.

"My mum's health has taken a turn. My father called last night, and we had a long talk. I'm going back to be with her and help daddy," Alicia said.

Leah walked around the desk and put her arms around Alicia. "I'm so sorry. Don't worry; I'll take care of these," she said, pointing to the folders.

Alicia exhaled and sat down. "Thanks. They think she'll be all right, but she's in for a rough patch."

"When will you be leaving?" Leah asked.

"Pretty soon. I'm going to tell Wyatt this morning. I've got to settle some affairs before I leave, but I hope to be back in London by next week."

Leah gathered up the folders and glanced at the clock on Alicia's desk. "Alicia, I'm sorry. I've got to run and make a call. We can talk more at lunch. See you around noon?"

"Sure. I'd better prepare for my talk with Wyatt," Alicia said.

Leah walked back to her office. She took her phone out of her handbag and texted Doug, "Ask me again."

Leah placed the phone on her desk and picked up a photo, which she had taken at her grandmother's farm near Enid. Leah and her mother would visit for a few weeks each summer. The day she took it had been rainy, and she was bored. She and her equally restless cousin had had been playing a board game in the dining room, until they started to annoy each other and fuss.

Leah left the room and walked into the kitchen, where she found her grandmother reading a newspaper at the table. "Can I see the crossword?" Leah asked.

Her grandmother squinted over the top of her glasses and swatted at a pair of fruit flies circling her half-eaten peach. She turned to Leah and smiled. "In a minute, dear. I just have to finish this piece."

"Anything interesting?"

"I'm just reading about a neighbor, Tom Gant. He was working on his truck, and it slipped off the support and crushed him."

Leah drew back, startled by her grandmother's unexpected reply. "That's horrible."

"It is—what a queer way to die." Leah's grandmother set the newspaper down and took Leah's hand. "What is it, dear?"

"Jodie's driving me crazy. I need to get away, but where?"

"Honey, my grandfather built this farm. He came here during the Land Run and claimed this. He farmed it until the day he died. I've lived here my entire life, just like my mother and father. You can go anywhere, Leah. It's all right before you."

Leah got up from the table and went to her room to get her camera. The rain had stopped, and there was still enough daylight to walk down to the woods, about a mile away. She set out bare footed across the broad field in back of the farm house. The wet soil squished between her toes. The rain had not cut the heat, and fog was beginning to form above the wet ground. She reached the woods and walked a few more yards toward the stream. She could make out two forms, visible through the drooping branches. She moved in their direction and saw two blue herons, erect and motionless in the stream. She stopped and hoped they would not notice her and flee as she framed the pair in her sight through an opening in the trees.

Leah placed the picture back on the desk. She was fourteen when she took it. It was before Mitch and before Doug, when she stood by the water and felt the terrible stillness.

About the Author:

Andy Spisak attended Boston University, where he earned a BA degree in history. He also has graduate degrees in international relations and statistics. After a career in public policy and economics he has begun a new phase of his life in writing. He and his family reside in Virginia and Hawai'i.

THE FEEDING
by Tammy Huffman

His reach fell short. Just beyond his fingertips. He wanted the fruit in the highest branches. Only those apples would do for his seed — the ones that bobbled like rubies, the ones without blemish. Brice grabbed a limb and hand-over-hand bowed it toward him. Slowly, carefully. He was too greedy to let any drop to the ground and be wasted. The upside down cluster of apples opened before him. His for the taking.

He cupped the first apple, the best apple, in his palm. He held it before his eyes. Then he turned it in his fingers, checking for rotten spots and worm holes and blight. It was perfect. He placed that one in a jacket pocket. He made a pouch of his shirt front and stuffed it full. After he stripped the limb bare and was big with apples, he snaked down the tree. He poured the apples into a basket. It was his mother's laundry basket with stave-wire sides and metal handles. It would hold a good bushel.

He slithered back up. The trunk forked and he wedged one foot on each large bough. He got a leafy handhold and straightened, spread-eagled and shirt-tail winged. The rising sun had pried open the horizon to a red-rimmed slit. Mr. Johnson's pasture was on a rising plateau. With little chance that his invasion would be discovered, Brice took his time looking around. He could see his father's farm just across the fence. The house and barns and cribs looked gray-smudged in the thick morning mist, like the charred hulls of a flotilla. The wind picked up and he swayed on his crow's nest of branches. The distant farm seemed to roll and recede. For a moment he felt let loose, floating away and free. He fancied the galley slave had turned mutineer and brigand. He'd boarded, ransacked, and burned the ship of his captivity and now he watched it sink from afar. He was glad beyond measure to be rid of its sweaty, unbearable, suffocating hold.

Brice quit his fantasizing and dallying and repositioned himself and continued after the fruit. He worked quickly, diligently and without pause — until the wild dogs set in. They were very near and he shrank inside the tree, holding an apple against his chest, feeling it quiver against his own hard-beating heart.

The coyotes were hunting just down the bluff at the drainage ditch. One of the coyotes yipped and the whole pack yowled and all of the dogs on the neighboring farms started up. The coyotes were on a chase and their howls were a mix of ecstasy and mournfulness that thrilled the boy to the marrow even as it chilled his spine. The howls reached to riotous and became blended screams streaming in a whirlwind. Then the pack fell perfectly still. The beasts had made their kill. Brice was awed by a gluttony so consuming it devoured its own tongue, but he was also relieved, and he moved the apple from his heart to his stomach. He got down to empty the sagging bag.

On the ground, he stretched and yawned.

Mr. Johnson's herd of purebred Angus were stirring in the pasture. The cattle swished tails, chewed cuds, grazed the green grass on the pond bank.

Brice spotted his father's runaway sow drinking at the pond. The old hog seemed to feel the boy's eyes on her. She quite her guzzling and raised her dragon head and stood frozen, listening, smelling. Brice could hear the water dripping from her jowls. She turned her head and stared at him for a moment. He thought he saw curiosity in the black, bottomless eyes that blinked at him, and he imagined he glimpsed something else in the high way she held her snout and snuffled and turned away from him, something like contempt. But he forgot about her as he went back again and rustled inside the tree's veil and plundered the fruit.

Bow the limb, twirl the thick stem, pluck the fruit. Brice's system for ravaging the apple tree became tiresome, mindless, and his thoughts drifted.

His folks had lusted for the apple tree.

That was yesterday, when the four of them, him, his mother and father and little brother, had been bucking hay in the hay field. In the sultry heat the field of yellow stubble had blistered and bruised Brice's tired, sneakered feet.

His mother drove the tractor that pulled a flatbed trailer. In low gear, the tractor-trailer waddled like a wind-up bug between the endless rows of green stippled hay bales. His little brother Zeb sat on her lap and pretended to steer. He gripped the wheel and made his own engine noises, "Vroom, vroom, putt, putt, putt."

Ahead of Brice, his father's hay hook flashed. He snagged a seventy-pound square bale and tossed it onto the flatbed on top of the other bales already stacked and wobbling. He moved to the next bake, spiked it, wheeled and pitched it. He dispensed with the bales

with the same ease Samson's jawbone made short shrift of the Philistines.

Not strong enough to carry a bale, Brice drug it by its strings as close as he could get it to the path of the passing flatbed. The bale was bundled tightly by two strands of twine wrapped around the ends. The strings pinched through his gloves and left deep red welts on the inside knuckles of his fingers where he gripped. By the time he yanked and drug it over the rough field to the trailer, the strings loosened and the bale split apart like flayed hide.

"That's my boy," his father said, barely glancing at him, and with no hint of disappointment. He heaved the bale atop the other bales.

Your boy, thought Brice. How did that ever happen? His own hands clamped to rebellious fists doing the backbreaking farm work — hoeing, fence mending, ditch digging, brush cutting — chores he loathed and his father relished.

Like today. In the breath-taking heat under a pounding sun his father was bareheaded. His skin was tanned the dark brown of boot leather and he went barebacked. The muscles in his arms were like cable and his palms were so calloused he went barehanded and the heavy iron hay hook was light as a toy in his grip.

Brice, on the other hand, was wearing long johns meant to ventilate perspiration, under a long-sleeved shirt meant to save his pale, freckled skin from burning. Every exposed bit of him burned anyway, and sweat soaked his clothes till they chafed and the elastic band of his billed cap until it smelled sickeningly of older sweat and the spicy odor of aftershave. The flies and gnats and mosquitoes that his father didn't seem to notice or mind absolutely ate him up. Every so many steps, his hands beat to slap his face and neck and arms, as though he were a self-punishing fanatic and could pound out of his own flesh notions that lit and bit and galled him.

At the end of the field his father bellowed

for water and his mother braked the tractor to an abrupt stop that threatened the bales with capsize. She cut the engine and swung Zeb over the tractor tire to the ground. Rubbery-legged from the vibrating tractor seat, Zeb went weaving, lost his balance, and plopped on his behind.

"He's drunk," his father said.

His mother climbed down. She took off her straw hat — she called it her Minnie Pearl hat — and horse-lip whiffled to them. "Vhew."

They collapsed in the grass of the road bank with only the tractor tire for shade. His father brought the water jug from under the tractor seat. He drank in a steady sluice that made his neck cords stand out.

His mother passed the jug to Brice. "Give your brother a drink, too, please and thank you."

Brice drank his fill. Then he interrupted Zeb's picking dandelions to help him tip the jug while he held the bottom for balance. Zeb swigged and swigged until his mother said, "That's enough, Brice. You don't want to make him sick."

You don't want to make him sick, a voice inside his head mocked. Please. And thank you.

"Brice."

Brice jerked the jug away and the icy water splashed down Zeb's chin and neck and he clawed at his wet shirt front and scowled.

"That'll cool you off, idjit," Brice said.

His mother fanned herself with her broad-brimmed hat. Her face was flushed from the heat and her eyes watery from gas fumes and ragweed. Her hair was bunched on top and strands hung down in tentacles so that her hair looked like a squid sitting on her head. She wore a loose, oversized blouse handmade from a bolt of cotton print. She wore blue jeans and long socks and heavy men's shoes. My clod hoppers, she called them.

"It's so pretty," his mother said. "Like an oasis in a desert."

She was looking at the apple tree, just across the fence in Mr. Johnson's pasture.

"Know what I see?" his father said. "Hot apple pie fresh from the oven with a dollop of vanilla ice cream and a cold, cold glass of milk."

His mother brought a rust-seamed can of bug spray out of some deep pocket and ordered Brice to use it, saying he looked like he'd gotten the chicken pox, then told him to spray his brother, too, please and thank you. Brice grabbed Zeb by the wrist and gassed him. Zeb tried to hold onto the dandelions and said "Leave go!" but Brice shredded the heads and told him "She won't want those weeds."

"How does it stay so pretty and green when everything else is as dead as dead from the drought?" his mother said.

His father stretched out and put his head on her lap. "Runoff from the pond. Pond is spring fed. Mr. Johnson sank his well just below it. He never runs out of water."

"He won't pick the apples. He won't make pies or applesauce." Her voice had an unusual petulant note and Brice's head cocked and swayed on his neck as he listened more closely. But "Too bad something so fine has to go to rot" was the only other thing she said. His mother folded her arms under her head and her eyes grew droopy staring at the tree. She breathed deeply as though she were breathing in a nectar of apple blossoms. "I could just bathe in it," she whispered.

"It must be nice to afford to be so wasteful," his father said. His father squinted at the neighbor's farm. Brice looked where he looked, at the tall stone silos, the red barns, the split rail fences, the paved driveway lined with dogwood. The house, a two-story brick, was plain as an old school house, but stately and imposing. His father's eyes fell on the apple tree as though it were the crown jewel of the larger estate.

"It's really too rich," his mother said, and her voice had gone one note beyond petulant to bitter and Brice heard it and his eyes flicked back to her and focused to pinpoints. "Almost makes me sick."

His father stood up, and he blinked at the hot sun and brushed hay seed off the back of his neck and seemed tired all at once, and said, "Come on. Let's get back after it. Watch for snakes."

And so it was, trudging along the field, that Brice glanced again and again at the flaming apple tree. Because of the look that had been in their eyes, he could not keep his own eyes off of it.

Using his free hand to break their tumble, Brice poured the last apron of apples into the basket. He picked it up and started for home. He thought to hurry now that it was past daylight. But he had not gone far when he stopped and set the basket down and backtracked. He had scaled the walls of the mighty and spoiled his treasures and now with one final act he put down his confidence and strength. Leisurely, not at all urgently, Brice peed on the apple tree's naked trunk.

He came up behind the house and left his hoard, save one, by the machine shed. He sauntered around the house into the front yard. He tossed the prized apple proudly from hand to hand.

His father was sitting on the porch rail with a cup of coffee. Zeb was squatted on the porch steps, poking at something with a stick. Brice could hear his mother in the kitchen, humming as she fixed breakfast. He could smell breakfast smells, coffee and sausage and biscuits and gravy.

"Those are fine looking apples I saw you with," his father said. "Where did you get them?"

"Off the ground."

"Off the ground. Mr. Johnson will not take kindly to having his apple tree looted. In the end, you have only saved him the trouble of picking them himself."

"He wouldn't have picked them," Brice said. "He would have let them go to waste. You said it yourself."

"Then it would be Mr. Johnson's waste. Not ours. He might have given them to you, Brice, if you had asked. Why didn't you just ask?"

Brice hid the apple behind his back. "I brought them for pies. Hot apple pies with ice cream. Homemade ice cream."

"Throwing words back isn't going to help, Brice."

"They're a gift for mom. To make her feel special. A nice surprise."

"Trespassing. Vandalism. Stealing. Your mother will be surprised at you, all right. And troubled. As I am."

Brice slipped the apple into his jacket pocket out of sight, lest it too should be stripped of him. He met his father's eyes. His father's eyes were cold and hard and unblinking and reminded Brice of a marble he owned and kept with his other trinkets in an old cigar box.

Zeb tugged at his father's pant leg and the man broke his stare and looked down. Zeb had a worm in his outstretched hand. It was fat and swollen green and seeping brown juice with spiked hair and a tiny horn on its tail.

Brice saw his father's eyes soften at his brothers gift. His own eyes smoldered behind half-lowered lids and his face grew pale as the worm of envy coiled around his heart squeezed tight.

His father thumbed the worm's prickly spikes. "Thank you. They call that a tomato worm."

"Why?" Zeb said.

"They call that a tomato worm if it gets in the tomatoes and a corn worm if it gets in the corn and a silk worm if it gets in the silk and down south they call that a tobacco worm if it gets in the tobacco."

"Why?"

"Because a worm can get into anything."

"Why?"

"Put the apples in the cool of the cellar for now to keep, Brice. And then you will give them back to Mr. Johnson to do with as he will. That's how worms feed, Zeb. They gnaw from the inside out. Go show it to your mother. She'll get a kick. Don't let her use it to spice my eggs."

Coming around the machine shed, Brice heard the sow mashing and slathering over the fruit before he saw her. He yelled and chucked a rock and the sow lumbered off. Her rolling lard-layered backside was stained with something that looked like tar and her heavy teats nearly drug the ground.

She'd tipped the basket over. Brice saw the damage was not that bad. She had eaten only one apple and tromped a few others. Brice started to put the apples back in the basket, but stopped. Then, calmly, almost serene in his violent decision, he picked up an apple and slung it at the sow. And then another as he poured out his wrath and another so that the red balls flew out rapidly as from a repeating gun. The startled sow trotted off towards the woods.

When Brice reached and felt nothing and looked and saw the apples were gone, he was surprised and disappointed that the apples were spent and his fury was not. But when he saw the bright, shiny apples strewn over the pasture, he was mollified. They would soon rot in the sun and they would be meat for the birds and the rodents and, yes, the worms. Brice turned to leave. A smile tugged at his lips. There would be no taking anything back now.

"She had her babies last night down at the drainage ditch," his father said to him when he came back around to the porch.

The sow was waddling down the path through the timber. And Brice realized that what had looked like tar on her backside was the issue of birth.

"Take some corn to feed her from now on of the mornings."

"From now on?" Brice sat heavily on the porch step. His late night foray that had crested to zealousness now sank to sloth. He yawned and his stomach rumbled.

"She won't forage of a night now. She'll want to stay close to her young. I'll bring her down a bale of straw in a while for her to line her bed. By the time you are done feeding her, breakfast will be ready."

"She's a stupid old rip for having them out in the woods instead of inside the barn," Brice said. "She's just asking for the coyotes to get her babies."

"She will get the coyotes first. She will make short work of anything that threatens her young."

"She's nasty," Brice said. "She eats garbage and cow flops and maggoty gross stuff. Why does she get the run of the place, anyhow?"

"Because she's too smart for a pen to hold her. She's a maverick."

"She's ugly," said Brice.

"She's a beauty," his father said. "She had twelve little ones."

"Twelve little ones," Zeb marveled after him.

"She's a monster," Brice said to his little brother. "She could eat you whole."

"Could not."

"She's a gentle old sow and a good one," his father said.

"She could swallow you alive," Brice said to his brother. "Chomp, chomp, chomp."

Zeb looked at his father's face to see if that were true.

But his father was looking into the face of his oldest son. "Take her some corn. About a pound coffee can worth. Brice, I will not tell you again."

Brice shot to his feet and stomped off. Zeb followed him to the wagon of corn parked by the grain bin. Brice slashed savagely at the corn with the scoop and hurled the grain at the mouth of the chore bucket. Zeb had a little sandpile bucket and he grabbed fistfuls of corn and threw it in. Brice jumped out of the wagon with his bucket and opened the gate. Zeb ran after him.

"Where is she?"

"Out there."

"Why?"

"Why, why, why. Why did you have to come along?"

Brice walked through the barn lot and down the path through the bluff of oak and maple and his brother followed. The narrow path was packed hard by cattle and deer and went down hill. Brice carried his near empty bucket easily, swinging it along. Behind him his brother's pail was growing heavy. He switched its hooped bail from hand to hand.

"You're spilling it," Brice said. "You're stringing corn all over the farm."

"You carry it."

"I'm not carrying it."

"Carry me."

"I'm not carrying you," Brice said. "Who asked you to come?"

He'd reached the drainage ditch at the bottom of the hill. His brother followed at his heels as Brice forced through a cattail stand and slogged through waist high swamp grass.

"There she is," Brice said, only to himself.

The sow had burrowed out a mud hole at the edge of the marsh. She was lying with only her snout and gristle-ridge of her back above the water. She watched the boys through eyes matted with gunk. Her eyes were tiny and black and deep as dates skewered into raw dough. She wallowed in the mire and snorted bubbles through her nose.

Brice poured out the corn on dry ground and it fell into a sliding heap.

The sow snorted eagerly as she struggled to get up. She pitched and rolled this way and that and got her legs under her and gave a heave to her feet with one ponderous movement that made suction noises and slapped the brown water in drudging waves. Another lumbering heave parting sludge and she was on the bank. She stood dripping filthy water and the mud caved off her sides like sloughing scales. She sniffed at the corn and then began to eat.

The sow was a brood sow. She was four hundred pounds of blubber on disproportionately tiny and fragile hooves. She was solid white with bristled hair rubbed bare in patches and quickly drying to coarse-grained dander. A stalk of Jimson weed was stuck between her huge back teeth, cockleburs knotted her tail like a bola, one ear was notched with a metal tag, and a ring glinted in her nose.

Brice glared at her with wholehearted disgust and it did not occur to the boy that she was a wise and clever brute; that she laughed at fences and the men that made them; that she counted poisonous weeds and venomous snakes as trimmings; that she had tromped the earth fierce and fearless and had survived fangs and claws since the ice age. He saw only that she was fat and filthy and ugly and all the world held her in legendary scorn.

"You smell," Brice said to the sow. "Like you just fell off a gut wagon."

The kernels powdered to meal between the sow's sharp yellow teeth and her mouth frothed and drooled.

Brice stood with his hands in his pockets and watched the sow eat. When he looked, Zeb's pail was there but he was gone. He saw him moving in the woods. When Brice came up, he found his brother squatted on his thighs. He was unmoving as he peered through a thicket of gooseberry bushes. Brice heard a faint mewling. He shoved his brother aside roughly and lifted the vines. The litter of slumbering piglets was pink and tan and almost merged to vanish -- except for a kick and twitch and squirm -- in the bed of leaves and twigs and rooted, red clay clods.

He counted eleven piglets. His father had said twelve. Brice began to search the ground, stooped over and intent as a bloodhound to find the lost pig. Separated from the others, it would chill, starve, be eaten. He had hardly begun looking when Zeb stumbled across the newborn. Frustrated, Brice kicked dirt at the both of them, and said, "Big deal."

The pig was curled in the roots of a sawed off tree stump in a clearing of what had once been a logging trail. It was sound asleep. Zeb brushed the pig's tight, milk-swollen belly and its ears wriggled and its wet, flat, black nose flared, but it did not wake up.

"He's lost his mommy," Zeb said. "Little runt. I'll take you to your mommy."

"Go ahead, idiot," Brice said. He walked away and snatched up the chore bucket. "Pick her baby up. See what mommy does."

Brice stopped in his tracks and turned when Zeb did immediately as he was told and picked the animal up. At first the pig, still mostly asleep, only wriggled in the little boy's grubby hands. And then it awoke fully and grunted and squirmed. Zeb gripped it tight around the middle so as not to drop it. The pig thrashed and began to squeal in high, hair-raising shrieks.

Brice shifted his glance to the swamp. At the panicked trilling of her young, the sow's head came up with the force of a sledgehammer. There was a brief pause for honing, then she wheeled and charged. Brice was amazed by the speed of the animal. She plowed a furrow through the soft marsh grass and crashed through the thick stand of cattail reeds.

Zeb did not have sense enough to let loose of the screeching pig. Instead he shook it, to get it to mind. The sow came barreling steady and fast through the underbrush of the timber. Brice watched the ground narrow between his brother and the enraged sow. He saw his brother's eyes startle wide with terror when he saw the huge sow coming straight at him. The big eyes, as big and blue as any marble he owned, turned to him for help. Brice opened his mouth, but only a grunt escaped him as the wind was knocked from his lungs.

His father slammed him out of the way. The straw bale the man had been carrying burst apart and Brice saw through the dust that his father had skidded into the path of the sow that was now mere feet from Zeb. He smashed his heavy work shoe into the sow's snout, jolting her around.

"Drop the pig!" he shouted at Zeb.

But Zeb was fuddled and peevish in his confusion, wanting to bawl. The pig paddled air with its front feet, squealing to beat thunder. The crazed sow lowered her head like a battering ram, but before she could lunge the man whipped round, slapped the pig out of Zeb's hands, picked the boy up by the nape of his shirt collar like a cur, and leapt to the safety of the stump.

The sow circled the stump and took stiff legged jumps at the man and boy, snapping her teeth, slobbers flying. She stood suddenly still, her snout way up in the air. Rumbling grunts came loud and deep from her belly, like a challenge. Then, satisfied, she turned to her baby.

The little pig was sitting on its haunches, stunned. The sow sniffed and huffed and bumped it around and off the ground with her nose.

The man jumped off the stump and sat Zeb on the ground. "Are you hurt?"

Zeb shook his head.

He felt over the boy. "Are you sure?"

Then in a few quick steps he crossed the ground between him and Brice. Brice jumped to his feet. He saw the look on his father's face and glanced frantic all about him, like a cornered animal. His father grabbed him by the shirt front and shook him. "What is the matter with you?" he said. He shook him again. "Why didn't you help your brother? Why did you just stand there?"

Brice wrenched free of his grip and staggered back and his face was flushed bright red and scrunched. There were tears in his eyes, not of hurt or anguish or remorse, but of outrage. "Those were for seed!" he shouted. He smote his chest with his fist. "My seed!"

"What?" his father said. His eyes were narrowed and pained and searched hard.

He waited. Brice only stared, blinking back the hot tears and snorting the run from his nose, lips quivering.

His father looked away and focused on nothing for a moment and then he let Brice go with the slightest push and turned and went back to Zeb. Zeb had taken off after a grasshopper. The man picked him up and put him on his shoulders. He took the path for home and did not look back.

The sow was eating a dead frog or lizard that had dried to green leathery skin and white hollow bones. The little pig was under her feet, spinning in circles, making grunting sounds in his throat.

Brice sat on the stump and watched the little pig for a while. He reached in his jacket pocket and brought out the apple. It had not bruised when he hit the ground and he saw in the vanity of his own sight that it was still perfect. He thought to tear out chunks with his teeth, spit out the pulp, and save only the core, the seed. But it was all spoiled for him now.

"Here," he said. "Take it."

Brice tossed the apple and it rolled to the sow. The sow sniffed it once, blasted it with a disdainful mist from her nostrils, and turned in preference to the dead thing.

The End

About the Author:

Tammy Huffman has a degree in English/ Journalism and has worked as a reporter on a home-town newspaper for 25 years. She lives in the rolling hills of northwest Missouri. She currently resides on the same farm she grew up on.

MOVING

by Tali Treece

I tie a bandana around my face and Johnny, that's my husband, he swings me close and pinches my rear and tells me I'm Rosie the Riveter turned bandito. I'm allergic to dust, is all, and there's dust everywhere because we're moving day after tomorrow, and almost everything's packed away. The furniture I inherited from roommates Freshman year of college, and which I carted from dorm to dorm, and finally lugged into our apartment when we got married our Senior year? We hauled it all to the dump, and you wouldn't believe the dust bunnies and cobwebs under the green velvet chair and the old gold couch. And I thought I was tidy. My mother, she used to say what a good wife I'd make. "She can clean," she'd say. "And cook!"

But we order pizza because every pan and plate — why did we already pack the plates? — is taped into the boxes I scavenged from the recycling center. I'm heaving a stack of books across the floor when Johnny circles his arms around my waist and twirls me to him and tugs down the bandana to kiss me. I sneeze. He laughs, happier than he's been in months, ever since he graduated with the philosophy degree that flung him up and sent him spiraling down and out like a maple seed caught in the wind. He says, "We're moving! A new start," and I press my lips against his, my tongue in his mouth, and we're sinking to the floor, right there amongst all the cardboard and cobwebs and dust mites, when someone knocks at the door.

"Surprise!" they say.

My mother-in-law and sister-in-law. Johnny makes a face at me like, *What the hell?* but we both smile as they bustle into our apartment. My sister-in-law pecks my cheek. She smells of lavender and soap, cool and fresh, even after a flight from Texas to Wyoming. "You've got dirt on your face," she says as she pulls away. "And, oh dear, a cobweb in your hair." She snatches the strand and lets it dangle there for a second before flicking it to the floor.

"How do you stand this heat?" my mother-in-law asks, digging her boarding pass from her purse, and fanning herself nonstop. "I'd die without air conditioning."

Johnny hates it when she's passive-aggressive like that, and he looks at me and flares his nostrils, but to her he says, "I'll get you a glass of water." He has to dig through three different containers to find a cup.

It *is* hot in here, and I tie the bandana over my hair and hope I really do resemble Rosie. My in-laws sip at the tap water while we all perch on cardboard boxes and shuffle our feet over the hardwood floor. That's something about this apartment: it's smaller than most couples find livable, and all the window sills are peeling, and the bathtub is so short I can't stretch out my legs even when I'm sitting up, but it's got these wonderful old heart of pine floors, and a ceiling that towers above us, and I've loved it here, very much.

I try to sweep some of the dust behind me while pretending to pay attention to my mother-in-law, who's telling us about their flight, and the nasty stewardess who scowled at her when she asked for a bottle of Aquafina. "A paying customer!" she says.

I catch Johnny's eye and he winks, like, *We're fine, we'll get through this.*

My sister-in-law bangs her heels against the box she's sitting on, and I pray it's not the china my grandma left me when she passed away last year. It's very fragile. I try to peer around her sandals to see what's written on the side, and she hops up and says, "I'm in the way, I'm so sorry!" and I have to say, "No, no, sit down, be comfortable, you're fine, everything's fine." And she does, but holds her purse on her knees and shifts from one butt cheek to the other, back and forth, like she needs to pee. Johnny nods at his mother, smiles at his sister, and doesn't wink at me again.

My mother-in-law launches into some saga about her cracked crown, and I say, "So why are you here?" and they all stare at me with their dark brown eyes, and Johnny says to me, his wife, "They're here to help, of course."

"I need to go lie down," I say, and stretch out on the bare mattress on the bedroom floor. I tie the bandana over my eyes.

Through the thin, ancient door I hear my sister-in-law ask, "Is she all right?"

"Yeah," Johnny says, and part of me hates myself for giving in so easy, and part of me wants to scream, *No, I am not all right!* I haven't been for a long time, months now, ever since we finished college and Johnny started working at the lumber mill, because what good does a philosophy degree do in an old railroad town that's dying? He *hated* that job, so they fired him, and he got worse than he'd ever been. All tired and confused, fading away like fireworks that hang in the air for just a second after they explode and then you blink and they aren't there anymore. But I don't scream, of course. I get off the mattress and go into the

bathroom and scrub that dingy little tub, because I am just like Rosie the Riveter, and no matter what happens, no matter how sad and distant Johnny gets, I can take it. I'm the strong one. I've got to be.

A tap on the bathroom door, and my sister-in-law pokes her head in and says, "I'm so sorry, but I need to use the restroom."

So I retreat to the bedroom, but Johnny and his mom are in there now, and she says the only way to truly get the walls clean is with a feather duster.

"Except that we don't have one," I say.

"I'd love to buy you one. Just a tiny gift." She's still holding her purse and she shifts it up her arm, like she's about to whip out her wallet.

I look at Johnny, wait for him to grimace. He gets it, how crazy it is to give us more stuff when we've just packed up everything to move across the country. But he slings his arm around her shoulders and says, "Thanks, Ma, that'd be great." And then he turns to me, finally. "Listen, they're hungry, so I thought we'd take them out for a bite to eat," he says, his arm still around her. His sister steps out of the bathroom and flanks his other side.

I say, "Go wherever you want."

"Don't you want to come?"

The sun is setting and a beam catches on a spiderweb dangling from the ceiling. I blink at Johnny. "No," I say. I'm being ridiculous, resentful, I know that, but I shove my hands in my pockets and say again, "No, I don't."

"Suit yourself," he says, and ushers his mom and sister out the door, without so much as a glance back at me.

I haven't packed my clothes yet, and I *still* haven't gone through the junk drawer, but nonetheless I sit on the floor and gaze out the window. There's a fly stuck in the screen, wings broken, but shining in all that golden light, as if any second he might wake and fly away. Back in high school, my friend Nathan and I would sit on the roof of my old treehouse and watch the sunset, just like this. That was in Florida, and we'd be sweating and slapping at mosquitoes. It always seemed worth it, though, the way the oaks and the palms turned orange, and the rooftops shone copper. Sometimes I'd dance over the shingles, like I was commanding the sun, and he'd lean back on his elbows, lanky legs hanging off the edge, and whittle a stick with his teeth, laughing at me with just his eyes.

I haven't told him we're moving back to Florida, for Johnny's new job teaching philosophy at the charter school where my uncle's the principal. I think about texting him, but I can't remember where I put my phone, and that feels all wrong, anyway. I wish I could send smoke signals.

I open the window and poke the fly back through the screen, and a wind catches it up.

*

By the time Johnny gets back, I've gone through the junk drawer, and packed up my clothes, and put on my pajamas, and gone to bed. The pine boards creak as he steps into the room. "Baby?" he says, but I pretend I'm asleep, and then I really am, and I dream about Nathan.

I want to say it's never happened before, that I've never once thought of him since falling in love with Johnny, since getting married last year and starting this new bare and beautiful life. But, truth told, I do dream about him, sometimes. We're usually on that treehouse rooftop, me and Nathan, just sitting there and watching the sky. Tonight we're in the ocean, and he swims over and pulls me under the waves, and everything is warm and salty and wonderful, until I can't breathe anymore, and I wake up all damp with sweat.

It's dawn, pale light trickling through the blinds, Johnny's face on the pillow next to

mine. He hasn't shaved in a few days. I love that, and the way his beard doesn't grow where a scar squiggles along his jaw, and his slightly parted lips, and the whisper of breath from his nostrils. I roll close and he sighs in his sleep and drapes his arm over me, and I love the smell of him.

*

I must have fallen back asleep, because I wake up later that morning to Johnny squatting next to the mattress, tracing his finger down my nose. "You ok?" he asks. "Seemed kinda restless last night."

I stare into his eyes and they're brighter than they've been in a long time, and I don't want to mess that up, so I don't say anything about my dream. Or about all the little hurts that have added up to one great big ache in my chest after months of being so careful with him. Strong for him, always there for him as he tore himself up asking why he'd ever decided to go to college in some nowhere town in Wyoming. And why he'd studied philosophy, and why he'd let himself get to be twenty-four years old without a marketable skill to his name. And sometimes just sitting there questioning the meaning of life.

"I'm fine," I say. "Just anxious about the move, I guess. We've got so much left to do."

"Sure, but first…" and he kneels over me and kisses my cheeks, my eyes, my lips, his hands on me.

"Come on, Johnny," I say, swatting him and rolling out of bed, even though I *know* rejection always makes him get quiet, kind of gone. But this morning he just hops to his feet and starts tossing shirts in a suitcase, humming the entire time, and I trudge into the living room, and pack up my Lit books. He sounds so cheerful I wish I hadn't pushed him away.

"Knock, knock," my mother-in-law says as she shoves the door open.

"We brought breakfast!" my sister-in-law chimes in, a tray of coffee cups in one hand, a bag of muffins in the other. "Cute pajamas," she says, and I wish I'd gotten dressed before they came over.

"Tell us what to do," my mother-in-law says, and I ask them to finish with the books while I work on the bedroom. Johnny takes the pictures off the living room walls and wraps them in plastic. "Oh, you're taking all those?" his sister asks, and the way he's humming I think maybe he'll say something snappy and sharp, all smartass like he used to be, but he's silent.

I brush my hair and change my clothes before I go back to the living room. It's bare now, nothing but cardboard towers and cobwebbed corners, my mother-in-law and sister-in-law standing around, staring at the dust that shadows the floor in the exact shape of the couch. If they'd simply leave, Johnny and me, we could scrub and dust and shake it up to Billie Holiday and Ella Fitzgerald until every square foot is sparkling, gleaming. And then Johnny could take me to the floor, where there won't be a speck of dust, and this time I'll hold him for all I'm worth.

"I'm famished," my sister-in-law says.

"I've got sandwich stuff," I offer.

"Oh, no, no, we couldn't trouble you," my mother-in-law says. "I'd love to take you out. My treat."

"That's sweet," I say, "but we've seriously got so much to do still. We have to leave the place spotless if we want our security deposit back."

"It'll take no time at all with us here to help," my sister-in-law says, smiling so big I can see the pink flesh of her mouth.

"Johnny," I say. "Really."

"How about we make it a quick lunch," he says. "And then we'll tackle this together."

"I'm not hungry," I say, and they all protest, tell me a little muffin wasn't nearly enough, and I hold up my hands and say, "Honestly. I'm fine. Please, just go."

They all file out, Johnny in tow, and I tie the red bandanna over my face again, put on an old playlist, and take a rag to the walls. It's all going well, I'm getting lots done, pissed off and cleaning fast, when "Hey There, Delilah" comes on. That was our song, mine and Nathan's, one we used to listen to on road trips to the beach, and I dig around for my phone and dial his number.

"Nathan," I say.

"Hey, what's up!"

"Why didn't we date?"

"What?"

"In high school. Why didn't you ever ask me out?"

He doesn't say anything, and I could kill myself for calling and talking like this, but I can't make myself stop. I blurt, "I would have said yes. If you'd asked."

Still no response, though he was always like that, so quiet people'd forget he was in the room.

"It's not like I've thought a lot about this or anything, but looking back it's clear you did like me. Right? Something more than friends."

I can hear him breathing. I say, "I think I was in love with you."

He sighs, the sound of it like wind in the trees. "We were so different," he says. "I knew it would never work out."

"Of course it wouldn't have worked," I say. "Not for long, anyway. I mean, I definitely never would've married you."

"I wish we had anyway," he says.

"Me too."

He's quiet for so long I think he might've hung up, but finally he says, "How's Johnny?"

I'm not really sure how to answer. I could tell him he's been depressed, not doing well at all, but somehow that feels like betrayal, so I just say, "He got a new job. In Florida. We both did, teaching at my uncle's school. So we're moving back."

"Then I'll see you."

"Sure."

"I'm glad you called."

"Me too."

After we hang up I stare for a long time at the blank screen of my phone, and I'm not thinking about Nathan anymore, I'm thinking how I wish Johnny was home. If I told him I talked to Nathan, he wouldn't be mad. He'd understand, I know that, so why am I crying? I strip my clothes off, right there in the living room in the middle of all the windows, and the light pouring in so that the dust — why is there still dust? — dances in the beams of sunshine, and I walk to the bathroom, and sit in the tub, and let the discolored water run over my legs. I feel like that Van Gogh painting of the woman naked on the steps, her breasts wrinkled against her knees.

The door opens and Johnny enters and kneels beside me.

"Where's your family?" I ask.

"The hotel. I told them it'd be better if just you and me tackled the rest."

"I already did most of it."

"I'm sorry," he says.

"So am I," I say. I don't tell him what for, though maybe somehow he can feel it, because he takes up that rust-tinged bathwater in his cupped hands and pours it over my bowed head like a baptism. Sunshine streams through the bathroom window, and he raises his hand, and waves so that the dust flits and scatters, and I say, "We're moving," and he says, again, "A new start."

We laugh, and stand together, his arms around my waist, my head against his chest, bathwater dripping from my body and purling around our bare feet as we shuffle over the tile, slow and sweet, in all that dancing dust.

About the Author:

Tali Rose Treece holds an MFA in Writing from Pacific University, and is currently working on a collection of short stories, as well as a novel. Besides a handful of nonfiction publications, she has a short story in The Round, and another forthcoming in Bayou Magazine. She teaches first grade at a charter school, and lives in Texas with her husband and pup, and an ever increasing number of house plants and books.

A DUCK ON THE POND

by Fred Miller

What, pray tell, could eclipse the satisfaction of a stroll in the park on a summer evening, that is, once the hoi polloi scurrying about to late dinner engagements have all but disappeared. Nothing, I say, as I emerge from the flat at exactly eight-twenty, umbrella in hand for unforeseen showers or defensive measures if necessary. I'll return my door in precisely thirty -two minutes, every moment in timed sequence, every turn in specified order. Discipline is the centerpiece of my existence. And to those who might risk an obstruction or abridgement to my routine, I say, beware. Toleration has its boundaries. Count on it.

XXXXX

Ah, now to settle into my favorite chair with a preferred smoke and a vintage sherry and listen to the best of Beethoven on the parlor Victrola. A life of business dealings with nerve and cunning leads to rich rewards for those wise enough to toe the line. I know.

My word, who could that be at this hour? No one's expected, no appointments on the calendar, I'm quite sure. "Who is it?" I say.

"Police. Open up, Mr. Harman."

First to check my appearance in the hall mirror. Must stand erect, project confidence, exude an air of surprise. Ready.

"Why, Officers, won't you come in," I say. Two in blue flank the door, one with his hand on a billy club. Two wallets appear, badges flashing.

"Robert Harman?" the one with pinched eyes says.

"Why yes, gentlemen, do come in." Neither moves. One looks over my shoulder to confirm I'm alone. Best to remain calm, keep a serious demeanor. Sudden movements or visible emotions might prove imprudent in this situation.

"We'd like for you to accompany us down to the station for a few routine questions, Mr. Harman," the other says in an unassertive tone. He's had practice at this. Must watch him closely.

"Why, pray tell, officers? What's this concern?" Give them the innocent furrowed brow. Keep the voice evenly modulated. Not a hint I may know what this is about.

"Just routine, Mr. Harman. We can sort this out down at the station." There's a pregnant pause. No doubt, they're waiting to see if I'll make an ill-timed move.

"Are you coming willingly, Mr. Harman? That would be best, you know," the soft spoken one says. Ah, the expected challenge with subtilty. Shrewd, I'd say. These two are well practiced at this routine. Must play along, leave no ideas I may have anticipated this intrusion.

"I suppose so, but I'd still like to know the nature of this inquiry." I cock my head to one side and wait though I'm confident neither will reveal anything now.

Silence.

"Oh well," I say and turn back toward the hall

closet for my coat. But before I can take three steps, one of them grabs me from behind and pushes me to the floor, face down. This is quite unacceptable.

"Unhand me, sir. I'm no criminal," I say. My face is burning and I'm aware of a blush washing over my face. But I cannot help it. "This is quite uncalled for, officers," I say.

"Don't make this any more difficult than it already is, Mr. Harman. Best to cooperate, make it easy on yourself," one says as the other cuffs my wrists behind my back.

As they pull me upright I decide to make one final protest. "I've breached no laws, and I know my civil liberties. Uncuff me, sirs," I say.

They study my face for a moment, then force me out the door toward their waiting vehicle. It is at this point I elect to alert them to their judicial peril. "My solicitor will hear about this. You've overstepped your authority, officers," I say as I'm shoved into the backseat of their car and a door slams in my face. Uncivil, that's what it is, uncivil.

XXXXX

Plain white room. One-way glass on the wall. No doubt I'm being watched. Must remain calm and unmoved by their tactics. Be as still as possible and stare directly into the glass. I've planned well for this scene, I may add. They have nothing, nothing at all.

Time passes, nothing happens, I can almost hear my heart beat. How'd I end up in such a predicament? T'was his fault, Nelson, that unattractive little man, that fastidious bore with an insatiable appetite for gossip. Just the thought of him makes my skin crawl.

Yet I must say, we did hold a tacit agreement between us: the park, his for morning walks, the evenings mine, and never the twain should meet. Until that night. How dare he, my path, my walk, my time. And to encounter that little wretch on the pond's narrow bridge. Mine, I

said, and said it clearly enough. And charged ahead.

But did he give way? Well, in a manner of speaking, I suppose. The scene unfolded with such abruptness. A solid blow to the temple with my umbrella staff and down he went.

From the edge of the bridge, I paused to look back. Just a duck on the pond, he was. Slow concentric patterns began to excite the lily pads into stately pavanes. A lovely sight, I say, quite.

Moving smartly up the path making up for lost time I mused, no villainy here, none at all. Just tidying the park a bit. Adolescent of Nelson to challenge me on my path and my schedule, adolescent indeed. No social rectitude to the man.

And if it weren't for the bobby, Officer Nick, with a courtesy nod at the park's entrance, t'would have been a flawless crime in every respect. The poor dear fellow must have slipped, hit his head on the rail, I'd say, and fallen into the drink. How lamentable.

Opportune for me that Officer Nick, cheerful chap that he is, has had recent financial difficulties. T'is a weakness of today's society, I say. No planning, no discipline, no keen sense of scheming. Well, the oaf is in my pocket now, so to speak. No worries from him, I'd say.

Hmm, no doubt those behind the glass wish to see me emotionally unhinged. They'll receive no such satisfaction. Posture remains important, erect, shoulders back, chin out. Fine habits, fine indeed. They'll get nothing from me, nothing at all. Yet somehow, I need to throw them off, sidetrack them from their planned strategies. Hit them with what they'd least expect.

Getting warmish in here. Wonder if they've deliberately cut the air. Wouldn't surprise me in the least. A bead of sweat scoots down the center of my forehead onto my nose and pauses on the tip. I dare not move. No satisfaction for the opposition, none, I say.

My wrists are beginning to throb. Cuffs are much too tight. Wonder why they chose to leave them on? Ah, further efforts to fluster me. The blokes expect me to fidget. Do not worry, my worthy foes, I can outwit you any day. Ha, you're wasting your time with this adversary.

Damn, it's been over an hour, and it's stuffy in here. What? Two suits stroll in and eye me. Took your jolly good time getting here, I'd say.

"And who are you?" I say with an air of controlled command.

I'm Detective Wolfe and this is Detective Hoppmann. Are you ready to talk now, Mr. Harman?"

"Of course, detectives. I'm Robert Harman, I live at 2435 Euclid Lane, Mayfair, I'm widowed, and retired from my investment business. And you?". I say this with a twinkle in my eye to throw them off. Now I'll look for nonverbal reactions and wait to see who'll choose to speak first.

"You want to tell us about it, Mr. Harman. You can save us all a lot of time. We've got a witness, you know." At this wild card he's played, I show no emotion. I know better. "First things first, gentlemen. I believe I have a right to know if I'm under arrest."

"You want to tell us where you were the night of July 16th, Mr. Harman?"

"You want to tell me if I'm under arrest, Detective Hoppmann?" He's taken aback I even remember his name. And they must wonder why I've remained unruffled. Meticulous habits, I say. Good for the soul. And with scrupulous care, I'm ready for them.

"No, Mr. Harman, you're not under arrest. Yet. Now answer the question: where were you the night of July 16th? And don't play games. As I said, we have a witness."

"That was some time ago, detective. How on earth should I be able to recall that particular evening?" I say. "Wednesday, two weeks back, Mr. Harman. Were you in the park?"

"Quite possible. I take a stroll every evening when weather permits." Now he thinks he's gotten a break. T'is evident in his face.

Now sloe-eyed, he leans forward. "Who did you see in the park that night, Mr. Harman?"

"Didn't say I was in the park, detective, just that it was quite possible," I say. He leans back, trying to regroup his tactics, I'd bet a quid.

"Tell us about that particular evening, Mr. Harman. Where did your stroll take you?"

"Not a clue, Detective. I've no idea the route of my walk that evening."

"Did you see a policeman that night, Mr. Harman?"

"No idea," I say and wait.

"Are you sure, Mr. Harman? There's a bobby on the evening beat in that neighborhood. Are you sure you didn't see him?"

"Ah, I see what you mean," I say. Both unconsciously readjust themselves in their seats. No doubt they're sure they're on the cusp of breaking the case open. "You want to know if I saw Officer Cochran that evening. Well, I can tell you definitively, I did not. It's been quite some time since I've encountered the good officer who patrols our neighborhood."

The detectives look at each other and frown. No doubt they wonder if I know that Cochran retired six months ago. They've painted themselves into the proverbial corner. Ha.

"Enough of this, detectives. Uncuff me and allow me to call my solicitor." One of them takes a deep breath and sighs. Not the piece of cake you thought it'd be, old chaps? I muse.

"Jim, take the cuffs off Mr. Harman." "But---" the other begins to protest.

"Take them off. Mr. Harman is uncomfortable." Ah, we're getting somewhere. Now I'm in the know on the roles each plans to play.

Wolfe takes the cuffs off, and I visibly rub my wrists. And make a face. " My hands are quite numb, gentlemen."

"Now, you want to talk with us, Mr. Harman?" "Why, yes, detectives, once I've had an opportunity to talk with my solicitor." Their faces look as if each has just been obliged to take a sip of soured milk.

They glance at each other and leave the room. The door slams. Well, at least the cuffs are off and the room has cooled down. And they still have nothing. Unless... unless Officer Nick let the cat out of the bag. But he couldn't. He wouldn't. He's been well paid. And I can prove it. No, that won't do. I need to speak with my solicitor, now, not later.

Hmm, how to handle them when they return. Candor and directness along with naïve innocence, of course. But once again I need to throw the blokes off balance.

Minutes pass. No doubt eyes are watching. Mustn't weaken, must exhibit a bland face, a man with clean hands, inculpable. When they return I'll focus on every gesture I see, every nuance. Stay one step ahead.

The door opens. A new face.

"I'm Detective Johnson. Sorry for the wait, Mr. Harman. If you'll just answer a few brief questions for me, we'll see that you're promptly returned to your residence, and you can then resume your usual evening activities."

Activities indeed. "I need to relieve myself, Detective," I say. Yes, it appears I've caught him off guard.

"Of course, Mr. Harman. I'll have someone escort you to the loo shortly. Now if you'll-----"

"Now," I say with some fervor. "And if I'm not under arrest, there should be no delays." My voice is insistent. Heads behind the glass must be turning. Must play the ruse out with self-assurance.

The door opens. Another suit appears and nods to Detective Johnson. He rises and says,

"come with me, Mr. Harman."

"Where are we going?" I say.

"To the loo. You did say you needed to be relieved, did you not?"

"Quite."

XXXXX

Thank goodness the fool's left me in here alone. Let's see, windows are too high to reach. No way out. But I do see a vent in the ceiling. Ah hah. No doubt there's a camera up there behind it. And they're watching me. Can't outsmart me for a moment, chaps.

Must make it look as if I did have a genuine need. The door behind me opens and someone shuffles in toward the sinks. I hear a water tap turned on, but I know better than to turn around. I pretend to finish, flush, and turn.

It's him, Officer Nick, lathering his hands, I see. And ignoring me, he is. Waiting to spring a trap on me, are we?

From behind him, I could easily seize his billy club from his belt. But there's a camera on me, I'm quite sure of it. And he's the plant. Yes, they're expecting a friendly chat to erupt now while they record it. Shrewd chaps, they are, I'll give them that, but not shrewd enough.

I casually step up to a sink, wash my hands and turn. And without speaking I stroll out the door.

And in the hallway, I find several officers milling about. And in an instant, with astonished looks, they are transfixed on me. T'was a lark fooling you chaps, I muse.

And with a chuckle, I say, "Thought I'd pause for a chat with Officer Nick, did you?" At once I gasp at my faux pas, my face flushing.

"Cuff him. Book him", words that echo through my mind and haunt me still.

About the Author:

Fred Miller is a California writer who specializes in penning short stories with eclectic themes. His first was selected by Constance Hunting, the New England poet laureate in 2003. More than fifty of his stories have appeared in publications around the world in the past ten years. Many of his stories may be seen on his blog:
https://pookah1943.wordpress.com.

GRUNTIN' AND DEBATIN'
by Daniel Elasky

I was supposed to be attending the National Debate Tournament in Princeton, New Jersey. Instead, I detoured to the annual Worm Grunting Contest in Slapchappy, Florida. The good news and bad news: I won the under-75 class--I grunted up 482 worms--a new under-75 record (though admittedly far short of the over-75 record of 557 worms held by the immortal Harold Stank), for which I received the first place prize of $20. The bad news: I would have some serious fibbing to do when I got home. Fortunately, I'm very good at making up stories to cover my tracks. There was no reason this time would be any different.

In case you don't know, a worm grunter attempts to entice worms to come to the surface. To do this, you drive a wooden stake into the ground, which you then rub with a smooth piece of metal like an old saw blade. This creates a vibration which attracts a worm, and it quickly works its way up to the surface.

The WGC is the big event of the year in Slapchappy, population 302. This year, some forty people grunted, and nearly twenty more were spectators. In the nonstop rush of grunting and beer swilling, I wasn't even thinking of what I would say when I arrived back home. I started tossing it around in my head on the drive back.

Think about it: how are you supposed to explain to your parents, who have worked and slaved to send you to the best school, hoping that you'd become a successful lawyer or diplo-mat, that you'd rather spend your time rubbing a stick in the ground, trying to scare up earthworms?

The way I saw it, there were fifty million good debaters running around, but only a small, very select group of people could claim to be expert grunters--people like Garley Peffelfanger and Hilda Buffonk--and I surmized they made some serious money from endorsements.

So I was sure I could talk my way out of it, get a plausible story past Ma and Pop, using my trusty old tool, bullshit. I'd have to be in top form this time. I felt very good about my chances, though, as I was well-rested from the drive, and reality-based in my thoughts, as much as I ever am.

However, I knew I was treading on thin ice when I stood with Ma in the kitchen and she was icily silent. Pop came in from the front yard, where he'd just shot down a drone flying over our property ("That damn Amazon!") and stood with Ma.

Okay, Alex, this has to be convincing. Put on your debate face.

"So, how was the debate tournament?" Ma said.

"It was good," I said.

"Did you learn anything?"

Scramble, brain, scramble.

"Well," I said, "I entered the novice competition but didn't win. But I picked up a lot of pointers from the experts. How to come up with arguments, organize 'em, present 'em, stuff like that." That sounded quite good.

Pop said, "What was the debate topic?"

Make something up. "It was, uh, let me see if I can remember the exact words. Oh, here it is: 'Russia should be invited to become a full member of NATO.' "

"Those are the exact words, eh?"

"Yes."

"I don't think so. I looked it up. Here it is: 'Research on animals for scientific purposes should be banned.'"

I looked down at my shoes and Pop did, too.

"Look at the dirt on those shoes," he said. "They was new when you left. You ain't been to no debate contest. You've been gruntin' those damn worms again, haven't you?"

He had me. "Yes, Pop," I said.

"You'd rather hang out with night crawlers than learn how to debate, eh? Then s'pose you go sit in that hole in the back yard for a while?"

"You mean that pit they're diggin' to drain the septic tank?"

"One and the same," Pop said. "Now get your ass out there."

"But Pop, it's gross. . ."

"Get out there and sit in that hole."

"Yes, Pop."

I put on my oldest, crappiest clothes and went out and sat in the hole, which was filled with about seven inches of "wastewater." God, what a stench.

As I sat in the hole, I started to grow fearful: what if some of my college friends, home for the summer, came to the house? What would Ma tell them? Pop? "Oh, he's in the back yard,

sitting in a hole." The thought made me insane with terror.

No, this could not happen. I knew that the gods hated my guts, but surely they weren't this deranged, to let something like this happen.

It turned out, they *were* this deranged:

Stepping down the back steps and walking across the yard were the two girls I admired most in this town, Mary and Jenna, home for the summer. Oh, no.

Mary: "Hello, Alex. My, you're lookin' spiffy." Tryin to keep a straight face, but losing it.

Jenna: "Alex, I hate to use cliches, but you need to 'clean up your act,' as they say." She managed to get it out before she cracked up.

Mary: "Oh, god, this odor will permeate our clothes."

Jenna: "We're out of here! Alex, give me a call when I can't smell you five miles away."

Very, very funny.

Then Grandma came by.

"Glory, Hallelujah! Just look at you!"

When she stopped laughing, she put on a serious face. She said, "We had such high hopes for you, Sweetness. The first one in the family to go to college. And here you are, sittin' in a damn shit pit!"

"I'm sorry, Grandma. I'll try to do better next time."

"That's what you always say, you young jackass!"

"Yes, Grandma."

It was time to swing for the fences: "Grandma, do you think you could ask Pop if I can come out now?"

"I 'spect he'll let you out when the time is right."

"Yes, Grandma." I was raised to always remain respectful, even in the direst circumstances.

Well, Pop eventually did let me out, when a sudden tornado warning popped up, but Ma and Pop and Grandma made me sit in the opposite corner of the cellar from them, out of smelling distance. I hoped the tornado would fill the hole with boards and cows and stuff, so nobody could sit in it, namely me. But when I looked later, the pit was empty, almost dry. The tornado had sucked the shit out of our septic tank!

Well, as you can see, my cover story bombed. And so, from that day on, after I got the smell off, I pursued my studies with a single-minded passion, as much as I am capable of. I ask you not to divulge the foregoing history to anyone, as it would seem unseemly for the newly-elected President of the International Monetary Fund.

Ha! More bullshit.

Seriously, though, I am today the Secretary General of the Saskatchewan Lavatory Attendants Association. So, not a complete washout by any means.

About the Author:

A former staff writer on historical subjects at ProQuest, **Dan Elasky** left several years ago to try his hand at fiction. He's written two novels and recently completed a collection of golf stories, and finds writing short form fiction challenging and satisfying. He's especially drawn to unusual characters and situations. In addition to writing for publications, he's currently developing a partly humorous, partly serious series of podcasts for children. Dan is a member of the Old Town Writers group in Alexandria, Virginia and lives in Fredericksburg, Va.

YOUNG

by Nicole Reinholdt

Wednesday morning, when Kyle picked me up for school in his dad's grey Buick Skylark, he had Neil Young's *Everybody Knows This is Nowhere* playing over the stereo. Since the two of us had started seeing each other sophomore year, it had become 'our' album—he called me 'Cinnamon Girl' because I had red hair, and both of us loved the title track because we lived in a very small town that no one cared about. That's what was on when I got into the passenger's seat. "Good morning," I said to Kyle.

"Good mor-morning to you, too," he said. His stammer was always worse when he was tired.

I buckled the worn seatbelt as we pulled onto the road. Right on cue, Neil's mournful voice pleaded, *"Gotta get away from this day-to-day running around/ everybody knows this is nowhere…"* I squeezed Kyle's wiry right arm. "You didn't sleep well, did you?" I asked him.

He sighed. He was wearing his dad's sheepskin jacket, so he smelled (not unpleasantly) like cigarettes. "Not r-really. I woke up when Dad got home, and then I couldn't fall back asleep." Kyle's dad, Bill, was a cashier at the Holiday gas station, and lately, they'd been putting him on the night shift, eight PM to four AM. "How about you?"

"I was cold at first, but then Rufus came in and got on the bed." Rufus was the family dog—a four-year-old Wheaten Terrier. "He was

a good boy, he just laid there by my feet all night."

We drove on through the cold blue morning. There was frost on the aspen trees and the windows of people's cars. Some houses still had their Christmas decorations up, even though it was almost Valentine's Day. We pulled into the school's parking lot just as "Down by the River" was ending. That song had always made me uncomfortable; to me, it wasn't literally about murder, but about love turned into a destructive force. It was perilous territory.

Our school was pretty much the only impressive building in town—three stories, made of white stone. When it was built, it was solely intended to be the high school, and it still had 'Hepburn High School' in sharp black Roman letters above the main door. But these days, it served grades six through twelve, and I'd read an article in the paper saying it might merge with the elementary school soon.

Kyle parked, and pulled the key out of the ignition. "Well, here we go," he said. Then he yawned. "Looks like I'm sleeping through Algebra again." He ran a hand through his light-brown hair. Sometimes he put gel in it to make it stand up, but today it was just silky and clean.

I leaned over against him. "Don't do that."

"Why not? It's not like Janovich cares." Mr. Janovich was brusque and seemed frustrated with life in general. He was hard on Kyle, calling on him when he knew Kyle hadn't been paying attention.

"He does care, though," I said. "He knows you could do better."

Kyle frowned and rounded his shoulders obstinately. "I thought you were on my side, Allie."

"Kyle, I don't like it when you say things like that." He didn't quite understand how his words affected other people, so I tried to remind him as much as possible.

He put his hand on my head, stroking my hair. "Sorry. I just- I just- I hate it so much. I just want it to be over." We were seniors, but June felt like a long way off.

I cuddled against him for a second, and then straightened up. "I know. I'll see you on break." At 10:45 every day, the whole school had a fifteen-minute break—a holdover from the days when everyone smoked. It was a good chance to check in and see how things were going. I kissed him on the cheek, and then we went inside.

In homeroom, I sat down next to my friend Sarah Pulaski. Sarah looked like Patti Smith— wild, feathery dark hair, a thin face, and cool clothes. Today, she had on a Sonic Youth T-shirt, ripped jeans with black leggings underneath, and a loose green flannel shirt with the sleeves rolled up to her elbows, showing her gangly forearms. She smiled at me. "Hey," she said. "What's the weather report?" That was our code for talking about Kyle.

"Cloudy with a chance of Janovich," I said.

She quirked her lips consolingly. "Rough night?"

"Well, I wouldn't know. I wasn't there." Then I blushed, realizing the implication of what I'd said.

She pounced on it, her hazel eyes squinting with glee. "What? I thought for sure you guys were doing the blanket hornpipe by now!"

I clapped a hand over my mouth, trying not to burst out laughing. "The *what?*" I whispered.

"You heard me!" she whispered back. The bell rang, and we tried to get it together (or at least I did), but it was useless. Every five seconds, one of us glanced over at the other, each thinking of that ridiculous phrase, until we were practically bent over with silent laughter. Fortunately, homeroom was more or less a free period, so once Ms. Jenkins had taken attendance, we could talk again. Sarah started to form the word "Blanket," but I held my hand up to 'shush' her.

"Don't start!" I said. "I have something to tell you. Something serious."

She tilted her head, the mischief gone from her eyes. "What's up?"

I bit my lip. "I got into Whitman," I said. "Full scholarship for the first year."

She brightened up. "Congratulations! That's exciting."

"Yeah," I wavered. "Yeah, it's just... I haven't told Kyle. He knows I applied out of state, but I just sort of let him assume I'd be going to the university in Missoula."

Sarah leaned toward me, suddenly grave. "Allie, you need to tell him. And you need to do it soon."

"I mean, I might not go," I said. "There's nothing wrong with going to Missoula. That way he could come visit on the weekends."

Sarah folded her bony arms. "Allie," she said sternly. "Don't do it. You are going to go to Whitman College, just like your mom, major in English, and be a school librarian on the Oregon coast. You've been talking about it since I've known you." Sarah and I had only really started hanging out freshman year; it was through her that I'd gotten closer to Kyle. "Have you not talked about that with Kyle?"

I shrugged. "Yeah, but we've also talked about how I'm going to become the first woman president," I said. "I never wanted it to seem like that was the only option."

"So what's the other option?" she asked pointedly. "What, you go to Missoula, you see each other on weekends, you drop out because he says he misses you, you come back here and get married when you're nineteen?" She flipped her flat bangs out of her eyes. "You spend the rest of your life taking care of him?"

"You say that like it's a bad thing." I wasn't sure whether or not I was joking.

Sarah shook her head at me. "Allie, you're his girlfriend, not his mom. I mean that's-" She looked around, as if she were afraid he was in the room, and dropped her voice. "That's why I've kind of distanced myself from him. He's not a bad person, I still really like him and I want him to be OK or whatever, but he just *needs* so much from people."

My heart dropped, and suddenly, I thought I might cry. She was right. (She usually was.) It seemed different for me because I loved him. I knew I made sacrifices for him that I never would have made for other people, because lying on his narrow chest with his hand against the side of my head was the best thing in my world. Looking in his dark grey eyes and seeing myself reflected back as something special and beautiful, feeling his stubble against my lips when he kissed me... I kept telling myself it was worth it. But was it? I didn't want our relationship to end, but when I really thought about it, I didn't know how we'd make it work outside of the protective bubble of high school.

On break, Kyle came up behind me at my locker, put his arms around my waist, and lifted me into the air for a second. I gasped and laughed, swatting at him. "You're lucky I know you," I scolded as he set me down. Mostly I liked it when he did things like that, but it was a reminder of how much physical power he actually had.

He nuzzled his head against my neck. "You can say that again," he murmured. Then he let out a groan. "I wanna go home."

I turned and put my hands on his upper arms, lightly pushing him away so that I could look up into his face. "Kyle, it's not even lunchtime yet. And you don't want to miss Art, do you?" Our art teacher, Mr. Gregory, was one of the few teachers Kyle got along with.

Kyle sighed. "No, I guess not. But do I have to sit through English first?"

"Yes, and if you fall asleep, I'll whack you," I said playfully.

He made a pouty face. "You shouldn't hit people; it's mean." Then he yawned. "I need a soda or something."

As we walked down to the vending machines, we passed Ben Knudsen and some other jocks. Ben was J.C. Penney handsome—beefy and blond with a smarmy smile. "Hey Talbot," he said. "Saw your dad at the gas station last night." He emphasized *at the gas station* so that everyone could hear. (As if everyone didn't know that's where Bill Talbot worked; there were only 2,000 people in this town.)

Kyle stared at him impassively. "And?" he asked.

Ben tilted his head. "Yeah, funny thing. He wouldn't sell me a beer. What do you think about that?"

"He knows you're not old enough, *Benjamin*," I broke in. "Unless you actually are twenty-one, in which case, what are you doing in high school?" My heart was pounding.

I saw Rob Haniszewski laugh behind his hand. Ben just did a kind of theatrical double take. "Ooh, check out the mouth on Allie," he crowed. "*Damn*, no wonder you're with her, Kyle. What else she can do with that mouth?"

Kyle's face turned white. "You don't *speak* that way about my... my... my..." He tried to say 'girlfriend', but it came out all jumbled, more like 'grfllrr'.

Ben put up his hands. "Sorry, *no hablo El Spazmo*," he sneered.

Rob grabbed Ben by the shoulders. "Hey,

lay off," he scolded. "He's right; you shouldn't say stuff like that. Allie's a nice girl."

Ben retreated, but not before a parting shot. "Looks like you better watch out, Kylie. Han Solo here likes your girlfriend." As they walked down the hall, Rob looked back at us and mouthed *Sorry*.

Kyle slammed his hand against the vending machine. "Fucking *asshole!*" he growled. He punched in the code for a red Gatorade.

I pressed his back with my palm. "Kyle, take it easy, OK? We have to get to class. It's no good getting all worked up."

He grabbed the bottle of juice out of the slot and whirled around. "How can I not?" he yelped. "Talking shit about my dad is one thing, but about you... I'm supposed to protect you, supposed to... You sh-shouldn't have to hear those things." He had his hand on my upper arm, almost painfully tight, and there were tears pooling in his eyes.

I put my hand on his chest, feeling the thick red flannel of his shirt. I rubbed it gently up and down. "Deep breaths, Kyle. It wasn't nice, but it's over now. Just leave it, all right? Drink some of your juice, and let's go."

Soothing him like that, helping him control his oscillating moods, made me feel kind of powerful. I was, like Jane Eyre, 'poor, obscure, plain, and little', but I could do something that others couldn't. I remembered in elementary school, before I really knew him, being afraid of him. It seemed like he was always being hauled off to the principal's office, or made to sit in the hall. He was like a fox kit, small but fierce.

Everyone knew his story. One night, when he was just two, his mother had fallen asleep with a lit candle next to the bed. Somehow, the candle fell over, and soon the trailer was ablaze. A neighbor saw the flames and rushed over, pulling Kyle out through the window, but Delia was already dead, suffocated by the smoke. Kyle had burns all over his back, which melted and twisted into shiny ropes of scar tissue. The physical scars turned out to be the least of his problems.

In English, we were talking about Orwell's *Animal Farm*. Ms. Abbott got on a tangent about British writers and dystopian fiction— saying it was interesting because Britain had never been under that kind of dictatorship. To my surprise, Kyle raised his hand.

"Yes, Kyle?" said Ms. Abbott. She also sounded surprised.

Kyle cleared his throat. "What about... what about in the 80s? With um... that lady... um... Marg- Margaret Thatcher? I thought she was a f-fascist."

Ms. Abbott made an odd kind of smirk. "Someone's a punk fan," she observed. "No, despite what Johnny Rotten might have said about it, Thatcher was not actually a dictator." A few people laughed. She went on a little more, and then the conversation shifted around to something else.

When the bell rang, Kyle and I walked out together. In the hallway, I stood on tiptoe and put my arms around him, resting my head against his collarbone. "Forty-five minutes," I said. "Then we can leave." The school let us go wherever we wanted during lunch (not that there was anywhere to go, but it was a nice gesture).

He let out another groan. "I already know I'm stupid; I don't need to be reminded every five seconds."

I tucked my fingers into his hair, playing with the short fuzz at the nape of his neck. "You're not stupid, Kyle. Anybody could've made that mistake."

"You wouldn't have," he said.

"Well, not everyone's a big giant nerd like me." I started to sing in his ear—"Round and Round", the third song on *Everybody Knows*...

"Round and round and round we spin,

to weave a wall, to hem us in,

it won't be long...

it won't be long..." I was singing Robin Lane's harmony part.

He let out a long sigh. "Oh god, Allie, I love you. I love you so much." He squeezed me and let me go, and we walked hand in hand up to the art studio.

For lunch, we drove over to Kyle's house. Ever since Bill had been on the night shift, he would wake up around this time, and it had become a routine to sit at their kitchen table while Bill made 'brunch', drinking strong black coffee. I loved that cozy little kitchen, with the yellow curtains in the windows and off-white Formica countertops.

Bill was waiting for us in the living room, wearing a green Western shirt with pearl snaps. His craggy, handsome face seemed straight out of an old frontier newspaper. He bounded over and scooped his son up in a bear hug—Kyle was taller, but Bill was bulkier. "Hiya, kiddo," he said. Then he saw me. "Hey, Alley Cat!" he exclaimed, holding his hand out. When I took it, he spun me under his arm as if we were dancing. "But you're not an alley cat, are you?" he corrected himself. "You're too neat and tidy for that. I like that purple sweater; it's a pretty one." Bill's Kentucky accent had softened after twenty-five years in Montana, but his speech still had a lilting rhythm.

"Thank you," I said, smiling at him.

"Well, kids, what'll it be? Ham and eggs all right?" he asked. We nodded, and all three of us went into the kitchen, Kyle and I taking our usual spots at the round maple table. Bill put the coffee on, and soon had the skillet sizzling. He moved quickly, but gently, trying not to startle anyone. A few times, as he passed Kyle, he put a hand on Kyle's head, as if to reassure himself that Kyle was still there.

Once we'd been served, Bill asked me, "Now, Allison, have you heard from any of those colleges yet? Did Yale call up and say, 'Get on out here; we can't wait'?"

My heart hit my throat. "I got something from Whitman, but I haven't opened it yet," I fibbed.

He nodded. "Now, where's that again? The name is familiar, but I can't remember–"

"Washington," I said. "It's in Walla Walla."

Kyle snorted. "W…" He stopped and shook his head. "I don't think I could say that even on a good day."

"It's a mouthful, that's for sure," Bill said. "But that's not so far away. Nice drive, too— gorgeous country on the way there."

"Missoula's pretty, too," Kyle muttered.

"It is," I said quickly, "and I know I'll get in there."

Bill looked at the two of us. "Yes," he said in a neutral tone, "I'm sure you will."

When we finished eating, Bill said he had an errand to run and needed the car. It was only a ten-minute drive back to school, and we still had close to half an hour. He left, and Kyle and I began to clean up. I decided to tell Kyle everything, before I lost my nerve. "Kyle," I said, scraping out the skillet, "I have something to tell you."

He set down the plate he was holding. "What?"

I put the skillet in the sink. "I got accepted to Whitman. Full scholarship for the first year."

"That's nice. You're not going, though, right? I mean we talked about this." He crossed his arms and looked down at me, almost like he was scolding me.

I bit my lip. "Kyle, listen–"

He held up his right hand, stopping me. "No, you listen! Allie, I can't be without you. Nobody else cares about me, except Dad. People just give up on me. All the teachers, the doctors, even people who tried to be my friend, until you. Do you know why I pick you up for school every day?"

I shook my head, not trusting myself to talk.

"It's so that I have a reason to get out of

bed." He stretched his hands toward me. "Allie, without you... I'm nothing."

I wanted to take his hands. I wanted to make it all right. But I kept thinking of Sarah's warning. Did I really want to stay here *forever*? Did I want to be like my mom, working in that poky little real-estate office on Pine Street for the next thirty years? Or like my dad, having to drive the forty miles to the hospital in Great Falls four days a week? "Kyle, this isn't easy for me, either."

He shook his head and leaned back against the fridge. "Everything's easy for you," he mumbled. "You know what I hate? Ben Fucking Knudsen and those guys—they're not any smarter than me, but they've got a ticket out, just cause they can throw a stupid football and run really fast!" As if to support his point, he coughed one of the wheezy little coughs that came over him when he got excited. "But me? What's going to happen to me? Am I gonna trade shifts with Dad at the gas station, selling beer to those jerks just so I don't get my ass kicked?" He started to cry. "At least with you, I might have a future."

I didn't really believe in hell anymore, but if it did exist, it probably felt something like this. I took a deep breath, making my voice as slow and steady as I could. "Kyle, you're not stupid. Some things are hard for you, but you're not stupid. Anybody who loves and appreciates music like you do..." I clamped my mouth together before I lost control of my voice.

He put his hands over his face. "Who do you think I am? Rufus? You think if you say nice things to me, I'll just wag my tail and forget about it?"

"Kyle, please..." I stepped over and tried to put my hand on his arm, but he slapped it away. "Kyle, I love you, and you know that."

He stared at me, his grey eyes foggy with tears. "Do I?"

"Yes!" I exclaimed. "Yes, you do! And nothing will ever change that. There's a place in my heart that's all yours, that nobody else can ever

touch." Now I had to rip the bandage off. "But Kyle, this is what I want. I want to get out of here and see and do things for myself. The future's coming for both of us, whether we face it together or not."

There was a long, horrible silence. I thought of the chorus of "Cowgirl in the Sand":

"Old enough now to change your name,

when so many love you, is it the same?

It's the woman in you that makes you want to

play this game..."

The last thing in the world I wanted to do was hurt him, but here I was.

Kyle's jaw quivered, and his face grew red. "Fuck you, Allie," he whispered. "Get out of my kitchen. Go get that big shiny future of yours that I'm not part of!" He was yelling now. "Go!" He picked up one of the cups and flung it at me.

It hit me squarely in the cheekbone, and then dropped to the floor and broke. For a second, I was so shocked I almost laughed. I looked down at it where it lay, in shiny blue pieces on the brown linoleum.

Kyle's legs buckled, and he slid down to the floor, hugging his knees. He started whimpering, ratcheting up to a moan like a wounded calf.

Then I heard the car pull up. Bill's footsteps up the sidewalk. The door, and the rush of sharp winter air. He came into the kitchen, and I saw him take the scene in. Oddly enough, I wasn't crying yet. He went over and knelt by his son. "Kyle," he said, quiet but firm. "Kyle Christopher Talbot, get up off this floor and go to your room." He grabbed his son's hand and pulled him to his feet, leading him into the hallway. I got the broom and the dustpan, and started sweeping up the pieces of ceramic. When Bill came back, he strode over, put his hand on my shoulder, and took hold of the broom. "Don't worry about that, darlin'. I'll take care of it. What happened?"

"We had a fight," I said. "I lied earlier—I got into Whitman. I told him and… he freaked out." I raised my face and looked him in the eye.

His weathered face crinkled with tenderness. "Let's go sit in the living room," he said.

I started sobbing. "I'm sorry," I said, not specifically to Bill.

He led me to the couch and sat me down, clasping my hands gently in his. "Oh, honey. You've got nothing to be sorry about. Is anyone home at your place right now? I should call-"

"Probably just Rufus," I interjected. "And he can't answer the phone."

Bill's laugh lines deepened. "O.K. We'll sit here a minute and then I'll drive you home."

I shook my head. "I don't want…" I dropped my voice. "I don't think we should leave Kyle by himself. I'll walk; it's not that far."

"I don't want you by yourself either," Bill admonished. "It's twenty degrees out there, and a storm's coming in. I could see the clouds. I'll drive you; it won't take long."

I shook my head. "No, really, it's all right. I think I'd like the cold air. I think it'd feel good."

Bill brought me my coat, and wrapped my green scarf around my neck. "Have your mom call me later on, all right?" I nodded, and he took a bunch of Kleenex out from the box on the coffee table and stuffed them in my coat pocket. He looked close to crying himself. "You take care, sweet gal. Get home safe."

Outside, the air was crystalline—the blue sky looking like it would shatter if you touched it. Like the cup. No, don't think about that. To the west, a bank of violet-grey clouds obscured the peaks of the mountains. It smelled like woodsmoke and dead leaves. I walked along the cracked sidewalk on autopilot, my body propelling itself forward while my mind hovered somewhere… else. It hadn't hurt that much; possibly it wouldn't even leave a mark. And it had hurt him to do it.

Cruelly, a flood of happy memories flickered in my mind's eye. Dancing to "Have Yourself A Merry Little Christmas" at last year's Snow Ball. Lying on Kyle's bed, listening to Nick Drake's *Five Leaves Left* during a thunderstorm. Sharing fry bread at the fair over in Great Falls, strolling the dusty midway as the rides lit up under the evening sky. All that love, all that joy… how was I supposed to walk away from that?

A shiny white Subaru honked and pulled up a few yards down from where I was walking. When I got up close, I realized it was Rob Haniszewski. He rolled down his window. "Hey, you need a ride?"

I hesitated. "I'm not going back to school," I said, swallowing the tears.

He shrugged. "It's cold. Just tell me where you need to go."

I opened the passenger door and climbed in. He had the radio playing—Grateful Dead's "Box of Rain". "You listen to the Dead?" I asked.

"I like the oldies," he said. "Where are we going?"

I told him where I lived and settled back against the plush seat. Phil Lesh's voice, earnest and aggrieved:

"What do you want me to do,

to do for you, to see you through?

For this is all a dream we dreamed one afternoon long ago…" I sniffled and turned my face toward the window.

"Hey, what's wrong?" Rob asked after a minute or so. "Are you OK?"

"I don't want to talk about it," I told him.

He adjusted his mirror. "Listen, I'm really sorry about earlier. I told Ben not to be such a dick."

"He's always treated Kyle like that," I said.

"I don't really know Kyle that well. But he

must be pretty cool if you like him." I couldn't respond. Fortunately, my favorite verse of the song came on:

"Walk into splintered sunlight,

inch your way through dead dreams to another land.

Maybe you're tired and broken,

your tongue is twisted with words half-spoken and thoughts unclear..."

I held my breath so I wouldn't sob out loud, exhaling as slowly as possible. I peeked over at Rob. He was handsome—there was no arguing that—with his dark curls and his freckles. And he'd always seemed genuinely nice; actually popular rather than just loud and dominant. I saw, briefly, a different world for myself: being on the prom committee, going to soccer games (I'd always liked soccer), maybe even going to one of the parties in Mary Halvorson's basement...

But I was leaving. That was the root of this whole mess. In four months, I would graduate. A month after that, I would turn eighteen. And in September, off to Washington. This imagined teenaged idyll had already passed me by. I had to turn toward the world, and see what I could make of it. *"Such a long, long time to be gone/ and a short time to be there."*

"Is this it?" Rob asked, shaking me out of my reverie.

Yes, this was it—my little brick house, with the weeping willow in the front yard and the chain-link fence. "Thanks," I said, unbuckling my seatbelt.

"Sure thing," he replied. "I hope you feel better."

I smiled weakly and dashed into the house. Rufus was lying in the green chair by the window, but he sat up as soon as I shut the door, his cropped tail wagging. He followed me into the kitchen as I filled the red teapot and set it on the stove. In that brief space of time, absorbed in my task, I wasn't upset—just neutral

and concentrating. Get down the bag of Red Rose tea from the cupboard. Put the bag in the green souvenir mug from Glacier National Park. Wait for the water to boil. Sometimes I had to break things down like this for Kyle, when he was at his most dysfunctional. Who would do that now?

I knelt down and scratched the silky curls behind Rufus' ears. "Oh Rufus," I said, trying to cheer myself up, "who needs a smelly old boyfriend when they have a smelly old dog?" He looked at me, his deep brown eyes full of doggy adoration, and bumped his shaggy head against my shoulder. The teapot began to whistle in G major, so I stood up, turned off the heat, and poured the water into my cup. Then I sat back down on the kitchen floor, pulled Rufus into my lap, and cried into his downy blond fur. The future lay ahead of me, as vast and formless as the oncoming blizzard. But it was *mine*. I could be my own person for the first time. Was this how freedom felt

About the Author:

Nicole Reinholdt was born and raised in Missoula, Montana. She currently resides in Brooklyn, New York, where she is working on her first novel. Her fiction has appeared in The Marymount Manhattan Review, and she has written about music and film online at Hitsville UK and Love Letters to Rock 'n' Roll.

A.J. AND CRAZY WOMAN

by Linda L. Dunlap

On her drive to work in the morning rain, A.J. hears on the radio that a helicopter just dropped out of the sky into the meat department at Davis Market. With everything else that's going on, she scarcely blinks an eye. After 40 years of threatening to, her daddy left her stepmother a month ago and moved in with A.J. He didn't take so much as a toothbrush with him when he left and had hardly hit the street before his wife had changed the locks on her house and taken out a restraining order on him. Her house, as she liked to say, with the emphasis on *her,* because she'd inherited it from her own mother. After all these years, hers was still the only name on the deed, even though he'd rebuilt the house when it burned in '89 and his name was on the mortgage.

But then everybody knew it wasn't about the house.

A.J. had sloshed down Pine Bluff, then maneuvered thru the downpour to Captain Mike's Liquor Store. Now she stands, watching from behind the counter at the torrents of rain that sweep the sidewalk in front of the store. Rain has fallen for three days, leaving a permanent feel to the moisture that seeps into her forty-five year old bones. She smells the electric crackle of the heater fan that clicks on in the back of the store. It's cold for mid March, ordi-narily the cusp of spring. When she flips on the florescent light overhead, a layer of faint lemon light blankets the counter. She lifts the dust cover from the cash register. Reaching behind her, she stuffs it between two of the stout white bottles of crème de cocoa that line the shelf like too many false teeth. There, she says, brushing her hands together and looking around. In five more minutes, she'll unlock the door.

Some people are born to work at Wal-Mart; some are born to work in a liquor store. A.J. was born to work at Captain Mike's. Her silver linings are this job and Mandy, her seven-year-old niece. Before them, it was riding behind Suitcase on his black Harley. He was called Suitcase because of the one he kept packed ready to leave his wife--but never did. When A.J. told him she was pregnant, that was the last she saw of him. She wound up having an abortion, something she'd probably think twice about now, since Mandy has arrived, plus A.J. has taken to dabbling in the church next door--but only dabbling. She knows it's easy to get caught up in religion in ways that are difficult to back out of.

When her brother Tag was in high school, he was seized by a religious fervor that sent him on a search for truth and wisdom. Nothing wrong with that, but zealous on the scale of

Jesus Christ? In the end the only thing he accomplished was to teach Nero, his Alaskan Elk Hound, to make the sign of the cross. Fortunately he came to his senses when A.J., who is 2 years older than he, pointed out this only proved the dog was the smarter of the two.

Still, the church next door offers a lot of comfort. The congregation is a laid-back bunch that meets in the Tidy Bowl Bar so that they can smoke and drink while they commune with the Holy Spirit. Last Christmas, the minister, a robust lesbian with good intentions, brought A.J. a little wooden cross. Our last one, the minister said, and we want you to have it. On the front was a perfect replica of a dogwood blossom carved into the wood with a heartbreaking finality.

A.J. wears it around her neck now. She's seen a lot of damage done in the name of good intentions, but not this time. Christmases are hard and the cross helps.

Still she can understand how the church would object to some things in her past. She finds herself objecting to them too. In fact, some things she's doing now--such as overdoing it again last night with the gin and breaking into houses.

A.J. unlocks the door to let in Miss Clara, the deaf alcoholic who's always her first customer of the day. Still slightly drunk from last night, Miss Clara had overdone it, too. Now she was in need of a morning drink.

A skin bag stuffed with sharp bones, Miss Clara is more of a mess this morning than usual because of having to wait outside in the rain. The brown finch feather on her once fine Shetland cloche droops soaked and limp. Walking on timid feet, she creeps toward the pyramid of vodka bottles just inside the front door. She gazes up at the intricate stack, her tongue, worrying the bits of food caught in her teeth from last night's taco casserole. A.J. knows it's taco casserole because that's what Miss Clara's husband, Butch, a buck-toothed man almost as thin as his wife, cooks for dinner every night.

A.J. feels lousy this morning and tells herself if she ever gets as bad as Miss Clara, she'll lay off the gin. She can do it anytime she wants; she's just going through a bad patch right now and has trouble sleeping.

Miss Clara stands staring at the vodka bottles as if she's asking herself how she'll ever do this thing that needs doing, when Tag pulls up to the curb outside in his white Jeep Cherokee. Both the old lady and A.J. smile to see Mandy's little blond head poke up from the back seat. They adore the little girl, but A.J. still hates when Tag drops her off at the liquor store. Some would call it child abuse, a seven-year-old in a liquor store. But today is a school holiday; Tag has a meeting and Mandy's mom is at the dance studio.

"So here I am," Mandy says, skipping in with a smile and cheering on the meager fistfuls of light in the room. "How are you, Miss Clara?" She nods to the old lady, who stops her fidgeting and smiles back. "And you, Auntie A.J.? Why, you look just beautiful today." Mandy has Tag and A.J.'s eyes, a hazel-blue that picks up the color she's wearing. Today it's a frosty-green hoodie that makes her eyes sing.

"Your red hair is so curly and bouncy," Mandy goes on now as if she's describing a character in one of the stories she writes when she's tucked behind the counter out of sight. She's amazing. One day after her mother had picked her up, A.J. pulled the wadded pages from the trash and read the tiny too-neat handwriting.

Since Granddaddy left Mee-Ma things are funny around here. Granddaddy just sits and stares at the wall. Mee Ma never was my real grandmother, just my step. Granddaddy says now she's not nothing and I get to call her anything I want to. He calls her Crazy Woman. He started calling her that after she chopped up his Bay Hill golf shirts and tossed them in the front yard where him and Auntie A.J. live. He calls her Crazy Woman all of the time now. But she's not crazy. She's just mean as hell.

A.J. chuckled when she saw how Mandy, on second thought, had scratched through the *as hell*. A.J. itched to correct the double negative, then remembered those days were over.

Tag comes in behind Mandy, his shoulders filling the doorway. He's become a regular at the gym and it shows. He smiles at Miss Clara, then turns to A.J. "Daddy says you broke into the house."

"It wasn't breaking in. She forgot to change the lock to the sliding glass door and I still have a key to it."

"Sure, sure," Tag laughs, "tell that to the police chief. But who cares how it happened? What I can't believe is what you took once you got inside."

"Daddy misses his train set. I thought having the engine might help. As for the clamshell dishes, he likes Oysters Rockefeller for Sunday supper. Do you have any idea how hard it is to find something to serve them in? Besides, he's so lost now, he needs some of his things around to comfort him. You know how this has blindsided him."

"You could have picked up his car registration. He'll need it to get his new tag."

Hesitating, he looks down. With the toe of his tennis shoe, he scrubs at a spot of stubborn gum on the tile floor. Finally he says, "I never thought he'd do it, did you? After all the years he said he would and didn't."

"It's not over 'til it's over. He could go back. I've heard it said when you've lived with crazy so long it becomes normal, then sometimes it's hard to live without."

"Well, let's just hope he left in time. But why now?"

She shrugs. Yes, why now? She's asked herself that question a hundred times in the past month.

"Remember how she used to tell everybody she took those two little deserted children in when their own mother left them," Tag's words

escalate, tumbling out one on top of the other. "She didn't take us in. Daddy got struck with a sudden attack of stupid and married the bitch. Oops! Sorry, Mandy."

"That's okay, Daddy," Mandy says, never missing a beat on the purple octopus she and Miss Clara are coloring in her coloring book. Mandy has her hand cupped around the shaky liver-spotted one to help Miss Clara stay in the lines.

Meanwhile Tag stands with his hand in his pocket jangling his keys. The look in his eyes is one A.J. has come to dread.

Finally almost in a whisper, he asks, "Do you think we'll ever see Mother again?"

A.J. feels her chest cave in. "Don't start, please. Okay?"

"But don't you still wonder?"

"Come on, not now."

"Okay, okay," he says. He takes a deep breath and adds, "By the way, where is Daddy?"

"He's down in the dumps at home. I remind him of how you might think things can't get any worse, but they can."

"And probably will."

"Oh, come on!"

Laughing, he scoops up Mandy in a bear hug. "See you, Sugar. He waves his keys at A.J. and heads for the door. Behind Miss Clara, he stops. Pointing down, he grins and pantomimes, "He could have married her!"

"Get out of here," A.J. yells. She knows he's kidding but hates the mean streak that sometimes flashes thru her brother's humor.

The octopus is finished and Mandy settles on her stool behind the counter. With tremulous hands, Miss Clara eases a vodka bottle from the poised stack. She's turning toward the counter, when the bottle slips from her hand and crashes to the floor.

By some miracle, it doesn't break. This is the third bottle she's dropped in the past two weeks. The others have smashed into a thousand pieces. When they break, it takes A.J. half the morning to clean up the mess and the store still reeks of vodka. But she refuses to fetch Miss Clara's bottles for her. Foolishly A.J. thinks this somehow absolves her of contributing to the old lady's drinking problem.

Miss Clara was once A.J.'s high school English teacher before she woke up deaf one morning and took her first drink of vodka the next. If A.J. brought up the subject of her drinking, which of course, she would not, and if Miss Clara were not deaf and it was a day when she could put a subject and predicate together, she'd have said, "Why Alice Katherine, darling, I can't imagine what you're talking about."

Now when the bottle hits the floor, she makes a tiny yelping sound. Her hands jerk about attacking little handfuls of air. She sees A.J. watching her and tries to hide. When she fades like a shadow into the corner, A.J. has to look away.

Before the drinking turned her into a zombie, Butch used to say he wouldn't mind Miss Clara's drinking so much if she'd just get drunk. The problem was she got drunk and did something. One winter night, before he'd learned to confiscate her keys, she came out of a blackout while driving her car down a railroad track. Two weeks later she fell into the Thunderbolt River wearing her new suede coat with the fur collar. She was rescued right away but the coat was ruined forever.

Now she spends her days and nights staring down the throat of a vodka bottle. Fun drinking, Butch calls it. At the end of the month, he drops by Captain Mike's and pays for her bottles--the ones she's drnk and the ones she's dropped. He finally surmised it was easier to stand on the bank than it was to wade through the quagmire of shit to the other side, his words. It's hard to picture Miss Clara as the Charleston debutante she once was, who'd married down~~when that sort of thing was important.

In A.J.'s senior year in high school, Miss Clara said she'd help A.J. get a scholarship to a college that had good English and Creative Writing programs. She said A.J. had a gift. But when she brought up the subject at home, A.J. was informed if she wanted to go to college, she'd go to the community college just like everybody else. Besides what made her think she was too good to just get a job? She wound up working on the South End at the Tastee Freeze.

A.J. adds water to the coffee pot and flips a filter into the holder. The wheels Tag set to turning in her mind won't stop. She remembers that last morning, the frog Daddy brought in with the firewood. Mother was quiet, bundled up on the couch in her furry new robe. Before they could catch the frog, Tag and A.J. squealing as they tried to hem it in between the couch and coffee table, it had dodged across the polished tiles to the foot of the Christmas tree. Gazing star-struck for an instant, it suddenly reached up and gulped down one of the blinking lights as if it was a tasty ladybug. They'd watched the bulb settle with a dim glow in the frog's stomach before it blinked out. Daddy pulled it out but the frog died anyway.

A.J. and Tag gave it a suitable funeral because long ago, Mother had taught them that frogs have mothers, too. That morning her hair was pulled back from her face, the pile of fluffy curls that ordinarily tumbled down her back reduced to a clumsy knot at the nape of her neck. When she spoke, it was in a hushed whisper. Her eyes had the look that said in her mind she was already someplace else.

When they woke the next morning, she was gone. She'd stayed until then so she wouldn't spoil their Christmas. Never mind that she'd now spoiled Christmas for them for the rest of their lives.

A.J. is pulled from these thoughts when she sees Mandy ease off her stool and peek at Miss

Clara. The old lady huddles still trying to shrink out of sight. Smiling at her, Mandy scrambles across the room and retrieves the bottle that's rolled beneath the lip of the counter. When she holds it out to the old lady, A.J. is about to say, "hon, what are you doing?" but something stops her. She watches Miss Clara clasp the bottle tightly around the neck and together, she and the little girl guide it carefully to the countertop. Then Mandy giggles and gives a thumbs up at what a fine job they've done. Miss Clara giggles, too.

Later when Mandy is scribbling away, A.J. glances over her niece's shoulder to see what she's written. *Captain smells like orange juice today but it must be from the bottle Miss Clara broke yesterday. It didn't break today.* Below that she'd added, *Like everybody doesn't know a bitch is a dog without hair.*

A.J. has almost finished adding coffee in the Mr. Coffee when Pete ducks through the door out of the rain.

"You're not going to believe what's happened," he says.

Her heart gives a stutter and the scoop of coffee in her hand tilts, speckling brown pimples across the counter. Uh,oh, this can't be good.

"What? she asks, then reminds herself that what Pete says is often biased. After all, he is Daddy's best friend. In fact, she isn't sure how her father would have survived through the years without Pete. But A.J.? Pete and his philosophizing can drive her insane.

He seems to think over her "what?" for a minute. In her mind she begs, No philosophizing now, please! Just give me the facts.

"Crazy Woman is in jail," he says finally.

"You're kidding!"

"Nope. You know life, it just keeps happening. It's like a box of Kleenex. You pull out one and up pops another and another--"

"--does Daddy know?"

"He's the one put her there."

"Why?"

"She shot him, that's why?"

"Daddy's shot? Is he hurt? Tell me! Tell me!"

"I did. I am. No." Pete says in a bluster.

"Where is he? I should have known something like this would happen. She's crazy! The woman is crazy!"

"He's outside in the car."

"Pete, why didn't you. . .forget it, forget it." She dashes to the door, then stops. She needs to make sure her father is not hurt. She really needs to do that now. But what she needs first is a shot of gin.

When she was still trying to help Miss Clara, A.J. had picked up a brochure from an AA meeting that asked 20 questions. Number 3 was *Do you drink before 5p.m.?* Hesitating, she stands undecided, then turns back into the store. Surely, it's 5 someplace.

Skirting fat drops of rain, A.J. reaches the car to find her father slumped in the backseat with his head in his hands. A meager stream of blood has leaked around a band-aid affixed over his bald spot. Her heart wrenches at his defeated look. When he left Crazy Woman, he never reckoned it would be like this.

Why did you wait until now, Daddy? Why now when I'm almost forty-five and finally no longer flinch when she reaches up to brush back her hair? Why not when I was twelve, when it would've counted for something? Why not when she slammed me in the mouth with the tennis racket and my braces cut my lips and blood sprayed everywhere? Why not when she yelled, "Now look what you've done. You've splattered blood on my new white couch? And you!" she'd turned to you and pointed. "Don't you say a word."

And you didn't, Daddy. You didn't say a word.

A.J. slides into the back seat beside him. Cradling him in her arms, she smoothes the nervous tic that's misshapen his face. Then her breath blossoming with gin, she whispers, "We're going to be fine, Daddy. We're going to be just fine."

For her to say anything more would be like the helicopter stalling over the meat counter at Davis Market then plunging down, ribeyes, T-bones, prime rib, porterhouses, pork roasts, baby backs and lamb chops flying in all directions.

A.J. pictures in her mind's eye, Miss Clara at the front of the classroom, the finch feather in her English cloche perky and spry. Miss Clara waits patiently for the slow student in the back row to look up. Then as if she's delivering a Shakespearian homely, she says, "What's important is not what you say. What's important is what you don't say."

A.J. had thought Miss Clara was just talking about literature. A.J. didn't know she was talking about real life, too. .

About the Author:

Linda L. Dunlap began a second career as a fiction writer in the late eighties after a successful career as a registered nurse. Her first story, "I'm Here, Mr. Sullivan," was published by Pencil Press Quarterly in 1987. Since then, she's had numerous short works published in literary and university presses across the country including The Crescent Review, Florida Magazine, RE:AL, Timber Creek Review, and Savannah Literary Journal. She was awarded artist's fellowship grants from the Florida Department of Cultural Affairs in 1996, in 2000 and again in 2010. Her short story, "Goldenrod" was nominated for a Pushcart Prize in 2010. A collection of her short stories entitled Rail Walking And Other Stories was published in 2015 and is available at Amazon.com in the Kindle version as well as print. Ms. Dunlap is a proud native of Georgia and lives now in Winter Park, Florida. She tries to write every single day. She can be reached at ldunlap@earthlink.net.

DORA THE EXPLORER

by Terry Engel

I used to watch the news all the time, especially this little blonde girl that covered the afternoon shift on CNN. Her name was Selena Cassaday, and she read the news like she knew me and I was the only one could hear her. She read the news like she spent her whole life waiting for two o'clock, when she knew I'd be turning on the television. She'd spent the morning in wardrobe and makeup, and when she looked at me, I knew that every story was written just for me. She didn't joke about the stories, or make small talk with her partner, sharing private meanings like lovers under the bed sheets. I liked looking at her. I'm not a fossil yet. Sometimes I'd even think about what it would be like to have her come home to me at night, after the news, and how I could take care of her and help her wind down from the stress of being the person that tells everyone else about how the world is going to hell.

To be honest, if she didn't look the way she did I wouldn't know anything.

For years the news has been the same. It has always been bad. Having someone decent to look at, though, made the day go by quicker. Someone pretty, someone with a little bit of class. Someone that might have given me a second look forty years ago. I don't tolerate abrasive shows on daytime television. You know what I mean: Shows with judges who think being a smart-ass is more entertaining than upholding the law; white trash flouncing their cleavage and tattoos, bleeping out every

other word; talk show hosts moralizing about stray dogs and dog pounds and the "objectification" of women in society, whatever that means. I just flip through the channels until I find a woman it don't hurt to look at.

The day I want to talk about, Selena Cassady was the only thing going. Rain rattling on the roof of the trailer drowned out her voice, which badly disappointed me, so I just watched her and tried to ignore the words running across the bottom of the screen. It was hard to do. Like trying to watch a TV show when someone has the captions turned on. You can't pay attention to what the people on screen are doing and read at the same time, and what they type never matches exactly what they say. Even I can tell that they don't always get the spelling right. Point is, if the words are on there you can't not read them. I don't need the words. I just turn the volume up to 30 and that works fine. There's nobody here to complain.

Sometime during that day Hannah called to talk. I mean Hannah's mother called and handed the phone to Hannah, my great-granddaughter, who is three years old. Her mother does that almost every day, usually about the time Hannah gets bored with television and starts tugging on her mother to pay attention to her. Truth be told, I'd just as soon talk to Hannah as I would her mother. Ginger never was a very bright kid.

I turned down the volume on the TV and tried to talk to Hannah, but even without the rain, I usually only get every third or fourth word, which, according to Selena, is how a dog hears humans. Hannah was full of news: Best I could tell she'd seen a cat outside her window and there was a mud puddle where mommy parked the car. She'd gotten a free cookie from the Wal-Mart bakery, where she and her mother had gone Christmas shopping.

"What's Santa Claus going to bring you?" I asked.

"Dora the Explorer."

"Who's that?"

I picked out the words "backpack" and "map." "You want a backpack and a map?" I asked.

She tried to explain, but I couldn't figure it out. I hung up knowing about as much as I did when I started, so I knew I'd be heading to Wal-Mart sooner or later to find out exactly who this Dora was. Hannah was talking about a monkey and a fox now, and then she blurted out: "Daddy's going on a long trip," real loud.

"A long trip? Where?"

"Eye, Eye. Eye-something."

"Iraq?"

"He rides a hummerbird."

"Where's your mother. Put her on the phone."

"She said I should talk to you until she gets back."

Ever since Hannah was big enough to pay attention to her mother, Ginger'd stopped smoking in the house. Now she just called me up and handed the phone to Hannah while she stepped outside for a couple of cigarettes.

We talked about tea parties, and after a while Ginger finally got on the phone.

"What's this about Tommy going back to Iraq?" I asked.

Ginger coughed in my ear and cleared her throat. "The 39th got called up last month. Don't you ever watch the news?"

"I must have missed it."

"Christmas in Falujah," Ginger croaked. "I cry my eyes out ever night after I put Hannah to bed. I wasn't cut out to be no soldier's wife."

Over the next couple of days I couldn't get Tommy out of my head, and I spent ever minute I could glued to the television, trying to figure out what was happening in Iraq. It didn't really matter to me if Selena was giving the news or not, but it made it better when she did.

I don't want you to take this wrong—it wasn't about Tommy. He had narrow-set eyes and a slack jaw that made me question exactly how faithful my granddaughter had been to him every time I looked for his face in Hannah's. Tommy was about as smart as the gear shift on my pickup, lazy enough to make a city employee jealous, and just enough of a jackass to make me think a tour in Iraq dodging road-side bombs and jabbering with camel jockeys might make him a better human being when he came back. Three years ago I wouldn't have cared if he did get killed. Fact of the matter, I would have been happy for Ginger to have a chance to do better. But now that Hannah had come along, I couldn't stand the thought of her not having a daddy, even such a daddy as God had chosen to give her.

It hurts me to think about how I didn't do right by my own family, years ago, when I was the age of Tommy and my girls were a few years older than Hannah. It was drinking that done it. My wife left me and I ended up with an old girl with bad breath and the law breathing down our neck over her bad checks. My girls grew up without a daddy. It never bothered me about the way I done my wife. She had faults of her own, but what killed me was I used to come riding home after work and my girls would bubble out of the house to see me. I was better than the ice cream man and a trip to the dollar store with money in your pocket to burn. My oldest used to just light up when she'd look up from playing and realize I was watching her. It'd melt my heart. But after I moved out and her mother got through talking about me, that girl wouldn't look at me at all. I was dead to the oldest, and the youngest never knew me for more than a stranger. I was lucky that my ex-wife let me get to know the grandkids once they started to come along. She'd invite me over when she was keeping them. Ginger especially took on to me. She let me come to her high school graduation, invited me to her wedding, and even let me get to know Hannah. Hannah's voice would light up over the phone when I talked to her, and I imagined that same look my oldest girl used to give me.

I figured out who Dora the Explorer was by accident. I was watching Selena one day when she did a story on defective toys being recalled. The toys had been manufactured in China, of all places, and there it was on the screen, big as Stone Mountain, a Dora the Explorer bedside lamp. The toy itself was frightening enough, let alone the defect. Dora was this little Mexican girl with a giant head and eyes ten sizes too big. I mean her head was as big as the rest of her body—It was like the lamp shade I guess—which was attached to a spring so it jiggled when you touched it. Selena had a toy safety expert on the show with her and he said the toy was dangerous because it could tip over easily. Selena was horrified. She actually said, "that's horrific."

All I could think about was Hannah lying in her crib with flames spreading up the slats. I thought about it a long time. Then I decided to drive down to Wal-Mart and take a look for myself.

The parking lot was crowded and I got stuck behind some fat old lady who parked in the middle of the lane and waited for somebody in the first couple of slots to come out and leave, so she wouldn't have to walk an extra hundred feet. I don't know what the woman thought she was going to do once she got inside the store. The store looked as big as the Astrodome to me. She'd probably borrow one of them little mechanized scooters I guess. After a minute or two I whipped around her and then had to slam on the brakes to miss some kid rolling in a string of empty carts. He gave me a look and shook his head and then bent back down to his work. I finally got a spot to park and nearly got run over ten or twelve times just getting to the front door.

I hadn't been in a Wal-Mart for fifteen years. Back then, everything they sold was Made in America. Now you can't buy anything not made by the red Chinese. I've been in a big place or two, and noisy at that, but I hadn't been in anything bigger than Fred's dollar store since my last trip to Wal-Mart. I had forgotten how many things there were in that world that a person could buy, given enough money, time, and the inclination. At first I just wandered around, staring like a country boy on his first trip to town. Now there was a hair salon, an eye doctor, a bank, and even a medical clinic. The grocery section was bigger than my trailer park. I got nervous at the sheer energy and size of the place. I waited patiently at intersections, assuming the rule of the four way stop more or less applied. But women nearly ran me down with massive carts loaded down like the radio had predicted a winter storm, simultaneously pulling cartons off shelves, talking into cell phones, and shoving bottles in their dirty babies' mouths to make them shut up. Greasy looking Mexicans chattered at one another like bickering squirrels. Troops of teenage girls took up the aisle and wouldn't break ranks to make room for an old man. Happy looking men pushed flat bed carts loaded with television boxes the size of my pickup, usually with an angry looking woman not far behind. Wal-Mart even had their own television station beaming from TVs mounted to the ceiling, just in case you had missed a chance to buy one more thing.

The toy section was right where they left it the last time I was here, but I wandered another thirty minutes before I found what I was looking for. It looked harmless enough, there in the package. The lamp I mean. I couldn't imagine having that little Mexican girl all lit up on my bedside table though, staring at me through those giant eyes. I looked around but there was no one on the aisle with me at the moment. I took out my pocket knife and slit the tape and pried the box open, only to find the lamp was wired to the bottom of the package. I slit the edges of the box open with my knife and peeled them back like a banana. A couple of the wires still kept the spring from working, so I untwisted them and freed Dora. The lamp felt top-heavy, but I couldn't be sure, so I cleared a spot on the shelf and set it there, then pulled the lamp cord. It tipped right over. There were about fifteen of the lamps left, at $12.95 each. I wasn't sure what to do, but I knew I had to do something.

I took the lamp and went wandering until I found someone looked like a manager. He was a short little fellow in a blue employee's vest, and I guess he'd been working there long enough to spot a customer who wanted to ask a question, because he shifted his gaze and put his head down and tried to sneak past me. I reached out and grabbed him by the vest.

"Excuse me, Sir," I started. "Are you aware that CNN News listed this toy among the top ten most dangerous toys of the Christmas season?"

"What's it doing open like that?" the guy said. "Did you tear the packaging?"

"Uh, no. I found it like that."

"We got surveillance cameras if you did," the guy said. "That means you have to buy it."

"I can't afford that. I'm on a fixed income. I'm just trying to report a safety hazard. I thought your bosses might like to avoid getting sued."

The guy looked at me a moment, sizing me

up, then glanced both ways down the aisle. "Okay, let me go check on this with my boss," he said. "I'll see what we can do about clearing the shelves. Just wait here." He took the lamp and walked off fast without looking back to make sure I was waiting.

I sort of needed to go take a leak, but I waited anyway. The shopping around me picked up, then lulled, and picked up again. I was getting close to the point of losing control. I thought I saw the guy I'd talked to once, ten aisles away, but I couldn't be sure and I didn't have the time to go looking. I headed for the restrooms. By that time I knew the employee had been jerking me around. He'd probably headed off for his break and stuck the lamp on the first shelf he came to. The more I thought about it, the madder I got, and by the time I got back from the restroom I knew I had to do something.

There was a little girl holding one of the lamps when I got back, showing it to her father. She was a little older than Hannah, but not by much I guessed. I stopped short and pretended interest in some god-awful ugly doll dressed like a prostitute, another toy with giant eyes—and listened to the girl. She had curly red hair and wore house shoe slippers. It was clear her parents didn't have sense enough to even dress her well in winter, let alone protect her life.

"I want it," she said. "This will help me go to sleep at night so you don't have to keep coming into my room and telling me to hush up."

The father, another slack-jawed, pimple faced kid like Tommy, having kids before he's old enough to call himself a man, took the package and eyed it like it was a piece of machinery he couldn't quite figure out, shrugged his shoulders, and handed it back to the girl.

"Whatever makes you happy," he said. "Come on and let's get out of here."

"Hold on a minute, Sir," I said. I reached down and took the package from the little girl. She didn't let it go easily.

"What the--?" The father looked at me, and I knew that if I hadn't been an old guy I'd be lying on the floor by now. No one wants to be seen beating up senior citizens. I knew I had one chance to say my piece.

"I know this to be a dangerous toy," I said. "It's a matter of life or death."

"There's a dozen more on the shelves," the father said. "Go get your own."

"No. This toy is on the top ten list," I said.

"I'm scared, Daddy," the little girl said. "I don't want it. Can we go home now?"

I could see the girl meant it, and I gave her a smile meant to be reassuring. "It's made in China anyway," I said.

"Everything I own is made in China," the father said. "Come on Carley."

He grabbed the girl's shoulder and backed her down the aisle, watching me like he might watch a snake or a pit bull. They got to the main aisle and disappeared, and I looked down at the toy in my hands.

I carried the lamp to the front of the store and held it while I waited in the express check out lane. When it got to be my turn the girl reached for the package to scan it without even looking at me or wishing me a Merry Christmas or anything.

"I'm going to take this outside and stomp it on the sidewalk," I told her. "You can call the police and I'll be waiting out there."

"What?"

I repeated myself, then pushed on out toward the door, holding the lamp slightly away from my body like the dangerous thing it was. On the sidewalk I peeled away the packaging like before, set the lamp on the ground, and stomped the evil smile off the little Mexican girl's face. People hurrying into the store barely paused to see what I was doing, but they gave me a wide berth. A little boy pulled away from his parents and tried to pick up a fragment of Dora the Explorer, but I warned him away, telling him it was a dangerous toy.

"Sir. You'll need to come back inside with us," I heard a man say, and when I looked up I was surrounded by four men holding Walkie Talkies. They looked angry.

"I told the girl I was going to do it," I said.

"I know, Sir. You'll need to come back inside with us and wait on the police."

"Yes sir," I said.

A crowd had gathered, and even though one of the store detectives was trying to break them up, they were all of them looking at me. I'm sure some of them saw a monster, and some of them saw a confused old man. One little girl smiled at me and I heard her tell her mother, "That man looks like grandpa."

I felt good about myself at that moment, but then the men led me to the back of the store, past row after row of bright shiny things that can destroy babies and people and children.

Writing is like Breathing you cannot do without.*

ABOUT POETRY, ITS THERAPEUTIC EFFECT, IMMORTALITY AND THE SOUL
by Dr. Raymond Fenech

Whether messages were conveyed in prose or poetic form, I always knew that there was something special about writers. Since I started writing poetry and keeping a journal when I was 13, I had heard someone say that writers were among the lucky few who could achieve immortality because what they thought and said would be around long after they had crossed the lighted tunnel.

Yet whenever inspiration dictated my hand to take pen and paper and to scribble my thoughts, I felt as if the information I was receiving was not entirely coming from inside my head, but from beyond. It was as if it was information received through channeling.

Then as I took up writing as a profession, I learnt about automatic writing. This sounded very much a realistic phenomenon because many writers and poets use this as a normal exercise to fight writer's block. It is also used to bring about higher awareness, which helps a writer dig further beyond the normal human perception. Unknowingly, free writing can trigger off a direct link with the higher self. Personally, I know from experience because there

have been times when I would drift into a spell-like trance and commence writing in a frenzy. The results often times have been very amazing. The following poem, which I wrote in a few seconds falls into this category. It was like an invisible hand guiding my pen.

The Ghost in the Inkpot

The ghost in the inkpot
guided my hand
into the yellow light
of the desert,
then into the mirage
where the water
welled in my eyes
like a fountain
of mineral crystals.

Suddenly I was
outside a world
of dimming lights
where the sun was masked
by damask,
and when it tired
simply laid down to rest,
cooling its fury

into the sea
sizzling as it sank
deeper in the deep.

The inkpot's ghost
leaves his mark
like the Scarlet Pimpernel,
in pulsating handwriting
in words from within;
flowing senseless,
or meaningful,
with calibrated rhythm
or rhyme, like music
sound spilling,
splitting silences.

When I embarked on my writing career as a roving reporter aged 17, it hardly ever occurred to me that writing was actually also therapeutic. What I knew at that time was that I enjoyed putting words together, expressing myself and letting it all out. I also believed that poets were privileged because of their exceptional capability of observation, sensitivity and a determination to change the world. That was over 43 years ago and I still believe this wholeheartedly.

In those days, I was at an age when I could easily be hurt by the afflictions of young

love and each time it happened, my heart was in shards. Journaling my feelings used to make me feel better. Whether I let it all out into my journal, or wrote a poem it didn't really matter. Then, I was very much under the influence of my favourite poet, John Keats. Whilst other young people of my age had rock band musicians as idols, mine was this poet who was everything I would have wanted to be. He was as courageous and good with his fists as he was good with words and when I read about how once he beat up a bully who was kicking a puppy, he won me over heart and soul.

Becoming a journalist and a poet eventually

proved to be the ultimate baptism by fire, but I set off chomping at the bit with more determination than ever. I was then attending science classes, but we still had English Language as one of the main subjects, something I excelled in. One day when I was 13, we were given an essay to write on the subject, *Snowstorm*. I went about it very seriously and came out with almost a short novel. My English teacher Kay called me aside after class and pointed out that I should reconsider and perhaps change to art and language classes.

I took her advice and did this at a great cost because my parents were not in the least bit impressed about my change of heart. In those times, journalism and writing were not even considered a profession and finding a job with one of the only four existing newspapers was like wishing to travel to the moon and back. But as they say, it takes 10 per cent inspiration and 90 per cent perspiration to become a writer and in the end my dream came true and at 20, I was one of the youngest reporters working for the leading English newspaper, The Times of Malta.

As I wrote more and more poetry, I started to realize that the way inspiration seems to come to the poet was in fact like a sort of miracle. It was like a transcendent state of mind that bequeathed lines of words that at times I hardly realized I was actually writing. Sometimes, I didn't even get the meaning and to understand what I wrote I had to re-read more than once.

Then I concluded that poetry comes from the spirit, the very depth of the human soul.

Hence, why it is so perfect and divine. Perhaps it is also the reason why poetry can help man to remain human. Every poet is allowed to write only a little portion of all the poetry that comes to his mind and this is a privilege in itself..

Poetry is the only form of art that can actually serve as a constant reminder that there is more to life than the eye can see. Keats claimed he was *God's spy..* Plato defines the poet as, *A light and winged and holy thing*.

If man is to stay human, then poetry must become an integral part of his life and poets must be given more credit and respect. For this to happen, children must be taught how to love and appreciate poetry. Most children cringe at the very mention of the word, poetry. Most young people also bear a dislike to poetry and those who don't, are indifferent to the art. America's poet Laureate Rita Dove once said she intended to change this situation in her country. In an interview, she had stressed she wanted,, *to set Americans at ease with poetry, especially those bored by the whole subject during school days. They've been frightened away either through some luckless encounter in the school system where they were required to ... interpret it first, let's say, instead of learning to enjoy it first*. I would add on that critics and academics have contributed a great deal towards rendering poetry so unpopular.

The era of critics serving as a sieving system between writer and the public has come to an end. With desktop and self-publishing technology available everywhere, writers and poets are finding easier access to publication, without the need to go through the parochial systems of publishing that used to be determined by leading academics, critics and editors. Thanks to this modern age, a lot of talent, which otherwise would have been lost has come to the fore and acquired the recognition it deserved. Now, readers have the opportunity to decide for themselves what is good and what is bad, the results obtained sometimes going directly in the opposite direction to what academics and critics would have otherwise predicted.

Some poetry books are bought because of the influence shed by leading critics telling people how good they are. Other books sell because of the reputation of the authors, even if the content is not worth the paper it is printed on. The truth is that most readers fall victims of these critics and waste good money on books that serve no other purpose except that of gathering dust, forgotten on shelves, or in some remote drawer. This is one of the reasons, which has earned poetry that certain unpopularity which is constantly plaguing our society today.

Poetry strikes when you least expect it. It is a lightning of inspiration that must be vented forth from the poet's system. It froths and bubbles; it kicks the poet to a higher level of consciousness and makes him the number one thin-skinned human observer, with extremely sharp hyperactive senses, volatile, almost spiritual. Poetry is a bridge between mankind and everything else. It calls as loud as silence and no real poet can refuse to be the medium.

Poetry is the strength, the fiber behind humaneness, sensitivity and behind the greatest privilege men has, his spirit. Without poetry men would be missing an important link, that which makes them complete, in full synchronization and one with nature, the environment and last but not least, the soul.

In 2004, I was diagnosed with Hodgkin's Lymphoma. I was 46 and at the peak of my writing career. I was editor of two nation-wide distributed magazines and a managing director of an in-house advertising agency of Malta's largest travel agency. All this suddenly became in the past. I was confined home for almost two years, fighting for my life against cancer, a fight during which I looked death straight in the eye so many times. But even as I lay dying after a very long and delicate operation, inspiration came to me during the voyage towards the lighted tunnel and when I was resuscitated I wrote the following poem:

**Operation – Traveling Towards the Light
(To my lovely wife, Angela)**

Eyes travel ahead
like spotlights;
lasers fencing with darkness,
and the unknown.
On this cold metal bed
identity is on a plastic bracelet
and silence converses with itself.

I am no longer within
and the pain is gone.
For the first time
I am at peace
in a waking deep sleep.

Then a light appears
through closed lids,
blood red like a sun.
A sea in dreams
leaks through my eyes
staining pillows.

Time freezes in my veins.
The Siberian cold chatters
with death until it leaves the room.
But only this time.
Life flows back
from the refrigerator
into red roses in the vase,
and the warmth of my wife's hand.

It had always been my dream to undertake a degree in creative writing and in a desperate attempt to regain some of that joy of living, which I was losing quickly due to the illness itself and the devastating side effects of chemotherapy, I enrolled for an online BA degree with a concentration in poetry. Throughout my

life as a child and eventually as a young man, my dad used to tell me, *Everything happens for a purpose, even the worse thing one can think of – if it doesn't kill you it will only make you stronger.* Well that dictum was about to come true. I was also about to realize poetry/writing could be used to cure people with serious psychological problems, something I had already experienced in heartbreak as a teenager and when unknowingly, I had self-administered journal or poetry therapy.

As I was deciding what theme to choose for my thesis, I came across a title of a book, *The Healing Word* by Fiona Sampson. I didn't know what the subject was all about but on reading the book, I became interested and decided to research poetry therapy for my thesis. One thing very much led to the other and suddenly I found myself wanting to undertake a basic course in poetry therapy simply to be able to know the subject better and be able to present my thesis in a more professionally way.

Most of the replies from institutions I wrote to that offered such courses were

discouraging, because the fees per credit hour ran into thousands of dollars, which at that time I simply couldn't afford. Then, in 2009, out of the blues I received a letter from the *Creative Righting Center* at Hofstra University of New York informing me that I was being awarded a full scholarship in writing therapy.

Now, I know for a fact that writing in which ever form it comes gives the writer that extra superhuman strength, which makes him move forward regardless of any obstacles, allowing the inner spirit to guide him forth. Poetry is the vibrating energy without which the difference could be as distinguishable as that from night and day, life and death, water and fire, the invisible and the visible.

Poetry is in all and everything. The poet is needed as a medium to channel this form of art from life and its surrounding. For poetry means living, appreciating life, nature, all that is earthbound and even that which lies beyond. Poetry is forever and belongs to mankind. Without poetry mankind would be soulless.

Writing is like Breathing you cannot do without.*

This special column in Adelaide Literary Magazine will not be dwelling on one particular subject but several – anything that's under the sun. There will be articles about the benefits of creative writing as self-therapy, journal and poetry therapy, journalism, including poetry, short story, and article writing, the supernatural and interviews with people who have come very close to death and experienced what is known as Out of the Body Experience (OBE). There will be articles on several other subjects, nostalgia, memoirs, stories about very special or heroic animals, special people, but not necessarily famous, legends, history, as well as research on interesting scientific research, parapsychology, and onsite investigations in the paranormal world by famous scientists and paranormal investigators.

About the Author:

Raymond Fenech embarked on his writing career as a freelance journalist at 18 and worked for the leading newspapers, The Times and Sunday Times of Malta. He edited two nationwide distributed magazines and his poems, articles, essays and short stories have been featured in several publications in 12 countries. His research on ghosts has appeared in The International Directory of the Most Haunted Places, published by Penguin Books, USA.

MY BROTHER

by Lisa Reily

Huge, swollen knees stare us in the face, only partly hidden by a nylon floral hem. We follow the flowers up to a mouth filled with random teeth and an olive-skinned face framed by dark hair, pinned to one side with a single bobby pin. Two children stand next to the enormous knees, a girl and a boy. The girl is smiley and the boy is little, and he looks a lot like Brennie.

Back in the car on the way home, Brennie whispers in my ear. "She's not my mum. My new mum's nicer."

I follow his pointed eight-year-old finger. It's right on Mum. Our mum. "Yep," I say.

We both smile at each other and that's that.

Brennie, Brendon, had already been to two foster homes before he came to live with our family. I was two then, and he was five. So in my mind Brennie was always my brother, no questions asked. It was only when I had to tell people how many siblings I had that I reeled off what I'd probably heard from my parents. "I have three brothers, well, two real brothers, really—Mike and Lucas—and a foster brother, Brendon."

Mike was the eldest child in our family; then Brennie, who was a year younger; then me; and then my baby brother, Lucas, who came along as a last-minute accident. There was always a joke in our house about that. When you planned, you got a girl. Boys just turned up when and how they wanted. I was planned.

Before I was born, I think Mum wanted to do the right thing and help a child in need. She thought fostering a boy around the same age as Mike would give him and the new little boy a playmate. And they did become playmates, happy ones—most of the time. But they enjoyed beating the crap out of each other on occasion, too. Sworn to secrecy, they would biff and scuffle as quietly as possible in their room downstairs, only stopping when Mum yelled down the stairwell. Or when she came down in person with a fierce look on her face.

"What are you two boys up to?" she'd say.

"Nothing."

Brennie was really my favourite brother most of the time. He was the kindest and most gentle. I reckon Mum thought so, too. When ever she brought in groceries, Brennie would rush to help her. When he got older, he'd mow the lawn and wash the car—sometimes without even being asked. Mike'd just whinge or sulk. If Mum had garbage to take outside, Brennie would always say, *I'll do it, Mum!*

He was the most fun, too. When we had cracker night, he'd always help me light my sparklers and run with me to make patterns in the dark, away from the other kids and Dad's enormous, crackling bonfire; the sparklers worked better at a distance. And next to our place, there was an empty plot of land with a concrete slab on it. Brennie and I would go there, to play air guitar and scream our guts out, singing *Jailbreak*, that old AC/DC song.

We'd act out being shot and everything. I remember Brennie loved chocolate cake—and he'd eat a whole one if Mum didn't stop him! My funniest memory, though, was when lemonade spurted from his nose, he was laughing so much at the dinner table. Mum had a fit at him, but we still couldn't stop giggling!

Us kids had heaps of holidays and birthdays together with our cousins, Jake and Rosemarie. Jake was my uncle and aunty's only child. Rosemarie was adopted. Sometimes Brennie and I wondered why he wasn't adopted, too. Then we found out it was because his real mum wouldn't give him up. We were really sad about that and never wanted to visit her again. But Brennie loved having a new little brother who looked like him, and a half-sister, and we even got to see them a few times.

Once we had Brennie's birthday at Adventureland. Jake and Rosemarie were there as usual, plus Brennie's little brother and half-sister, and most of the kids from Brennie's class at school. We had loads of fun! Lots of mums and dads came to help—so we had to wait ages for our turns on the flying fox, because all the dads wanted a go. (More than some of the kids!) Mum made a massive red skateboard cake and Brennie got a new red skateboard—exactly the one he wanted. It was the best day.

I remember a man called Mr. Bromley sometimes came to our house for cups of tea. He had skinny, freckled legs and long socks. Also a red beard. One day, he was talking something serious about Brennie to Mum, and our dog, Lulu, who was behind him, jumped out of her basket and fanged him deep in the calf. Mr Bromley held his leg up and Lulu just dangled from it, non-stop growling. She'd never done anything like that before and Mum was really sorry. I reckon that was the day Mr Bromley was trying to get us to visit Brennie's big, fat mum. And I reckon Lulu knew it was a stupid thing to do. So her bite was worth it, because it stopped Mr Bromley from coming round so often. Brennie and I felt safer that way.

One thing that was weird about Brennie was that he wasn't the same as Mike and me. When we were little, and Lucas was a baby, I remember coming home from school and hearing that Brennie had messed his pants in class. I thought he was smarter than that. It happened a few times, but Mum was really quiet about it and cleaned him up real quick. I sometimes heard her saying stuff on the phone about him having some sort of problem, or something. He also had trouble with homework and Mum always had to help him. Mum said Brennie was better with more practical things. And she reckoned he could sometimes be too trusting.

My brother, Mike, was the complete opposite. He could be sneaky and a bit of a trickster—you had to keep an eye on him—but he was usually good to Brennie and didn't take advantage of how gullible he could be. Other times, he just couldn't help himself. One time, Mum and Dad put up our out-of-the-ground pool for summer and we were all having a swim. Brennie was crouched down, snorkelling—looking at I don't know what—and Mike was throwing leaves out of the pool. Then Mike got the idea of putting a leaf into Brennie's snorkel. Nearly choked him to death! Brennie should have known that he needed to keep an eye on Mike. But Brennie was always forgiving.

I'm glad now that Brennie tricked me with some matches one day and I ended up with half my eyebrow missing. He called me round the back of the house, knowing full well that I couldn't resist a box of matches. We lit them one-by-one; I just loved lighting them, their sizzling sound and smell. I can remember the smell of my burnt hair, too. I don't know what he said that made me bring a match so close! Anyway, now I just think that's one point to him.

When Brennie was in high school, he did really well in his woodwork class. He even made Mum a table with special French polish, but he had a lot of trouble with Maths and that. He also had a job at Franklins, the supermarket, and he taught a few kids guitar after school. He was raking it in! Mum and Dad had got him a guitar and some lessons and he took to it all like a fish to water. Teaching other kids to play was easy for him. Mostly, I just loved how he played really cool songs, like Neil Young and stuff. He could even play *The Needle and the Damage Done* just like on the record! He sang it, too. Really well.

It all looked good for a while. Mum and Dad were really proud of him. But then Brennie took to hanging out with some stupid kids in his class. A couple of them were real dopes, my father used to say. And when Brennie started roaming around with them on the weekends, he got into all kinds of shit. It went on till Dad said he'd have no hair left. One time, one of Brennie's stupid mates stole a car and he and Brennie got caught. But they got let off after Dad went to the coppers and had a chat.

When Brennie left school in Year Ten, it was hard for him to get a job with his marks, so Dad got him one at work. Dad was the head of accounts in an air-conditioning firm and he used his weight to get Brennie a job in the sheet metal factory—above other boys who applied, who were a lot brighter. It was all good at first. Then Brennie started smoking dope with the dopes and got himself into trouble again. Dad wanted to kill him, 'cause he'd let those other good boys go. And that was the tip of Brennie's downfall. From then on, he just got worse. I think it was around the time he found out his real dad was dead. His dad had only just got out of prison. But then he got shot during a robbery or something. We never got to meet him. Only got to see a photo.

After that, Brennie ended up bonging on all night, and sleeping in. Not turning up to work. Getting warnings from his supervisor. He wouldn't shower much either and you could smell him all about the house. Mum would try to talk to him, order him into a shower and shave. Dad'd threaten to kick him out. Nothing worked.

One night, Mum and Dad had an argument with Brennie. His supervisor had called 'cause he hadn't turned up for work again. Brennie had left that morning, acting like he was going there. Mum was fuming and when Dad got home, they told him that if he couldn't be decent and have a shower and turn up for work, he couldn't stay with us anymore. I thought Dad was going to throttle him! Brennie stormed out. A few days later, he moved out for good.

I don't really know what happened after that, except in the years that followed, Mum and Dad spent years losing their minds over their divorce. Dad moved out. Then Mike got an arts scholarship somewhere in Melbourne and moved out, too, leaving just me and Lucas at home with Mum. In that time, Brennie lost his job and only came by now and again, mainly because Dad wasn't there. (He would have shitted himself if he was.)

Brennie just kept finding new drop-kick mates to hang out with. Most of them were pretty sus. One time, after Brennie came by to visit with one of his new loser friends, our house got robbed. Mum put it down to Brennie and his mate. We got robbed a second time, too—straight after Mum had everything replaced. The new TV was gone and everything. To this day, Brennie reckons it wasn't him, but he couldn't say for sure about his mate.

I remember one good time, when Brennie came to visit Mum for Mother's Day. He arrived with a Mother's Day card and a little Buddha wrapped in pretty paper. He was a few weeks late, but Mum was thrilled anyway. He was really happy to see us both, and we were glad, too, because we had lost track of him. He was always losing his mobile, or leaving it somewhere. (I don't know how many times he put his phone through the wash by mistake!) He was always moving to different housing, so he'd change his home phone number like nobody's business!

That day, I told Brennie I'd got into uni and I'd bought myself a cheap car. When I told him, he was ecstatic and he raced down to the garage like a maniac to check out my new wheels.

"I knew you'd make something of yourself," he said. And later that afternoon, I came downstairs to find my car sparkling. Brennie was just that kind of person.

Mum cut Brennie's hair—and his beard. He started off looking like he was from ZZ Top, only with a shorter, blacker beard. When Mum cut it all off, his hair was everywhere on the kitchen tiles and he looked bloody terrible. His face was all gaunt and his eyes looked hollow, and a bit yellow. He was skinny all over and had lost all his muscle. Mum ended up giving him some of her tight jeans and a few T-shirts. Everything he tried on sort of fell off him, but he was happy with his new second-hand clothes. And when he talked, he was the same old Brennie.

Mum, Brennie and I blabbed on until way after dinner, then I left them him alone to chat with Mum. I knew he wanted help, to start up a lawn mowing business. He told me he wanted some money to finance the set-up. After he told Mum, she thought about it a bit and agreed—but she wasn't about to hand over any cash. She told Brennie he'd have to move back in and clean himself up. Then she'd help him. But Brennie wanted none of it, so the whole thing went by the wayside.

After Brennie left that night, I had a massive blue with Mum. I felt like she and Dad had let Brennie down. That he felt different to Mike and Lucas and me. Like maybe he didn't feel loved or something. That he didn't belong anywhere and he needed a chance. Mum cried and told me that she wanted to help him, but he needed to come her way. My blood boiled like crazy about it. Brennie was my kindest, nicest brother. He deserved a chance.

After that, I know that Brennie spent some time in prison for stealing, and I think for dealing drugs. He ended up in rehab—for alcohol and heroin addiction. He had a baby with a girl named Janelle, who was a smackie and real trouble. Worked at some guy's marijuana plantation in the country somewhere, but got ripped off. One night, Mum told me that Bren-

nie'd changed his surname back to McDermott, his real dad's name. At first I was hurt, but then I realised he was just changing it to get further away from the cops, and some scary blokes he'd met. He needed to start again, kind of with a new identity. But it still wasn't a good one. It was all a big, stupid mess.

By the time I hit thirty, Brennie became a distant memory. Mum tried to chase him up a few times, but with no luck. I nagged her a lot about it one day; I thought we should try to find him one last time. Mum got straight onto it. She spent weeks searching and ringing everyone she could think of, and finally she got a hold of him. We found out then that, around the time Mum got a new phone number, Brennie had tried to call. When he couldn't get through on her old one, he thought she didn't want to know him anymore. So he'd stopped trying and disappeared. Mum and I felt terrible.

After that, Brennie came around once or twice in the next ten years or so before Mum died. If I didn't chase him up again, he wouldn't have known. I invited him to her funeral and he was really sad. I made sure he came up to the front with Mike, Lucas and me and I invited him to Mum's place afterwards. He ate heaps of chocolate cake. Heaps of it. I kept giving him bigger slices and he just kept going. "I've always had a sweet tooth," he said, winking at me.

When Mum was in bed, dying, I asked her if she wanted to see Brennie, but she said no. She got sick very quickly and didn't want to see anyone. She was in a lot of pain. I felt guilty, not letting him see her. But I had to listen to her. Heaps of relatives wanted to drop in all of a sudden, too. Just nosey. I acted like a bodyguard at her bedroom door. Took all her phone calls for her.

Mum didn't leave anything for Brennie in her will, so I went to visit him. I took the little Buddha he'd given her, and the French-polished table he made her when he was in school. I shouted him dinner with his girlfriend, too. Spent heaps on Chinese takeaway, so he could have enough meals for a week in his fridge. It was nice hanging out with him again, but he looked and sounded really different.

Brennie was now in his forties and had got himself some false teeth. His voice was rougher, more country-like, and not as well-spoken. He was a bit more like his old self, body-wise, but he still didn't seem completely healthy. He told me he was taking methadone to keep him on track. He had Hep C. He was in housing and getting a carer's pension for looking after his new girlfriend, who had liver damage. She was also bipolar. But she was the one who saved him, so he wanted to look after her.

He told me that he had a job working as a mechanic and he worked really long hours. He was doing the job of a head mechanic, but he wasn't fully qualified so his boss didn't pay him much. He was getting cash most of the time, so his boss had him over a barrel. Brennie said he felt used, but he was glad for the routine. He told me he liked looking after his girlfriend, and doing the lawn and the edges round the house, and tinkering about under his car. "It's all keeping me alive," he said. "I like me job anyway."

Later that night, Brennie and I had a cup of tea and I asked him if he still played the guitar. He got up, went to the bedroom, and came back with a brand new one. I asked him to play and he played *The Needle and the Damage Done* just like on the record. He sang it, too. Really well. And it made me teary.

He told me not to worry about him. That he was proud of me. That he'd made his bed and he'd lie in it. He told me he should have listened to Mum and Dad. That he'd messed his life up unnecessarily. But he was okay and happy with things now. *He was okay*, he said. And because he didn't cry or anything, I felt like he really was.

After that day, I had a few phone calls from Brennie. Once he put his phone through the wash again—yep, same old Brennie—and I lost contact with him for a while. I sent him a few Woolies vouchers and some overseas post-cards, but never heard back from him. Then I got a call out of the blue, just to say hi. It's hard to keep in contact now that I'm miles away. But at least I know that Brennie is out there, and happy. And I know now, that he's doing okay.

About the Author:

Lisa Reily is a former literacy consultant, dance director and teacher from Australia. Her poetry and stories have been published in several journals, such as Panoply, Amaryllis, Riggwelter, River Teeth Journal (Beautiful Things), and Magma. Lisa is currently a full-time budget traveller and her writing is often inspired by her journey. You can find out more about Lisa at lisareily.wordpress.com

WHY THE REVOLUTION OF MODERN LIFE IS INTELLIGENT, MORAL AND BEAUTIFUL
by Thomas Dexter Kerr

It is an exciting and hopeful time to be alive. A revolution is sweeping the earth, increasing intelligence by allowing, enabling, inspiring ever more people to make more decisions in their lives. Modern systems that allow people to think more in daily life are well known. Democracies empower people to choose governments. Markets are people deciding what should be made and done. Systems of rules that apply to all help keep things open and honest. Support for ability to think comes from family and neighbors, schools, hospitals, books and internet. Enormous dividends result from getting it right. But decentralizing decision-making is never easy because it means ever greater complexity and the empowering of inconvenient people. The best path forward is illuminated by the idea that people thinking more is good, right and beautiful.

Modern peace and prosperity has resulted from the ever closer alignment of social organization with ways people by nature maximize intelligence. Humans became the most powerful beings ever to exist by developing a new way of using information, the content of thoughts and feelings. The information system created as people mingle thoughts and feelings with those of others evolved to be the most intelligent entity ever to exist.

Survival of the fittest individual was not the primary force that crafted human minds. Incompetence in a wide variety of forms is an essential part of what makes us human. Individual people today lack the full range of mental abilities necessary to survive alone in a wilderness. I couldn't do it, nor could any of my neighbors. Instead natural selection resulted in something far more powerful, intelligent and beautiful.

Many creatures, from ants to dogs, evolved to gain power over their environment by cooperating and communicating. All lost the ability to live and thrive alone as individuals. Over eons, humans gradually took the use of information to higher levels. As individuals they gave up the full range of faculties needed for survival because together they developed something far more potent. The unprecedented power this gave them at each step is what drove the evolutionary innovations that resulted in today's world.

Human intelligence is collective in nature, talents not concentrated but dispersed in individuals who are all different. A revolutionary kind of mind developed in groups of a few hundred in which everyone knew each other, every voice added to what was being thought about. In everyday life people have always shared ideas, songs, stories, styles and a myriad nuances of feeling, passing them down through generations, improving and innovating. The information that is the content of thoughts and feelings mixes together in their minds and among them. Because each person's mind is different, enormous creative flexibility arises out of many sorts of thinking striving, sometimes clashing, always mingling. We spin thoughts out of the unknown and unexpected, finding depth and diversity with inauspicious people and rising generations breaking old patterns. So many things can be thought about. Human survival and success has always depended on the system of thoughts that all share and take part in. Our kind of intelligence is a category leap, rising far beyond what could ever evolve to be the smartest, most wily, most dominant individual beast. Every successful creature is over-endowed with the means it uses to survive, necessary to overcome extreme circumstances. Our primary means of survival blossomed into the wonder of the universe.

The details of how individuals think were shaped by the enormous force of their effect on our primary tool and weapon, the human information system. Its intelligence could increase only as its component parts became more finely tuned to add to the thinking going on. Many of the talents that make people together so intelligent are useless in isolation, essential when combined with others. Kinds of thinking are scattered, each getting a little of this, a little of that. Impractical musicians, non-athletic priests, groveling politicians help bring disparate folks together. Mechanics fix things, clumsy scientists invent, cooks devise food, athletes run and hunt, shoppers gather, some who can memorize, memorialize the past. Fearless and timid, quick and slow, passive and aggressive, skillful and clumsy, female and male, serious and frivolous, analytical and intuitive, speculative and methodical, mathematical or musical or not, all are found in every group across the globe. This deep reservoir of possibilities is made more potent by the creativity inherent in the fresh perspectives of each individual and new generation. The mix found everywhere today exists because it is the combination that proved to be most intelligent.

If individuality were not naturally configured to mesh with other minds, the results would be useless. An association of thinking animals with a purely random assortment of differences would produce the intelligence of a zoo. Mental individuality in humans has a purpose. All elements are finely tuned to create with others, each general type essential, every new addition a welcome extension of the ability of everyone to think. It is an inescapable truth of every person's life that their most intimate impulses, those feelings that are most certainly theirs and theirs alone, are shaped and channeled in subtle, mysterious ways to augment the functioning of the human information system as a whole.

The magic of the human information system lies in everyday life, the great generator and heartland of intelligence. When a good idea pops into existence there is no way to ever figure out exactly where it came from. Inside everyone the information that is the content of their thoughts and feelings connects and mingles. Music and sports mix with math, politics and sex. Interconnections multiply as thoughts and fragments spread out through friends and neighbors, reaching around the world. All ideas are composed of strands reaching far back in the past and over many lands, influenced by threads of rhythm, color and rhyme, outrageous mistakes and hallucinations. Even the loftiest, most abstract sophisticated concepts grow out of pieces rattling around coffee shops, nurseries and football fields, mixing with music, cooking and gardening. Every mind takes part, each one living in the thinking of the world. Together we create the mental output on which all depend.

Morality evolved as an inseparable part of intelligence. In order to think together, people have to get along. This is not automatic. Our existence through the past has always been dependent on a balance of genetic and cultural supports for moral behavior that maximizes the creative intelligence of the human information system. We are genetically predisposed to empathize with others, fall in love and like things like music and sports that join people together. But we also need ongoing streams of new ideas in all areas of life, good and bad, to be dreamed up and tried out. Our collective creativity is generated by a diversity of individuals in all walks of life making different choices, going their own way. So a measure of wildness, especially by teenagers, is built in. The resulting instability requires a lot of work. We inherit culture as much as we do fingers. Moral concepts in multiple forms have been passed down and improved on from primordial times in the same way as technical ideas like the use of fire. Without morality, just as without fire, everyone dies. Embedded in every culture is a way of understanding the information realities of life, some picture of lives connected by invisible ties in a common endeavor and fate, the furtherance of which is everyone's responsibility. This is contained in direct explanations as well as music and art, sports, humor and a thousand tales about others and the past. The enormous success of the human endeavor owes a lot to the efforts of so many through the ages searching for ever better ways to convince people to live together wholeheartedly.

Though it can be hard to include those who are different, closing eyes to them shuts off communion with thought itself. To regard anyone at all as unworthy of recognition is to turn away from intelligence, which exists in pieces scattered everywhere. Every face is a unique shining facet of the most complex thinking entity ever to exist. The greatest impediments to human potential are institutional, philosophical and viscerally emotional objections to getting little voices raised and heard. It seems so easy to disregard the shy, odd, peculiar and strange, both rebellious and those that sound the same, voices small and lonely, the less talented and nonpolitical. But they are us and we are all there is.

The revolution of modern life is vastly expanding intelligence by turning on its head traditional notions that the source of wealth and power is the best and brightest. What is emerging instead is a world in which every mind is acknowledged as an important contributor. Particular individuals are useful for any one task at hand, and when they manage to do something special it is a wonderful gift to themself and everyone else. But no matter how impressive, every success is the result of a limited, particular vision applied to resources drawn from the vast sea of human thought. Mental or character perfection is an attribute of people as a whole. Individuals are expressly designed not to be that way. Every individual can be described as 'flawed' or 'not perfect'. This is a good, not bad thing. The largest are dependent, the smallest have something to add. The most striking thing an honest person sees in mirrors is the amazing ordinariness of uniqueness. So-called ordinary people exist only because we were over eons in the most severe circumstances in fact essential to the intelligence of the whole. The most important and potent attribute of human intelligence is not that some are all-encompassing geniuses but that none are.

In the practical world of everyday life, people thinking is people making decisions. On a large scale decentralizing decision-making so more are thinking is difficult. As individuals choose who to marry, where to live and what to do for others they create ever greater complexity because they are all different. But only when they go in their own directions is the intelligence of society enriched by their diversity. For them to be allowed do so, they need to be trusted to make reasonably good decisions. Most people have to believe in doing the right thing. Their activities will at times need to be nudged or constrained in more positive directions. Growing a beautiful garden takes a lot of work.

Individual initiative would look morally suspect if human minds evolved mainly to compete against each other. Then their inner being would be suffused with primordial impulses to do so at others expense. Even if not in fact stealing, their motivation would be tainted with it. From that perspective, morality would be an overlay designed to counteract human nature and attempts to achieve general fairness would struggle against the tide. Such concepts provide handy excuses to keep people from acting, to confine them in a static order that is supposedly more moral. But because human minds did not in fact evolve to oppose others, exactly the opposite is true. In the practical world, this distinction has a huge effect, changing the role of rules from constraining people's base nature to facilitating greater activity with helpful guidelines and admonitions. Taking initiative is people thinking. Intelligence is the source of morality.

A functioning system of separate and independent organizations has an inherent beauty and morality that is lacking in the only alternative. The appeal of centralized systems is the supposed comfort of enforced fairness. Their slogans through the ages can sound idealistic: a place for everyone and everyone in their place, and we think and you do and we'll take care of you. This has been most attractive to those already privileged or who suppose themselves superior. It is just so hard to imagine what good could come from having stupid people think. But imposed absolute fairness is a state of standing still, bereft of creativity and initiative, missing the point of life. Visions of everyone nicely quiet and in order are nightmares not dreams, horror not paradise. Their imposition has resulted in police states and mass murder for they directly contravene the most fundamental human reality, that our destiny is to think. The great counter-revolution of modern times was communism, which sought to infuse old ideas with more effective means of control. Substitute a unitary bureaucracy for kings, emperors or caliphs and the concept is the same. In recent times it has been shown that more open systems are far more accountable, productive, able to experiment and vastly improve life. The reason it works better is be-

cause it is more intelligent. More people are thinking.

Capitalism is the use of math for the purpose of decentralizing decision-making. Math is an impartial tool for opening activities to anyone who wants to take initiative. To measure whether they are doing something worthwhile it empowers the most dispersed, appropriate and severe critics, customers. Pricing includes the user in the decision-making process, enlisting their mind to help make systems more intelligent. When people pay the true costs of the things they use, it is then they, instead of someone else, who is deciding how much and when. They have most say when they can choose from the widest selection in the world. From single entrepreneurs to enormous organizations, the proper use of math makes possible the most active use of people's minds. When capitalism strays too far from its decentralizing purpose it becomes dysfunctional and inefficient. When working well it is beautiful because it is intelligent.

Essential to success in business is finding the right balance between making money and serving others. Actually doing something worthwhile is hard, failure a constant shadow. All kinds of people need to be made happy enough to voluntarily cooperate. Customers, workers, neighbors, a variety of government folks, competitors, suppliers, contractors, all must get along. Every day brings hard choices between scarce resources and quality of output. Everything takes longer and costs more, no one is paid as much as they think they should, and temptations abound to take shortcuts. Episodes of winning the lottery and successful cheating make fun stories, but that's not where the real money is. Real business success is never only about maximizing profits. As human beings, business people connect with their world in many ways, have multiple interests and goals. Their job is to make an enterprise work as a whole, otherwise all is lost. Success requires doing and caring about two things at the same time. Many people's desires need to be filled and it all has to add up. Serve to make money, make money to serve, chew gum and walk.

An open democratic political system is a necessary component of an intelligent society. There will always be those tempted to recentralize decision-making in order to grab advantages for themselves or a select group. Democracy empowers the majority who are less interested in gaining power and dominance over others. However, their ability to make decisions in their own lives is very important to them. This can lead to wild cultural expressions because it is central to self worth and identity. Secondary objects like guns and cars can represent the rightness of individuals thinking for themselves. And in believing it is both moral and productive for them to live actively thinking, they are right. The greatest beneficiaries of a decentralized society are its less important members. Democracy puts the right hands on the tiller, those most directly and personally interested in greater intelligence.

It is easy for initiatives to get out of hand, go in destructive directions. For capitalism to function it must have rules and guidance provided by an active democracy. All entrepreneurs, small to large, require ongoing adjustments to rules protecting their projects from theft and interference. They need an environment with sufficient infrastructure and healthy, educated citizens. They need the peaceful ways of solving problems that can thrive only in a functioning democratic political system with the good will of most of the people most of the time. Democratic capitalism is millions of people voluntarily cooperating and taking initiative to make life better for each other.

Democracy is commonly slandered as the worst system of governing except for every other. It involves a great show of shouting and grandstanding, confusion, indecision, delay, some cheating and lots of inconsistency. But the mess and confusion of a functional democracy are exactly its great strength, more people thinking. All other political setups explicitly seek to stop thinking. That is why they some-times appear clean and efficient. Intelligence is a state of motion, the opposite of keeping everything the same. Creativity always has an element of disorder, whether in one mind or that of many. Democracy is beautiful because it is active, alive and intelligent and deserves respect for it.

A widespread improvement in moral behavior is a necessary part of the success of capitalism and democracy. This is a long, slow process, as individuals gain new freedoms and learn from them. Increasing morality means people thinking more, not less. Progress results in an increase in general activity and the pace of change. Humans are not designed to sit still but to be intelligent. Together our destiny is to wonder and speculate, create and explore, seek truth and solve the riddles of the universe.

The image of humans as entities that exist separate, alone and inherently in conflict is an insidiously corrosive illusion. Its great attraction is support it lends for comparisons showing one worth more than another. As individual items, there is a scale handy to prove anyone better. Whether best mechanic, politician, musician, cook, mathematician or athlete, a soft cocoon of superiority beckons. Excellence then isolates instead of broadening life. Individual arrogance also decreases intelligence by working against the decentralizing tides of democracy and capitalism. People keep inventing ingenious ways of explaining why they should decide instead of others, why they are smarter and better and so more deserving of the perks and trinkets of life. But if theft is legitimate, then intelligence is not.

The most fundamental fact of human life is that we evolved to maximize the intelligence of the human information system as a whole. We have never existed separate and alone but as intricately connected parts of that system, within which we live our lives. Individual intelligence was worthwhile and increased only in ways which complemented our source of power. People do not exist on a linear scale from stupid to smart. They live in many dimensions, their value to the whole being that they are different. Supermen and philosopher kings do not exist. If they did our world would be much less intelligent.

Hatred is not about the victim, instead a category error in someone's mind, a voluntary severing of connection, a denial of the fact that all humans are intrinsically interconnected. People invent all kinds of ways to cut themselves off. Walking around measuring, categorizing and belittling others may seem a purely private obsession. But the artificial separation it creates decreases intelligence, just like lying, cheating, hurting and stealing. Even when they feel justified by real injury, those who come to hate always lose. Severing connections isolates each of us when we make this mistake from the millions of ways we are naturally linked to others with intimacy, substance and meaning. It is a personal failure to grasp the largeness of life. All forms of hatred are self-banishments from the community of life, alienation from the essence of the greatest intelligence ever to arise.

True intelligence is found not in any one person. It is the unexpected found in pieces everywhere, in every pair of eyes. Fulfillment in life is not a destination but a journey always in motion, mixing in with the world around. Love, the closest of connections, is the highest expression of intelligence, of our state of nature.

For little round billiard balls, equality is being the same and freedom to roll around is increased by taking others off the table. Since humans are not little balls but information entities, the exact opposite is true. Equality is being different and freedom is radically reduced by taking others off the table. People are equal in that each one is an element of the larger thinking system and all are needed to maximize its intelligence. Acts hindering others from thinking detract from the intelligence of everyone. Condescension is always obvious, as the perpetrator very publically makes their own life smaller and cheaper. Their victims resent it,

cooperate less, and close off in turn. Rising out of superiority to equality with all those lesser, acceptance to the core of humanity's great gift, the smallness and particularity of self, is the critical door opening to the wider world of intelligence, dignity and beauty. Freedom is the ability to make choices and move around in the vast information landscape of minds and lives. This requires participation in making things work, more giving than receiving. It is because the equality and freedom of individuals as information entities are essential to intelligence that they are inherent in human existence.

Because people are not objects but information entities, they are happiest not when cut off and alone but when their minds are best connected with the world. A drug induced blank smile is not at all what happiness is about. Whether it's baseball, another person, a job or a song they like, as they find fulfillment in their various peculiarities they are happier and their minds are more engaged. As long as they avoid harming others, this raises the intelligence of the human information system. More thinking is going on. Their happiness is the summit of life, peak experience and function, the highest expression of their unique contribution. Individual happiness is the source of collective intelligence. Can't have one without the other.

Fairness within the human information system is much greater than any list of physical items. Because it consists of enabling everyone to think and contribute it is essential to intelligence. No one can do so if starving or sick, ignorant or in chains. Everyone needs help to grow and flourish. Efforts to increase fairness, to better people's lives, are far more than feel good projects. They are for us, not simply for them.

In the clear cold light of morning the choice to live fully and behave in a moral fashion is obvious. People have invented lots of ways to explain why they should be nice to each other. But at root they all come down to individual awakening, opening to the information realities of life. Human beings perceive directly, without any explanation, theory or religion, that they are connected with others and the world. It is obvious in moments when an individual finds themself suddenly enraptured by another person. The illusion of separateness might unconsciously dissolve when encountering a song or a wayward glance, an ingenious machine or a football pass. It is the recognition of informational connection which inspires the look in a lover's eye, the visceral reaction to a baby's cry, the giddy feeling of a moving world when some work of art gets under the skin. Most people do not need complicated reasons to see grossly immoral acts as just plain wrong. Who has not been overwhelmed by the utter cuteness of a little child? Morality becomes self-evident with the experience of recognizing the warmth and light in another's eye, becoming much more than the right thing, the only thing to do.

Within every person lies a field of life full of hidden places, fuzzy feelings, acres of happenings and kittens and food, every corner filled with vastness, fluid motion moment to moment. Each comes with a mix of warm childhood memories, present experience and dreams of the future, all dense with nuance and impressions. Their information field is an extension and enrichment of all others. For anyone, the experience of recognizing this in one person and then another, a friend, neighbor or passerby, expands the boundaries of life. Multiplied by all those in a town, a region, the world, and the human information landscape seems to go on forever. The furthest corners of every mind fuel the most powerful and intelligent entity ever to exist. Its beauty graces all our lives.

Today awareness is spreading throughout the world of the myriad ways that participating in an actively intelligent society elevates every personal life. Individuals have ever more reasons to believe that their own peculiarities are good not bad, that it is alright for them to be more themselves. The variety of things they can do is expanding, with greater freedom, prosperity and people inventing new pursuits. Large organizations are recognized to be more successful when they enlist the minds of their employees instead of having them do only what they are told. The use of math to make it possible for everyone to make decisions is gaining acceptance. Ever more varieties of people are being allowed, enabled and inspired to participate. Democracy is spreading and theft by those who govern is receding. Even those with guns are slowly awakening to the fact that real power comes from intelligence, the secret to which is to be found in the sweetly innocent smile of a child. The modern flowering of the human information system is wonderful, moral and inherently beautiful.

CHILDHOOD AS OTHERWORDLY THINGS
by Emily Wilford

I'll be out of my mind, and you'll be out of ideas pretty soon

so let's spend the afternoon in a cold hot air balloon.

Owl City, *Hot Air Balloon*

I remember those days as shrouded in a thin veil of cool mist, visible but muffled, glinting silver and rainbow with tiny droplets of memories - weeks worth of memories, or months, or only a few days. Time seemed to stand still - or rather, time seemed to shimmer and waver and warp into something indistinct, raindrops slipping beneath the surface of a pond. I remember them sometimes as one day, a single moment during which everything felt inconsequential, except a small voice reminding me of the consequences of staying underwater too long.

I am a person who enjoys rain. I cherish every second decorated with pattering droplets against windowpanes; I stand with an umbrella in thunderstorms and watch until others start to wonder where I am. Eventually I tired of days when the sky didn't speak, and so my mother found the solution in the cheap yellow plastic of an old sprinkler. She set it along the rusted poles of our trampoline so that the water streams arced toward the empty sky and tapped against the black canvas with overjoyed, uncontainable whispers. My little broth-

er and I splashed and slid like little frogs in the rain until the days condensed into a single droplet of precious time.

~

He was a redhead, flaming orange hair burning from his scalp to his forehead, flickering away into faint cinders dusted across his nose and cheeks. His face was round, always smiling, even when there was every reason not to smile. He was a fire in every way, warm and frightening and always, always struggling. There was no way I could have known whether I should have doused his flame or given it more fuel to burn.

I didn't love him. We were only little kids, after all; how could I? I admired his smiles, and I edged close enough to him to feel the warmth that everyone else couldn't, from where they stood a safe, cold distance away. I suppose that was the reason I wanted to be close to him, because no one else did, because everyone else saw burning and chaos where I saw loneliness, a boy destroying himself because he didn't know any better. In the end, though, I don't think it mattered.

Brooding boy, gentle girl; it was the ubiquitous classic. That was why, as a child with a head full of fairy tale pages and TV screens, I thought it could work. I was the sweet, quiet girl, universally liked, or at least universally unknown. I had perfect conduct grades, knew my alphabet, and the teachers always adored me. I made my mother proud, and more importantly, kept my father from being angry. I had no reason to feel anything other than contentment and compassion.

He was the opposite; no mother's love or father's anger could contain him. I don't remember him as being aggressive, only excited. The only difference between me and him, between him and the good children, was that he wouldn't be subdued. His flame was too out of control, and we watched as it burned his green paper apple, the one that represented an A, into a deep red F, every day. Looking back, I think he was just a normal kid, one who refused to repress the energy and curiosity that came with being a normal kid.

No matter what the case was, I pitied him, watching him walk up to the front of the classroom to change his conduct grade every single day. I didn't know what to do, didn't know how to make him feel like he was a good person, even if the teachers said he wasn't, so I told him and everyone else who would listen that I had a crush on him. That's what little girls did to help little boys, right?

~

At times I would stop, bring my feet to a sliding halt, and watch. Even as I peered directly into the veil of sprinkler mist, leaning breathlessly against a cold trampoline pole, it seemed as though I was witnessing something from far away, just as intangible as a rainbow arcing through some unnamed distance in the sky. When we moved the droplets danced with us, flying into the air at every impact of our feet against the black canvas, glittering silver spheres like diamonds or stars. My mother's phone laid on the sparkling grass and indecipherable Owl City lyrics leapt into the air from it, intertwining with the rainbows in the water. Perhaps they were of the same world.

The saccharine notes of *Hot Air Balloon* flowed around us and slowly crystallized into a twinkling capsule of time, of elation so precious and intangible that it just avoided the ruin of reality. Every moment can be found within that song, within empty lyrics filled with meaning that is in turn so untouchably, delightfully meaningless. It floats somewhere in the realm of dreams and poems and light filtering through the other side of pale curtains.

~

My mother tells me that his mother told her that he got so much better. I didn't notice, or I don't remember noticing. He didn't know what to make of me, the girl who loudly professed to anyone who would listen that she was head over heels for the 'bad boy' of kindergarten. I remember being behind him in line one day, edging closer to him, and smiling as I said,

"Hi, Stephen."

"Oh, hey, Emily."

He said it nonchalantly, with barely a tilt of his head in my direction, before comically seeming to realize who I was. Though I had never heard the term back then, in the dictionary in my mind, that memory is the picture beside the term 'double take'.

"Wait- *Emily?*"

I giggled. By that time, he was already very familiar with the rumor that I liked him, spreading through the lunch tables like a wildfire, and he decided to take on a cliché as well: the bemused and awkward boy who didn't know what to think of the affectionate girl trailing after him. I didn't love him, but I appreciated his sense of humor. I realized then that I wasn't the only one of us capable of feigning emotion.

I don't remember anything else from that conversation other than looking at him and smiling, while he smiled nervously at me in return. I was aware even then that we were both playing roles, pretending to feel things we didn't feel, pretending to be people we weren't. But we were little; pretending was something to be enjoyed, something we did with sparkling eyes and little secret giggles when we were alone and broke character. Those days, there was something other than my mother's pride, my father's anger. I didn't love him, and he didn't love me, but we allowed each other to be kids, and that was where the love came from.

~

My little brother's rich brown curls danced alongside the sheet of droplets against the trampoline surface, his dark eyes taking in the gold and rainbow and silver of the world to reflect more sparkling joy than the lightest irises ever could. He giggled and babbled words so preciously meaningless that they evaporated into the air and formed fluffy clouds in my memory. I slammed my bare feet against the canvas of the trampoline to send both him and the water spinning toward the sky, prompting cascades of laughter as his smile pushed his reddened cheeks upward until his face was as round as a raindrop.

And so my little brother became a dream, a poem, a feeling of intangible elation swirling beneath the crystallized surface of a song. I wonder if I flowed into the water in his mind.

~

Now my father is disappointed in me, tells me that I'm becoming too selfish. He cites the coffee mug I gave my older brother for Christmas, the one he says I received as a gift from someone else. I didn't. I bought it. He tells me that he was so proud when I pretended to like that boy in kindergarten, just to make him feel better. I suppose that, since then, I have strayed too far from my role as a part of the

family unit, as sweet, as silent, as afraid. A little too focused on my own goals, my own dreams, my own life. Too selfish.

Stephen was expelled at the end of kindergarten for his conduct grades. My mother tells me that his mother told her that he improved so much at home, became so much more at peace with himself. But the teachers didn't want him to be at peace with himself; they wanted him to be someone else. They wanted him to be quiet, to settle down, to do what they told him and stop giving them a headache while they were trying to earn their salaries. They only pretended to care for us, to love kids, and they were adults. They didn't like pretending.

One day, when school was ending and we rushed outside to our parents waiting in their cars, I spotted him walking a few feet in front of me. I don't remember if I had hatched the plan earlier in the day, or if it occurred to me on a whim. I quickened my pace and grabbed his arm, whispering at him urgently.

"Stephen," I said, and told him something that no kid could ignore. "I have to tell you a secret."

His eyes grew wide, and he leaned down as I beckoned him closer, closing the head of height between us as I stretched up toward his ear. What valuable information, I wonder, did he think I had to tell him? What would I say now? Perhaps,

"It is never wrong to smile. No one should ever tell you that you can't laugh, or speak, or have a sparkle in your eye. Love the things you love, and never feel ashamed for it. It's not your fault. None of this is your fault."

Instead, I kissed him on the cheek, and he shouted my name in shock as I ran out to my mother's car, laughing.

THIS IS NOT MY BEAUTIFUL HOUSE

by Caleb Bouchard

What does one wear to the estate sale and auction of a well-regarded Atlanta attorney turned wife-murderer? This is the question I ask myself at six-thirty on a Saturday morning in August. I'm facing my open closet in my underwear. The open blinds letting in the pale morning light fail to faze me, despite the fact I'm almost fully naked. In my groggy, caffeine-deprived state, I've become absorbed by this issue of attire. Pictures from a Facebook album entitled "The Estate of Diane & Tex McIver" flash through my mind. An enamel wall plaque of a poorly drawn John Wayne is the first of the items to brand itself in my mind's eye, followed by a set of three country western themed throw pillows, and a set of five identical blue denim shirts with the words *Noddin' Down Saloon* in ropey script over the breast pocket. Since I've never been to an auction before —let alone an auction in the south — I consider the possibility that my subconscious is giving me fashion advice. I could take a hint from Tex's red, white and blue wardrobe — from what I've seen online, he owned more than a few shirts colored with a Texas flag motif — and assume the majority of the visitors at ranch today will be sporting attire appropriate for a square dance. Cowboy boots, leather chaps, brown suede jackets with fringe tassels. Were I a strategic dresser, I would pull out my blue denim shirt, but what to pair it with? I don't

own a single pair of leather chaps, and I'd rather not water down the cowboy aesthetic by wearing a pair of my khaki shorts or corduroy slacks.

But then, another auction lot pops into my memory: the wedding dress worn by Diane McIver on the day she married Tex. Should this be my cue to wear my Sunday best? Can I expect to be turned away if I don't arrive at the auction donning a black tie and jacket? I have no idea, but I suppose it's possible. The sprawling eighty-five acre ranch brings to mind visions of Jay Gatsby's mansion, had Gatsby considered himself a "good old boy," instead of an "old sport."

The smell of coffee which I've brewed wafts into my bedroom. Growing impatient with myself, I snag a white and grey striped t-shirt and a pair of shorts. Since the auction is to be held outside, under the minimal comfort of an open air tent, I figure it would be unwise not to dress for the hellish summer day ahead, which, I suppose you could say, is strategic dressing in a nutshell.

The grass is still dewey as I sidle up to a heather gray Chevy Impala outside the front gates of the McIver ranch in Eatonton, Georgia — a twenty minute drive from my apartment in downtown Milledgeville. Two middle-aged women in large brimmed hats sit statuesquely in the Impala. We're the first customers on the second day of this three-day long affair. According to everything I've read online, a tag sale of household items began yesterday at 10 AM and will run through Sunday afternoon at four. Items of significant value, though, will be auctioned off today. These lots include fine art, furniture, accent decor, china, jewelry, Tex's farm equipment, and, the biggest of the big ticket items, the estate itself. A large sign by the pokey two-lane country road advertises the real estate auction will take place on *Saturday, August 4th, at High Noon*. Considering the grisly circumstances that led up to this event, it's hard not to cringe when I see this. Like many, I've only followed the TV and radio reports on the McIver case with a passive, cursory interest. Yesterday, when I first saw a newspaper headline that read "Visitors see inside McIver ranch," I scratched my head and tried to remember where I had seen that name before. At home, I googled the name I had seen on the front page of the *Eatonton Messenger*. "Tex McIver sentenced to life in prison for killing his wife," read one of the top results, an article from the *Atlanta Journal-Constitution*. Within seconds, I had my friend Darian on the phone.

"Oh my *gah-ha-od*," Darian said. I could almost hear her jaw falling on the floor. "This can't be real life."

It should be said that Darian is the curious type of person that can binge-watch hours of *Forensic Files* and *Dateline*, then drift off to a sleep so deep and unperturbed it makes me wonder if these people actually take comfort in hearing about torturous trips down dark country roads, meticulously executed dismemberments, mold-speckled fridges stockpiled with human heads, bathtubs cleaned with bleach, and bed sheets stained with viscous mixtures of semen, blood, and tears. My mother, incidentally, is the same way. As a child, I was often lulled to sleep by the sultry voices of

Keith Morrison and Ann Curry describing macabre crime scenes involving electrical tape and chloroform. I suppose you could say I'm also a member of this screwy tribe, if only by proxy. That said, I'm only interested in murder on a circumstantial level. I don't care to hear about how the bodies were cut up, or the anarchist pap scrawled on the walls in the victim's blood. These details make my stomach turn, and I avoid them at all costs. Rather, I'm interested in context, as well as the mundane asides that tend to get left out the history books. (Forget Helter Skelter; I want to know more about Manson's perplexing connection to Dennis Wilson and The Beach Boys.) Darian knows this about me, and she was able to cater to my interests, mainly by focusing on the investigation and court proceedings following Diane's death.

"He told investigators, 'Guns aren't really my thing.' Can you believe that? He kept a revolver in the console of his car!" Just then, I received a Facebook message from Darian that led me to a photo album posted by the auction house handling the McIver estate. There, I had my first look of the items that would be up for auction.

"This is too rich," I said, chuckling. "Did you see the wall plaque that reads 'Honest Lawyer'?"

"Oh, that's nothing. Wait until you see the door sign that says 'We Don't Call 911.' I'd love to have that."

At 8:10, there are close to twenty people milling around the front gates. Our cars are parked in janky angles on either side of the driveway. Men in ball caps grip onto Yeti coffee mugs and grumble to their wives, who clutch their purses and smooth out their colorful summer dresses. Everyone seems ticked that the gates haven't opened at the advertised time.

"The website said the gates would open at eight for public parking," one of the ladies with a large-brimmed hat reminds a security guard in smug tones. The guard, a young guy with spiky black hair and a well-defined jawline, says there's a glitch with the remote that is keeping the gates from opening permanently, to let multiple cars in.

"We'll have the problem fixed very soon," he says, "I appreciate your patience."

"I'm just reading what the website says," the women retorts, swiping at her cell phone.

This complaint offers an easy segue to other frustrations and perceived slights that will be in store for the day ahead. The 18% buyer's premium, for one, which will be applied to all auction items in addition to the hammer price.

"I don't understand it," says a woman in dark sunglasses. "Do they need that extra money? Really?"

Someone who was here yesterday for the tag sale mentions how awful the weather was. "Hotter than the devil's armpit, but that's Georgia for you. At one point it rained, so it was humid on top of that." This person, a frail-looking woman with deep lines etched into her flat, bronzed face, brings up the Porta-Potties that visitors are required to use. "I hope they cleaned them since yesterday. The smell in there is unholy."

At a quarter past eight, the gates open. We jump into our cars and a guard directs each driver to park on the grassy field surrounding a man-made pond. I peer into the brown water as I walk toward the house and spot a large catfish milling around the sandy edge of the pond. It grazes its back along the water's surface, then slivers back to the pond's muddy depths.

Underneath the shade of the expansive front porch, I take a seat on a white wicker chair that is most likely meant for a child. A heavyset black woman sits across from me in a larger, adult version of my chair; a woman I presume to be her sister stands beside her. She looks at me with kind eyes. She wears a stylish white pants suit and maintains a bob haircut with caramel highlights.

"Are you from Smyrna?" she says, sidling up beside me. I'm taken aback by her greeting words, though not necessarily in a bad way.

"No, I'm not," I tell her. "But I've spent a lot of time there."

"You look like one of my grandson's friends," she says. The heavyset woman in purple smiles contentedly at me, as if my face is a framed watercolor you might hang in your dining room.

"Are y'all from Smyrna?" The y'all is a new thing I've picked up since moving to middle Georgia for graduate school. The southern drawl spares no one in Milledgeville, even in the upper echelons of academia.

The woman gives me a look as if I've just challenged her to a game of Twister. This is a look I've seen a lot lately, when asking this a native middle Georgian. To be from anywhere else is an insult to them.

"We're not, no, sir," the woman with caramel highlights says, patting me on the shoulder. "We've lived in Milledgeville our whole lives. My daughter lives in Smyrna."

We get to talking, and she tells me she and her sister — the woman in purple — worked on the grounds of Central State Hospital as file clerks in a detention center. "We saw men like Mr. McIver day in and day out. So sad. She's dead and he's in jail. It's very sad."

I tell her I can't argue with that.

The middle-aged sisters pick up a new conversation between themselves, and I stand up to stretch my legs. Everything on the front deck that is not part of the house structure bears a red price tag, I notice. A life-sized driftwood horse sculpture. An antique dinner bell bolted onto a beam at the top of the front steps. Patio tables. The child-sized wicker chair I was just sitting in is one of a set of four. $85 is the asking price. Although nobody says it, nor is it printed on a banner in bold lettering, the message is clear: Everything Must Go.

It is not yet high noon, but outside it feels like it. The blinding yellow sun climbs higher and higher into the sky, sucking up the shade provided by large oak trees. Unseen cicadas buzz in their monotone, dread-inducing way. A bald man with narrow eyeglasses approaches the growing crowd on the front porch. He is wearing blue jeans and a fitted white dress shirt that exposes a tangle of silver chest hairs.

"That's the man in charge," someone whispers to their neighbor. "I've seen him on TV."

The bald man waves and introduces himself as the owner of the Montgomery & Marple Auction Gallery. He gives a brief run-down of the day's events.

"Please keep in mind that there are two lines. One for auction registration," he motions to a white tent behind the house, "and one for the tag sale. If you know you want to register for the auction, do so as soon as possible. We're expecting a big crowd today, and we have a small staff, so it might be a bit of wait, but we will be sure to take care of everyone. Thank y'all. We'll be opening up the house shortly."

The bald man walks off, and we split into two lines. Wives mumble to their husbands, unsure if they are in the correct line. A few bold souls wander around to the rear of the house, giving up their spot in line for the tag sale. A chrome food truck serving barbecue is stationed adjacent to the house; beside it, a man and women are in the process of pitching a rainbow-colored tent advertising Sno-Cones.

A skinny guy with tousled brown hair and green eyes smiles at me. He looks familiar, but I can't quite place him. His white denim jacket and pockmarks aren't characteristic of anyone I regular see. Perhaps I'm friends with his older brother or sister? I pull out my phone and pretend I don't know him at all. It's a low move, and it backfires immediately when he files in line behind me and says, "What's up man?"

"Hey!" I exclaim, overcompensating for my ignorance. "What brings you out here?" I assume he's enrolled at the same college I study at, but he isn't. He tells me he's grabbing audio for the Atlanta morning radio show he helps produce. I hit my forehead with my palm, remembering our mutual friends at the dive bar we used to frequent for karaoke.

"Trevor!" I blurt out, a complete non-sequitur.

Trevor chuckles. "Yeah man, it's me."

We move past my gaff, and I ask him how are things at the radio station.

"The whole McIver thing has been a big story at the station," Trevor tells me. "The hosts love to make him the butt of their jokes."

The line inches forward. The house is open for business. A white-haired police officer stands at the front door, counting heads as people enter. He holds up a large hand just as I'm about to cross the threshold.

"Only thirty-five at a time," he says. His face is the color of salmon. His eyes are black buttons, so perfectly round and stitched in. A doll's eyes.

While waiting, Trevor interviews the woman behind us in line, who says she is interested in picking up some "Indian artifacts." She also complains about the weather.

The officer pokes his head into the house. "Okay, five more."

Trevor and I shuffle into the foyer, followed by the woman on the lookout for Native American artifacts. The interior is like any other McMansion one might stumble into, however, here is the place has been halfway disemboweled. China cabinet doors and kitchen cupboards are wide open, their contents marked with orange price tags. A sign posted on a mahogany bookcase in the study informs shoppers that hardcovers are two dollars, paperbacks are one. *RARE BOOKS: INQUIRE.* In the living room, married couples sit on couches and chairs, testing for comfort. My eyes glaze over as I realize most of this stuff fails to fit into my obscure sense of style.

"There's nothing for me here," I tell Trevor, considering the overpriced china and outdated art prints. Then, out of the corner of my eye, I spot an animated Hank Williams Jr. action figure, decked out in dark sunglasses and lipstick red cowboy boots. I go over and press the button at the figure's base. It jumps to life, rigidly shaking its hips while singing "All My Rowdy Friends."

"Perhaps I spoke too soon," I say, transfixed.

Upstairs, we wander into a child's woodland-themed bedroom, furnished with a log cabin motif bunkbed and desk. Smiling bears and joyous moose fill the walls. Stuffed woodland creatures sit upright on the beds, price tags hang from their fuzzy brown ears. Later, I will learn this room belonged to Tex and Diane's godson, whom they treated like their own child. In court recordings, his name is evoked time and time again by the Bruce Harvey —Tex's defense attorney — as a means to shut down the prosecution's case that Diane's killing was intentional. Tex loved his godson more than anyone else in this world — the only exception, arguably, being Diane. Why would a rational man go out and do something that would jeopardize such a special relationship?

A strange, sad feeling coils in the pit of my stomach as I cross the hallway into the master bedroom. I hardly notice the bedroom itself, for I am drawn to the expansive open wardrobe on the far side of the room. Here, Tex and Diane's everyday clothing are up for grabs, from their silk underwear to their horse-riding gear. Picking through the tops and bottoms, the gravity and general surreality of the scene fully sinks in: the estate sale of a couple who is only half-deceased. It feels intrusive and vaguely pornographic to be here, fingering sports jackets and ogling neck ties and sampling perfumes — participating in the dismantling of a family, the commodification that resulted from

a horrible crime. I feel culpable, guilty in my own right. Just because Tex was convicted to be a cold-blooded murderer doesn't mean Diane deserved to have strangers pick through her bras and jewelry. Cringing, I squeeze my way out of the walk-in wardrobe and dash downstairs. Talk about airing out your dirty laundry.

Half an hour later, Trevor and I sit in foldable plastic chairs, underneath a large, white, Methodist-revival-style tent. The air is sticky and stifling as the August morning unfolds into afternoon. Many fan themselves with their bidding paddles. High noon—and the house auction—is almost upon us, but first there is the business of the regular auction.

Not a minute after eleven, Mike, the bald auction gallery owner, steps up to a lectern, accompanied by a athletic fellow with a trim red beard and watery blue eyes. He is dressed in a slim fit Oxford shirt and jeans of a hue so blue they inspire patriotic sentiments. He, too, appears to be bald underneath his mesh baseball cap — albeit, his look seems to be cultivated, while Mike doesn't seem to have much of a choice. After a few welcoming words, Mike introduces Ronnie, the athletic fellow: the auctioneer. It is Ronnie who sets the ground rules and expectations. Only raise your paddle or hand if you want to bid. The last person who raises a paddle/hand at the drop of the hammer is expected to pay for their item(s) that day, either by card, cash or check. There will be no waivers for the 18% buyers premium whatsoever. He's not mean, per se, but there is an undeniable intensity about him that tells me he's ex-military. Marines, probably. In his hands, the microphone appears to be less of an amplification device and more like a baton.

Once the crowd has been verbally domesticated by Ronnie's stern monologue, the bidding commences. The first few lots are nothing to write home about. Wooden duck decoys. A crystal decanter. Hungarian silverware. Trevor bids on a stuffed armadillo and I bid on the country western themed throw pillows. We're both respectively and swiftly outbid. When a series of firearms comes up on the lot list, I tune out. Guns aren't really my thing, and unlike Mr. McIver, I mean this sincerely. My eyelids flutter as Ronnie The Auctioneer spouts impassioned locutions during a heated bidding war over a single barrel musket, or a pair of 19th century dueling pistols. I can't remember which.

"*350!* Ain't no friends at an auction — even if it's your mamma! *375!* It's only money, folks! *400!* Last chance, hoss…"

Soon after this exchange, a gumball machine Trevor has been eyeing comes up for bid. We sit up in our seats.

"Alright," Ronnie says, "we've had a lot of folks asking about this one." He contemplates the screen displaying a picture of the nondescript red machine. He strokes his red beard. "Let's start the bidding at $100. Can I get one-hundred-un-dred-that's-one-hundo-hhh-one…" Trevor lifts his paddle. Ronnie acknowledges him.

"Yessir!Gimme-*one-twenty-five-ive-yyy-one -two-five*…" Ronnie's attention shifts to the other side of the tent. His eyes light up as he points out another bidder. "Now it's *one-fifty-iddy*—a fine piece of machinery, folks!—*kick-'er-up-to-one-seventy five*— yessir, thank you, sir—*TWO-hun'ed*…"

"I'm out," Trevor says, rising from his chair. "I'm gonna grab some more audio."

We shake hands, and as Trevor walks off, Ronnie shouts, "Sold!" The hammer price is half of my monthly rent.

A few minutes before noon, a group of men in blue polo shirts crowd around the edge of the tent. They all share the same high-and-tight haircut, the same taught lips and predatory stare. Their leader, a tall man with a beefy chest and hard blue eyes, has the build and machismo of a WWE wrestler, or a mechanic. Take away his business casual attire and put him in a jumpsuit, he would also fit in well at a body shop, barking orders and replacing transmissions at lightning speed. I mentally dub him "Motor Head." Compared to him, the other polo shirts are just goons, cronies, yet intimidating all the same. They're not here to play games. They're here to fuck shit up.

They're here to sell a house, goddammit.

When the clock strikes noon, Motor Head sends over one of his men to whisper something in Mike's ear. Mike nods, and Ronnie, without acknowledging Mike or Motor Head's crony, introduces Hartfield Auction Company for the handling of the real estate auction. Motor Head and his men march forward as Mike and Ronnie fade back. The big dogs have arrived. Motor Head takes the mic, looks the crowd over, and begins with general remarks and ground rules. This, I assume, is pure spectacle. Before the auction, I heard, prospective house bidders were required to fill out enough paperwork to make an IRS auditor's head spin. There have also been mumblings of credit reports and background checks. Perhaps Motor Head and his men personally collected blood samples and birth certificates? All of this is to say that when Motor Head lays out the terms and conditions, he's mostly preaching to the choir: an elite, invisible few of us who can afford an eighty-five acre ranch, even at auction. Those who need to know about the small print are already in the loop.

"We're here to represent the seller," Motor Head states for the public record. "We're here to sell this farm. We've met an awful lot of good folks out here. We've heard a lot of things. We know the good, the bad… but I'll tell you this the good far outweighs the bad on this property."

At this, the woman in front of me shifts uneasily in her seat, then leans over and whispers something in her husband's ear. Someone standing at the back of the tent asks Motor

Head about title insurance. The air feels heavy, and not from the humidity.

"A'ight. I'm gonna turn it over," Motor Head declares. "I've preached, and I've prayed. And now it's time to pass the plate. Here we go, boys."

Motor Head plods off with his clipboard and the auctioneer, a rotund man with a goatee, takes the stage. The men in blue polos wade out into the crowd, whooping it up, serving as the auctioneer's brash cheerleaders.

"Heyyyyy! What d'ya say?!"

"Hey hey hey hey!"

The bidding begins at $700,000. Not a minute later, Motor Head screams "QUARTER! QUARTER!" He yanks his fist in the air as if trying to start a chainsaw. The auctioneer acknowledges the $725,000 bid, then promptly nabs bids for $750,000 and $775,00. A one-two punch. A few feet behind me, a portly old man who bears a vague resemblance to Motor Head cries: "Hey! Hey! Hey! *Hey! Hey!*" His voice is reedy and shrill and cuts right through the swampy air. Motor Head points him out from across the room.

"Whatcha got, Pop?"

Heads swivel toward Pop. A pregnant pause envelopes the crowd. The persistent cicadas fill the silence as the old man catches his breath.

"Goodness me," he finally gasps. "One million dollars!"

The crowd explodes with cheers and applause. A blue shirt with a white mustache does a little jig. Motor Head bears his teeth and roars, *"Yee-aaaah!"* The scene is downright primal.

The auctioneer continues his feverish bid calling, first asking for a million and a half, then a million and a quarter. His eyes scan the room for any signs of interest from the previous bidders, but it seems they've all bowed out. "A million-twenty-five-twenty-five going ONCE..."

"Hey! Hey!" The portly patriarch barks. "They know the swimming pool goes with it?"

"The pool does go with it. We're giving 'em the swimming pool! Million-twenty-five going TWICE!"

"Last man bidding will own the property!" Motor Head reminds the crowd.

The auctioneer echoes this statement, then adds: "You know what's gonna happen, John?"

"I know what's gonna happen!" Motor Head hollers.

"Six months, eight months, two years from now you're gonna ride by this road, you're gonna ride by this farm, and you're gonna say 'I should've, I could've...' but it's too late!"

"IT'S TOO LATE!" Motor Head shouts in this Come to Jesus moment. But no one approaches the proverbial alter.

"Million-twenty-five!" Sweat cascades down the auctioneer's plum-colored face. "All in? All done? All satisfied? Last and final call, Burt, ya comin' in? A million-twenty-five..."

"Just give it to him!" Pop pleads.

"All in? All done?" The Auctioneer waves his finger one final time over the crowd as Judgement Day approaches... "Sold! For one million dollars!"

An edifying applause fills the tent. Blue shirts swarm the back corner of the tent, joining Pop as he jumps up and down like an elated child on Christmas morning. I turn in my chair to spot the new homeowner, but in the hustle and bustle of handshakes and hugs it's hard to see who is congratulating whom.

An exodus of people get up from their seats and wander off to the food trucks, leaving the tent half full. Those who remain are the seasoned, serious bidders, I gather — the ones who aren't here for the spectacle, but rather for the sport of the occasion. Their auction lists are heavily marked in pen, their legs are crossed at jaunty angles, their craggy poker faces betray nothing about their intentions or desires. Sitting among them, I feel a surprising sense of camaraderie, though distant. Unspoken. These are the men and women still playing the slot machines at three in the morning, the barflies who have to be shooed out of the pub after last call. The relentless romantics, the persistent, patient dreamers, the handful of humanity that keep their butts in their seats and their eyes tilted upward, waiting and hungry for the next thing up on the auction block. It may not be a big, beautiful house with a cobblestone swimming pool and the country western saloon erected by a calculating wife killer. It may not even be an eighteen karat diamond ring, like the one that is now being presented (starting price: $2,000). But are these the things that truly matter in life? Or is it simply having the courage to raise your paddle, nod your head, or look up to the man with the hammer and give him a knowing wink: the sort of small but meaningful gesture that says, unequivocally, *I'm in*.

About the Author:

Caleb Bouchard is a first year fiction student in the MFA program at Georgia College. His nonfiction has recently appeared in Foliate Oak Literary Magazine. He is a Georgia native.

LOUD MUSIC
by Leslie Tucker

He is mournful and scornful, bellowing about love in vain, alternating a velvet baritone with a nasal whine. Thick, damp hair flops at his shoulders. His ivory-colored sequined jumpsuit, open to the waist, reveals a gleaming chest as he struts and gyrates. He has been living in my head for fifty years and this particular 1972 performance, now re-mastered for DVD, lights me up like a used car lot. I manipulate the remote control with my good hand, thinking that even at sixty-five, my bones have healed fast with titanium plates and screws. The nerve damage, well…

My first glimpse of him on The Ed Sullivan Show in 1964 still flashes neon bright, how he pouted those pillowy lips and bulldozed J.S. Bach out of my brain for a decade. I was a coltish sixteen and he was a sinewy twenty. He belted "Around and Around," prancing and slithering like James Brown, whom I would learn decades later, had told him to loosen up his knees. He wailed that time was on his side and I thought I knew what he meant.

From the night I first laid eyes on his wiry body and rubbery face I have longed to be him, to be Mick Jagger. And sure, I know, thousands of guys all over the world have reverberated with the same longing for decades, but I was a goony, star-student girl training as a classical pianist.

I was primed for Mick by my nighttime radio habits.

Dad had given me a transistor radio on my thirteenth birthday for listening to live broadcasts of classical recitals from the Detroit Institute of Art. And I listened dutifully, but I also tucked the black plastic box under my covers and tuned in to The Big 8, CKLW, a Windsor, Ontario station. Marvin Gaye's fluid tenor and Ray Charles' raspy one crackled under my aqua chenille bedspread, and a decade of meticulously memorized Bach Minuets and Preludes splintered like kindling. The Kinks' power-chord guitar riffs ignited my emotional tinderbox and when Ray Davies yowled, "Girl, you've really got me goin', you've got me so I don't know what I'm doin,'" I surrendered the precision of polyphony.

As an ambitious piano student, I had been fascinated by the intricate fingerings and dotted rhythms of Bach Inventionen and Sinfonien. The mahogany metronome was compelling as I developed rhythm and small muscle memory to its ticking, that is, until adolescence. Suddenly, I needed release from rigid classical structures, and from honors courses at school too. I was crouched over quadratic equations that Sunday evening, on the verge of tears, when Dad's voice sliced the silence. "C'mon, Les, take a break. British rock band on Ed Sullivan."

Ed looked like an old vampire to me. Hair slicked down on a receding widow's peak, starched collar pinching his jowls, he clapped as velvet stage curtains swept apart revealing five guys with hair that moved when they did. Three of them held electric guitars and one sat behind a drum kit, but my attention stuck on the long lean guy with wide nervous eyes. He sidled up to the floor stand microphone, snapped his fingers and tapped one heel. Muscular emotional vitality beamed from his uncertain eyes, zapping me through the curved TV screen. I leapt across the room, cranked up the volume and tumbled into a lifelong fascination with a front man.

I came by fascination with music honestly and early. According to my mother, I'd been enthralled by the Grinnell spinet in our living room and had begged for lessons from age three, stretching my hand up and pounding out bass notes.

I was five on the day my first piano teacher showed up. Mother seated her in the velvet wing chair near the piano and I hopped up on the bench, trembling. I smacked Middle C, babbled that the eighty eight keys repeated themselves and that hammers hit strings to produce sound. My five-year-old brain was exploding, somehow knowing that the person who would unlock the keyboard mystery had arrived. We began.

The piano pieces I learned played themselves in my brain when I was away from the instrument. Clementi rippled between my ears as I skipped across sidewalk cracks and Hanon exercises haunted me as our family chomped popcorn during *Ozzie and Harriet.*

I easily identify two moments that formed my character. The first, when my piano teacher cracked the code, revealing that lines and spaces on a musical staff matched the keys on a piano, that white keys were naturals and black keys were accidentals, representing how pitches were altered. The treble staff was for my right hand, the bass for my left. Tumblers in my curious Kindergarten brain clicked into place.

The second moment occurred eleven later when I was sixteen, the night Mick's sultry baritone leaked through the nubby tweed speaker on our big fat TV. The stovepipe pants, those uneasy eyes, all that shaggy hair tossed at a girl who'd only known boys with brush cuts and creases in their khakis. I felt radiant and unstable. I loved it.

I believed I understood Mick's feral message because I harbored the same rebellious inclinations he displayed on stage. I knew I wanted to be just like him.

Yet somehow, I became a piano teacher.

Not that I was always proper. I gave birth to my first daughter as an unmarried teenager. I raised her alone, with some help from my parents, while hauling myself through a low-level business degree. After college, I held a fast track administrative position at GM for seven years, a lucrative career opportunity during the golden days of the Detroit auto industry and Affirmative Action. I forced myself to fit the professional profile, cut off my long braids and slept on brush rollers to make my hair flip up on the ends. I posed, dignified in Butte knit dresses and tailored jackets, tilting my chin and chatting with flannel-suited men. It went well until one frigid morning in 1970.

The night before, I'd sprawled on the sofa far too late for a woman with a day job, repeatedly dropping the needle on my new copy of *Let It Bleed.* Hours boiled away in the liquid of Merry Clayton's "Oooh-oooo's on "Gimme Shelter," and the following day at work I blathered about Keith's innovative tunings, the balls-out-brave lyrics on "Shelter," the cowbell intro on Honky Tonk Woman. No one spoke. They averted their eyes. I needed my job and controlled myself after that.

I met my first husband, a turtleneck-and-smock-wearing-Design Sculptor, at GM Design Staff and five years later, my second daughter was born. Life was good. Falling in line seemed to be working.

While on GM maternity leave, I attended a chamber music conference. My instructor, a brilliant concert pianist, was sympathetic to my conflict: an unwillingness to give up earning serious money, juxtaposed with the dread of returning to a gray metal desk. Why not teach piano lessons, lucrative in my city, while considering other career options? Sure, good temporary solution.

But who would take lessons from me, I wondered, squashing myself into a cap-sleeved peach knit, believing it to be proper teacher's attire. Yow! Then five students a week became ten, became thirty, became forty-five -- all levels of proficiency, first through twelfth grade. Adults too. I developed a waiting list of students and donated the Butte knits to the Salvation Army, got comfortable in jeans and boots, ignoring raised eyebrows from student's mothers.

I settled into the grueling, detail-oriented work of classical piano, returned to college for music degrees and publically performed limited repertoire, all while teaching thirty-five or forty hours a week. I survived on four or five hours sleep a night for a decade, discovering that performing by memory with so little rest was brutal. I had memory lapses during public performances, felt humiliated. There would be time later, I told myself, to refresh and improve my technique, to sleep well, to perform the Beethoven sonatas I would put aside temporarily.

I became a full-time teacher and took on even more students.

I dissected ornamentation on Bach Preludes and explained lyricism on Beethoven Bagatelles, but after dark, when the last student left and my daughters were in their bedrooms, my husband dozing in front of the History Channel, I sped around town. Windows down, a bedraggled ghost of a woman, my hair flying ragged, *Beggar's Banquet* blasting in the wind.

Something bucked inside my brain but I never missed a lesson. No one suspected that "Sympathy for the Devil" pounded between my ears as I counted Clementi Sonatinas out loud. Students sweated over harmonic minor scales without a clue that Bobby Keys' raunchy sax solo on "Brown Sugar" thundered in my chest.

Although I abandoned practicing music to teach it, I always assumed I'd play the piano in retirement. I would refine, maybe even get those Goldberg Variations up to tempo, and above all, learn the Beethoven Opus 81a sonata.

But I didn't practice when I retired.

My second husband and I left the Detroit area in 2004 and moved to the Carolina mountains and I couldn't resist the fresh air and lush topography. Knowing that vigorous physical strength dissipates with age, I went outdoors to hike, to raft and kayak, to explore zip lines and rope courses. I believed there would be time to polish my keyboard skills later, when I had to sit down, indoors. Since the accident, however, it's doubtful I'll ever extend my left hand enough to reach, much less strike the octaves necessary to nail the baseline on the 81a, ironically titled *Les Adieux*.

So what? I raised two daughters, formed strong bonds with thirty years of students, earned a fine living and most important, passed the music forward. I'm proud of that. But emotional retrospect is slippery, and sometimes my mind slinks back through those years, how I felt ensnared in the barbed wire of propriety necessary for a teacher, even one in jeans and boots.

Again, so what? Many of us in my age group have plowed through our lives on autopilot, accomplishing complex tasks with accuracy. That I could teach classical piano repertoire with rock music blaring in my head, while deciphering the individual parts of both may be strange, but it's not what strikes me as most salient. No, far more important yet not often recognized, is what we know about ourselves when we are young and how easily we ignore the information. How we squander time, energy, and the laser beam focus of youth in the name of a hard day's work.

I knew as a teenager in flannel pajamas during that Ed Sullivan Show, and was drop dead certain for seven years as a GM Administrator in pumps and pantyhose. Under the worn jeans of an over-booked piano teacher, it was clear to me every day: Although I never had the ability to front a band or be a guitar wizard, I wanted to be a rock star, specifically Mick, who let music and uncut human emotion rip. I wanted the high-octane life force I saw in him. And I want it now, more than ever because I've watched him grow old before my eyes and I like what I see. A man who has done the opposite of what we are all told to do.

The rain was steady that July morning in 2013 as I trotted down our steep driveway with my two Springer Spaniels. One of them bounded in front of me, as she does most days and I hopped backward to avoid a full face plant on the concrete. But this time, both feet slipped from under me and I broke my fall, instinctively experts say, with my outstretched hand.

The double distal radius fracture of my left wrist was diagnosed severe, with scattered bone fragments. The scapholunate ligament on the top of my hand was severed. The good-natured ER nurses called it "the full dangle" and the doc said I was fortunate to be healthy, to have such strong bones at my age, that I could have easily shattered my arm, shoulder and hip too. In the ER, through the fog of IV painkillers, I thought of Mick, yes, really, who is four years older than I am and has never shattered anything that I know of.

Bones heal well with titanium plates and screws anchoring them, but ligament surgery is tricky, and scar tissue compressing my radial nerve caused unpredictable, electrifying pain for months, then years. Icy Hots and Thermal Wraps comprised an unwelcome new vocabulary for a physically vigorous woman, one who took pride in planks and pushups and had made it sixty-five years without an injury. At my home I have an "Adventure Wall" of photographs of my outdoor exploits – bungee jumping, skydiving, rock climbing, hiking all over the world. Yet looking back wrenches my gut sometimes. I recognize myself as a woman who postponed practicing Beethoven to ramble around outdoors until she could no longer extend her left hand far enough to strike a simple triad on her piano.

In the mid-sixties, The Rolling Stones played Olympia Stadium and my boyfriend scalped fourth row seats. Olympia, then home of the Detroit Red Wings, was a small venue compared to today's arenas, and for concerts, the plexi-glass walls surrounding the rink were removed and a floor constructed over the ice. We chugged a couple of Stroh's in the parking lot and found our seats, anxious for the first glimpse of the band we'd seen only on black and white TV.

Keith slithered out in high-heeled boots and lacerated the screaming horde with the opening fuzz box chords on "Satisfaction." Mick materialized in the blur of sound, pranced over and kissed Keith, full on the lips. The room roared. So did I.

Nine months later, my labor room screams were even louder. Soaked with sweat and grinning like the fool I'd been, I felt the distortion infused opening licks of "Satisfaction" throbbing between my ears and legs as they wheeled me into the delivery room. It all seems ridiculous now, excruciating and obvious, but I didn't get it then. There is nothing coherent about rock and roll – it's shameless and unconstrained, slapping the demons in our bones, awakening and exploiting all our sensual desires.

I have experienced the hallucinatory intensity of music pouring effortlessly from my body twice in my life. I've felt the simultaneous rush of giving and craving, the ethereal magic in a hushed room when connection with the audience is complete, when listeners slip into breathless silence before bursting into applause.

I've pulled my own psychic plug and floated inside the sound I first imagined, and then produced. I have given in to and exploited my emotional vulnerability. One performance of the Schumann Piano Concerto, and one of the Op. 31 Piano Sonata by Beethoven, two prolonged incidents of purest ease after years of physical training and intellectual rigor. I'm betting Mick can't count the times he's let it all spill out, has entered that zone of euphoric mental and emotional release.

Hammers hitting strings on a soundboard produce the pitches that emanate from a piano and the instant a hammer strikes a string, the sound begins to decay. The only way to maintain the sound is to keep striking more keys, combining more pitches, to keep playing the instrument. Mick knows this and continues to produce the sound that has swelled his body and brain for over fifty years. He absorbs the risk of public performance, with supreme courage, preening across the world stage.

No more chugging beer in parking lots for me and I haven't seen the Stones perform live in twenty years. After swearing I'd never whine about traffic jams, concert mobs and unreliable acoustics at stadium shows, I've become someone who does. So I'm seduced by the intimacy of the big screen in my living room. I savor and internalize the interaction between the well-worn Stones – up close and personal. Camera angles on Mick's savage face are tight and I quiver, detecting each nod of a head or tip of a guitar neck as band members toss riffs back and forth.

In December 2012, friends arrived at our home to watch the Direct TV Pay Per View event, "Last Stop, The Rolling Stones Live at The Prudential Center." It was, at the time, the last scheduled concert on their 50th Anniversary Reunion Tour and I had over-hyped it to our guests. World media crowded the New Jersey arena and the advance press blitz had been scathing: Could the old men survive the pressure and live up to their reputation? Was the greatest rock and roll band in the world worth the exorbitant price of admission?

Hell yes. Three generations of fans were ecstatic as seamless vocals, tight ensemble and the flaming guitar solos that had awakened my mind and body fifty years before seared through the screen. And Mick, once a scrawny but sensuous young icon, radiating tensile energy, had morphed by force of his own will (and a Norwegian physical trainer,) into a muscular and magnetic old man, ever charismatic and feral. My emotional inferno raged. I was young and wild again. For three hours. And so was he.

It all made sense as I focused on the sweat-drenched, furrowed face. After ten or twelve miles of vigorous stage travel, a common distance for Mick, I finally got it. In the privacy of my living room, by the grace of high definition technology, I saw something I'd never seen before: euphoria in his eyes.

I also saw that his rapture doesn't last. Wrapped in a thick robe post concert, body guards supported Mick, escorting him to the limo. His staggering exhaustion was evident, his face crumpled into a grimace.

So here's what I wonder: with thumping electronics and lights swirling beneath his cushioned Nikes, how does he prevail with full voice and all the moves, seemingly unfazed by the hysterical crowd? Or does he, like many performers, derive energy from them? Sure, I'm aware he's deaf and wired for relevant sound, but is that easier?

How does he maintain the chronic intensity, the feline runway prowl to navigate a three-hour performance at seventy? Does he just keep molting, renewing himself with music and movement, shedding the husk of age each time he steps on stage? Can those of us who make music, or hear it in our heads, break free of our time worn physical and emotional exoskeletons? Or has he found the quiet at the center of the storm? Is he immutable now, inside the eye of the crossfire hurricane he and The Stones churned up half a century ago?

Fifty years after switching to CKLW under my blankets, my brain is auto-tuned to the same musical frequency. Loud. Rock. Music. I float from my leather chair during TV concerts as consonance and dissonance erupt from ceiling speakers. Indelible images of youth, vitality and excess come into focus with mind-bending clarity. My emotional swagger is gaudy yet private, a secret standing ovation for the woman I never became.

Perhaps it's just that my angle of perspective has shifted. When I was young, I would have cringed at Mick's wrinkled face blatantly displaying the atrocities of age. Now, the physical evidence, his triumph and anguish, the distillation of age and endurance he displays, enthralls me.

And lately, the silence is fascinating too. My mind's eye is imprinted with two photos of the front man that appeared repeatedly as press buzz of the Stones 50th Reunion Tour swamped media outlets. In the *Rolling Stone Magazine* photo, taken during the Stones London concert in the fall of 2012, Mick is muscular and vibrant, slinky in a black tee shirt, sleeves pushed up on muscular forearms. He struts on a runway, guitar in one hand, mic in the other, chin tilting upward. His gaze is Zen-like, yet I see the snarl of the crowd, the flailing arms, and can imagine the cacophony of the mob. He is exposed and vulnerable, yet fully in control of the elation and terror that defines public performance. And that's exactly what I want to be: exposed and vulnerable, yet able to control, or at least manage, the elation and terror that defines aging.

The other photo, from the *London Daily Mail Online*, was taken immediately after an unpublicized warm-up concert in LA. It exposes a sweat drenched, haggard old man with unfocused eyes under bushy eyebrows, hearing aids dangling from his ears. One photo is emblematic of all that is lost, the other, of all that is left. It is hard to determine which is which. After a fall in the rain, four surgeries and years of unpredictable, electrical nerve pain, I do wonder what is left.

Here's what I know: the sparkling magnetism that tugs me toward the front man remains strong, stronger than the calculated electronics of high production values, stronger than the thwanging of Stratocasters and the thundering of Gretsch vibrating through my body. Is he just an oracle, an intermediary between my everyday existence and my most primal cravings? No, it's more than that.

The secret is written all over Michael Philip Jagger's face, he's modeled it across the world stage for half a century: the lurid freedom of living his one life uncensored. He got away with it. He proved it could be done.

The night of the TV concert I scrutinize Mick's performance, cringing, imagining his exhaustion near the end. I want to wallow in the Technicolor mythology of the screen and yearn for a triumphant finish of his hero's quest. And holy shit, it happens, I see it: the unbridled joy stretching across the rutted face. Applause explodes and lights flash, yet there it is: tranquility in his eyes, profound satisfaction I think, after burning it so hard, so near the end.

After Spinning class the other day, I swung my leg over the bike seat and was stunned that it felt rubbery, not wiry and ready to run, as usual. The rock music fuel of our workout had clicked off and the silence was deafening. I thought of Mick, wondering how his life will change when those skinny legs of his give out. And even now, what must the post concert silence be like for him? What is the sound of exhaustion and exhilaration after his state-of-the-art hearing system is unplugged?

I'm betting that the music keeps roaring in his head, just like it does in mine, and that it will continue when he has to sit down. He has internalized the ecstasy of his most intimate gesture: of splitting himself wide open on stage, of resolutely splattering his audiences with joy and pain. The Schumann Piano concerto in a black silk skirt, or Sympathy for the Devil in a whirling red cape, maybe it's the same.

The ivory sequined jumpsuit from the Stones 1972 world tour is protected behind glass in Cleveland's Rock n' Roll Hall of Fame. But the man who wore it is still out there. He defies the transience of youth, strength, and desire, a vibrant personification of the myth I embrace: that musical energy is endless, that we can rock on forever.

About the Author:

Leslie Tucker, a Detroit escapee, lives on a Carolina mountainside and refuses to divulge its exact location. She is an avid hiker and zip liner, a dedicated yogi, an ACBL Life Master in Sanctioned Bridge, and enjoys anything that requires a helmet. She holds degrees in business and music. Her work has appeared in the 2010 and 2012 Press 53 Awards Anthologies, where her essay, "Lies That Bind" won first place for nonfiction. Her work has also appeared in Fiction Fix, The Baltimore Review, Hippocampus Magazine, So to Speak, Prime Number Magazine, and TINGE Magazine among others.

REHABBING RAIN: IN THE SHADE OF THE COTTONWOOD TREE

by Brianna Heisey

I was born and raised in the desert. Like most desert plants and animals, I love rain. I live for rain. I live because of rain. Rain heals me, as it heals and seals the cracked floors of sunbaked arroyos and limestone canyon walls. It peels back the membranes of seedpods, freeing them to the warm winds and porous soils to replant and grow—shallow rooted and thin bodied. Rain plumps up cactus flesh, sending a moist exhale of rescue breaths down the throats of desiccated, sweat-caked desert dwellers whose minds petrify as they stare

intently into the flames of mesquite barbecues. This collective gasp sweeps across the land. This forced air is said to be the origin of the infamous haboob, the monumental respiration of all living things in the desert when the rain clouds roll in and the infernal sun is finally blotted out. You probably didn't know this, did you? The power of breath in the desert. In close proximity to sand and the earth's core, breath is powerful. The air is heavy. Rain reha bilitates the desert world.

As a girl growing up addicted to biannual rain seasons in Tucson, Arizona—summer monsoons and winter maintenance rains—I loved rain so much, I decided to name my first-born human child Rain. Someday. When I had one. Then someday became today and I didn't have a human child, but instead, an immense love for wild things. For displaced wild animals. For the canines that walk the line between domestic and wild, not knowing their sure place, and for many reasons I will get to later, I can relate to these animals. The world made us as we are—compatible and cohesive—to gravitate together in a realm of dire solidarity, to pack up and survive. To thrive. And so I began to rescue wolf dogs in danger of euthanasia from the animal shelter. My first feral female I, of course, named Rain.

Rain arrived. There was nothing seasonal about her, accept that she arrived with the monsoons, and she was weathered. Withered. Scrawny, her fur matted and full of parasites. In spite of this, she was beautiful. A spirit animal from another dimension. A small, white, yellow-eyed, large-toothed wolf. When I took her home from the shelter and bathed her, she howled, she gnawed, she clawed me. She was so malnourished, most of her sinewy fur fell out. She had the beginning stages of an Upper Respiratory Infection (Kennel Cough), I could tell from the sniffles and runny nose. She fought me, just enough to show will, but she was tired. I lathered her up and scrubbed her down, as she finally submitted, stiff as a board. Fight or flight had passed, Rain was in shock and submission. The pre-stages of learning to trust and simply breathe in the desert.

When I finished, she stared blankly at the drain—immobile, hairless, eyes on fire, skinny legs and all. I wrapped a towel around her and lifted her from the elevated tub, her legs sticking straight out, all 35 pounds of her emaciated frame. Her hip and shoulder bones pierced my hands, leaving a lasting impression. I dried her gently with the towel, then set to clipping matted fur from her with scissors and feeding her tiny pieces of dried fish. This, I would soon find, was her element. Soaked to the bone and devouring protein. It would take months before Rain would gaze upon me with her full moon eyes, but she was already beginning to feel me. To lean into me and fight less. And it wasn't long after that, Rain was running, racing me into the revelation of ethology and the genius of all things wild.

We hit the roads. Rain darted every which way like a minnow, petrified of my footfalls. Each forward step I took, she took two to the side. I finally let her off leash and she began to follow. We also had Shooter, my male Mexican wolf mix and confident alpha in any pack, leading the way for us. Shooter found me in the

back country wilderness of the Tonto National Forest, as a young pup. But that story is also for another chapter. It was Rain—as Rain needed the rehabbing—that growled and lunged at Shooter, conditioned from her first year of life as a stray in the streets of South Tucson, to fight off all competition for resources. And I was her number one resource now. But Shooter saw her as damaged and not worthy of his time, snorting into the air with disapproval. So I ran between them. We took to the washes—in between floods—dodging Diamond Backs and chasing rabbits. And the monsoon rains fell. Every afternoon into the evening, like clockwork. It was an El Niño year, and the satiating season for rehabbing Rain had begun.

Our adventures rolled in like thunder. It wasn't an easy time, but miracles did occur daily. And the sheer experience of living in the Sonoran desert during monsoon season is exciting enough. If you aren't aware yet, in the summer time, in the Arizona desert, it's shade that all living creatures seek. It's shade—before the rains begin—that provides relief and rehabilitation from the relentless desert sun. The shade of a tree, the shade of a bush, the shade of a tiny blade of grass—anything to defer the radiant sun that seeks to infrare itself upon the earth, absorbing directly or becoming ambient heat. The luscious, liquescent flesh of animals—particularly the vulnerable flesh of humans—is the perfect surface to absorb the sun's rays and burn. The infamous sunburn. Rain and Shooter—my wolf pups—have no problem with this. They never burn, with their numerous layers of fur. Even their vision is protected by dark black rings that encircle wild yellow eyes, cutting back on sun glare and absorption when scanning the landscape for prey or predator. I'm not as perfectly created by nature to triumph in the open range, and the desert reminds me of this. I'm usually lathered in sunscreen, wearing a hat, and I'm always on the watch for confident predators that might land me at the bottom of the food chain. Thank you, large brain, for compensating for my weak, pulpy, defenseless composition and keeping me alive thus far.

In the Rillito River arroyo, there isn't much shade to be found. There are plants, but they are the usual desert brush, weeds, and small trees like Willow, Blue Palo Verde, Ironwood, and the highly invasive Tamarisk (Saltcedar)— the thirstiest tree in the southwest. But the arroyo is a unique wild landscape within the urban space of Tucson—a raucous space where rivers sleep, awaiting rain run-off and a majestic awakening and return to the efficacy of desert waterway. Here, in this sleeping river bed, the sand is deep and the sun beats without reprieve. It ebbs and flows in piles and waves— both sand and sun—hardening into a concrete-like mass in the center where most of the vegetation grows. The soil in this arroyo is so loose, so unsettled and exposed that roots run rampant, clinging to one another in anticipation of the next upheaval. The next accumulation of

hydrogen and oxygen molecules so rarely combined in this moonscape of a desert-ed land.

Naturally, this arroyo is the perfect unregulated corridor for rehabbing Rain and avoiding the throngs of people that casually jog the paved walkway, or ride their road bikes at break neck speeds along the edge of the river run. A place within the city where the rules of wilderness return, and the rules of humans dance in the distance like a desert mirage. Shooter, my six year old wolfdog, has also determined that the fast moving people on the running path are reminiscent of deer or elk, and he must lunge at each human missile that passes us, creating a game of chase in a space where it's not appreciated. So the empty river bed is where we go to rehabilitate Rain and run wild as monsoon waters might flow.

In 2012—an El Niño year with record monsoon rains—I lived in a house that backed to the Rillito. Next to my house was an open-faced culvert that lead run-off water to the giant anticipating arroyo. Each morning, Rain, Shooter, and I ran like water—like frantically moving and unstable molecules in a liquid state—through the culvert, searching for the lowest, remotest form of land to sink our feet and imaginations into. It's an interesting metaphor—to let energy build within one's body each night, restoring cells and flowing as fast as legs can carry, into the harsh landscape of the

Rillito. Just like rain. Just like water. Just like anything looking for escape.

We ran early in the morning like flood waters with sharp teeth and punctual cadence, and we ran fast—wolf fur thick and wavy in the warm desert winds. I had a bottle of water in each hand, mostly for my furry friends whose body temperatures were 3-4 degrees warmer than my own. The sun was milder in the mornings, but the air was still heavy and humid, already anticipating cumulus build-up over the local sky islands—the Santa Catalinas, the Santa Ritas, and the Rincons, to name the closest and largest. The wind rushes over these igneous rock formations (at approximately 10,000 ft.), building pressure systems in a time of year when moisture is spinning counter-clockwise out of the Gulf of Mexico, borrowed from the Tropical Cyclone season in the Caribbean and the heated ocean waters close to the equator. This is the monsoon season of the American Southwest.

My wolves ran beside me as we entered the wash. I had a remote shock collar on Shooter—who listened well unless the call of the wild superseded—mostly for coyotes known to beckon and lure animals to a playful, pack oriented death. Like the gingerbread house in *Hansel and Gretel* or the clown demon in the rain gutters of the horror movie *It*, the coyotes lured creatures away with their promise of song and dance. Then the pack closed in and tore the creature limb from limb. Nature is not nice. Nature is to survive and promote ge-

netics. I had to step in with the threat of handheld lightning in the instance of coyotes with siren-like song that held species survival and murderous intent for anyone less savage than themselves. My wild dogs could probably handle the coyotes, but I wasn't interested in finding out, only to return with a smaller pack of my own. This would not fare well for our genetics and species survival, either.

In the lead, Shooter flushed out a rabbit and Rain crept around from the side—as social predators, they began to pursue and hunt as a team. Not truly being hungry, they didn't catch to kill and eat. They chased and sometimes caught, as a game. And once the animal stopped moving, the game wasn't fun anymore and they left it. It was clearly all about the chase, as some humans can relate to, as policy and procedure and maintaining interest. On this summer's day, Rain and Shooter chased a rabbit into the dense, tall growth of weeds and shrubs in the median of the arroyo and disappeared. I didn't panic. This happened often. I jogged along and looked for an opening or path in the growth, as one usually appeared.

As I already mentioned, there are few large trees in the desert. It's not like a coniferous forest. And most trees are deciduous. In fact, most of the desert landscapes around the world are quite tree-less. The Sonoran Desert (in Southern Arizona) is lush when compared to other deserts. Arizona contains all four North American deserts – the Sonoran, the Mohave, the Chihuahua, and the Great Basin—and it's the only state where this occurs. But it's the Sonoran Desert that allows for certain deciduous, hardwood trees to flourish. The Cottonwood tree is the largest tree in Arizona. So in a state dominated by all four North American deserts, the largest tree to be found is something special. Something unique. As Cottonwoods are a part of the poplar family—closely related to aspen trees—they require more water than a typical desert area might provide. These Cottonwoods must grow close to perennial, intermittent, or ephemeral waterways.

Every once in a while you might find one of these larger trees in the Rillito—a rare instance in which a Cottonwood or a Sycamore took root and shot straight up into the hot, blue sky. Here and now—there and then—I found the infamous Cottonwood tree, it's large, green leaves whispering and fluttering, light bark beginning to grow thick and knobby around the trunk. To find a Cottonwood tree in the middle of an occasional river bed is truly rare, as most of the desert waterways have been invaded by the Tamarisk, which grows like a weed and monopolizes soil nutrients. Cottonwoods are in direct competition with the Tamarisk. This Cottonwood discovery gives one hope for a healthier desert watershed, as groups of these hardwood trees can be seen clustered together from a distance—a bright splash of green leaves and pale bark in a land of mostly blues and browns—and can always lead you to water in the desert. So the Cottonwood signifies a steady water source, which in turns symbolizes survival in the desert.

I was looking for my animals, but I was drawn to the Cottonwood, mesmerized by the absolute shadow it cast. The tree wasn't big,

maybe 15 feet tall, a young version of its future arboreal splendor. As I walked closer, I could see a lean-to beneath the tree—an empty shopping cart tipped on its side and several pieces of plywood propped against the tree. I immediately felt sorry for the tree, for a live tree is not suited to support human construction and utilitarian burden. Then I noticed the dark boots sticking out of the structure, attached to human legs. A man was laying inside. I stopped fast, scanning for the dogs, not wanting to wake or upset a stranger.

As I spun in circles, the wild pups appeared—over their rabbit hunt—and immediately discovered the motionless man. They were on his doorstep in seconds, sniffing and assessing. They seemed calm, so I strained myself to stay calm, too—a very human endeavor and foreign to most of the animal kingdom. They smelled his legs and torso, then entered the wooden tent and started licking his face—probably for the sweat and delicious oils there. I was nervous, but reacting would alarm the intuitive animals, so I stayed still and watched, ready to act or consider interceding if needed. It happened so fast, there wasn't much left for me to do, anyway. I was a spectator watching human and animal interaction, praying for the best. Willing a benign encounter, or better.

The man stirred. He had a faded blue baseball cap pulled low, a long-sleeve flannel and torn blue jeans. I called in a hushed voice to Shooter and Rain—"Come here, now!"—but they chose this moment for selective hearing, as the new man in the sand was more interesting and aromatically potent than I was. The man's eyes fluttered open. He slowly lifted his arm and let Shooter lick his hand. Then he began to scratch the large dog's chest—Shooter's favorite place to be pet, other than his hind quarters. Rain, afraid of a fluttering shadow—kept her distance, until she couldn't stand it anymore. She moved in closer and the man scratched behind her ear—her favorite place to be pet, besides her belly. She remained leery, ready to run at the slightest threat, but she let him touch her which was a sort of desert miracle.

Pretty soon the man was petting the thick, but thinned-out summer coats of both wolf-dogs. He sat up, adjusting his cap. I could see his face better. He had a dark beard, and dark brown eyes he kept lowered. He seemed to have an idea of what he was doing.

"Sorry," I called so he would know I was there and the animals weren't alone. I took a few steps closer, but I didn't want to throw off the balance of animal-human amorous interaction, or send them into guard-the-human-alpha mode.

"I thought the coyotes were finally going to finish me off," he said. He spoke gently, with a noticeable slur. He probably wasn't sober, but who knows. I couldn't make out his ethnicity, as the sun had made him a creature of the desert and he was a brownish-red color. He squinted up at me, then the canines. "These here are really big coyotes. Do you run with them?"

I was holding my breath, I realized, so I let it out and smiled. "Yes, they're my dogs and we run together."

The man smirked. "These ain't dogs."

I laughed nervously. A tinkling sound like rocks falling in a cave.

"Close enough," I said. "Ninety-nine point eight percent genetically close enough."

The man ignored my data touting, staying focused on the animals. "I used to have a dog," he said. "When I used to have a house."

I didn't know what to say to that, so I said nothing. But I knew. My roommate in graduate school digressed from genius to homeless in a matter of days, and there was nothing anyone could do. I know it's rarely a choice. And it's usually mental illness. She was schizophrenic and I didn't even know. Until she stopped taking her meds. That's when she unraveled and in a matter of weeks, was running barefoot around the university and downtown with the rest of the local, ephemeral population. The descent from normalcy was quick, and if she hadn't had a family that loved her and friends that cared, she would probably still be there, if not dead. I often think of Rachel when I meet homeless people. I think of her when I start to judge someone—how brilliant the human mind can be, how fragile and fleeting our entire existence. Seeing the world through the eyes of a schizophrenic—danger and death around each jagged, hallucinated corner—made me realize that most homeless people used to have a home. And they probably even used to have a dog. The mentally ill seemed to run in the gap between civilized humanity and the untamed world of wild animals. Like the world of the wolfdog and wild urban landscapes. Like the Rillito River arroyo.

It seemed like I watched for hours as the man pet Shooter and Rain. He stroked them and cooed to them like I wasn't even there. And incredibly, they stood still and let him. The man was lost in his thoughts, more so with each passing moment. Then, like a gathering desert monsoon, his earth-laden body flooded with emotion and he began to cry. His shoulders shook and tears streamed down his face. Now my Shooter dog is the most sensitive, unruly guardian soul I've ever encountered, and human emotion undoes him—the same as thunder. It troubles him to the marrow of his bones. So Shooter whined, in response to the man's tears, and licked his face with intensity—an act I'd experienced many times myself. Shooter licked his face with so much concern, the man started to laugh, as the wolfdog's earnestness and empathy forced a crack in the stone wall of human emotion. A life preserver in a sea of black.

Soon the sunbaked man was roiling with laughter, as Shooter's antics knocked his hat off, and Rain rolled on her back next to him, offering her belly, catching the playful mood and the need for comic relief. This was the first time I'd seen her vulnerable to anyone but me. The man buried his dark hands in the tangle of Rain's snow white fur. She wagged her tail and rolled around on her back, smiling upside down with crocodile-like, toothy wit. I'd never seen her do this, but she was enjoying the attention. The man was laugh-crying, so he wiped the moisture from his face, and took deep breaths. As he put his hat back on I could see that it was a faded University of Arizona hat—the red and white "A" now a dark brown. I wondered if he'd been to school, and what sort of events had landed him here, in the bottom of the Rillito River, in the shade of the Cottonwood tree.

With the break in human emotion, Shooter was restless and ready to move on. He was a practical counselor, and not one to dwell in the past. Rain was ready, too. She jumped up and threw herself into Shooter like a tiny wolf wrecking ball, and they were off and running again, kicking up sand in the man's bed cloths and spinning into the desert wonderland.

The man put his clay hands up in mock protest. He spit sand from his mouth, grinning and shaking his head.

"Sorry about that," I apologized, feeling self-conscious without the animals.

He slowly wiped sand from his shirt and pants. Then he stared at his palms, face up in his lap for several moments, as if they reminded him of the dogs. He rubbed them together, then, and laced his fingers behind his head. The man was still smiling as he lay back down into the sand. I watched him, wondering if he would respond to me without the animals around.

"Thank you," he whispered from inside the wooden tent.

I considered thanking him for being so calm. For his willingness to interact with the unknown. For playing a symbiotic role in the rehabbing of Rain. But I didn't.

"You're welcome," was all I said.

I followed in the wake of my ambassadors. As we ran in the raised center of the wash, away from the only Cottonwood tree in the Rillito River for miles, I could already see the cumulus clouds building over the Catalina Mountains. The relative humidity was on the rise and the air temperature would rise with it. Until it began to rain. I watched the fluffy tails of my wolfdogs disappear into tamarisk and willow scrub ahead of me and I couldn't help but wonder if our new sand man friend would find his way out of the arroyo before the big floods came. I couldn't help thinking that if he didn't, at least he would sink beneath the water with a smile on his face.

A HUNDRED PENNIES
by Christopher Major

Sundays are usually reserved for cleaning and nothing else. I'd made up in my mind that anything worthwhile happened between Mondays and Saturdays. It was this Sunday, however, that had gotten the best of me. I'd been thinking of shows I had to catch up on, my last living grandmother to visit, and a younger brother to check up on to ensure that he hadn't gotten as intoxicated on freedom from my parents as I did at twenty-one years old. The washer had stopped a full two songs ago, but Ice Cube's "Good Day" was so good to me that I had to replay it. It made me wonder exactly what made a good day for me. Sure the weekends were good—late sleep, nowhere to go or be, whole days at home with forgotten hygiene— but would they really qualify as good days? Since my financial independence from my parents, and consequently my absence from church in the morning, Sundays had been treating me unreasonably well (Sunday deserved a better version of Christopher, I must admit).

This Sunday was intriguing because I was to be paid a fraction of what I believed my time was really worth from my job that Monday, and money had been tight for a week. Just as the IRS would take a cut of my money, so would my landlord, the power company, and the guy (or gal) who owned the gas station that never gave me enough gas for two and a half dollars a gallon. My nicotine addiction was telling me it was time to resume the lifelong suicide mission when I found a washed, wet dollar bill hiding under clothes that were clean but not yet dry. It was all I needed to get a Black & Mild cigar from the same gas station that fueled my car. After digging my coloreds out of the washing machine I looked at that dollar, it being crumbled after having survived a spin cycle that would have surely torn my frail body to pieces, and remembered how many times I'd found myself in this position—a day before payday, just trying to light and inhale certain death.

That moment was a good day that proved to me that not all good days are created equal. I keep a change jar in my bedroom that I use to empty my pockets when I get out of my clothes for the day. I'd once had ninety-nine cents worth of pennies in that jar and would spend the rest of my evening avidly searching for just one more, only to find it and feel like I'd slayed a dragon that day. No, that dollar bill was good, but it didn't compare to the satisfaction of knowing that I had to scavenge for one cent in order to pay for my untimely death. That dollar asked me, as it drowned in laundry detergent, "Does one really big joy really equal one hundred small joys?" My Sunday was ruined.

Change is pesky, and weighs down your pockets, but always makes the world of difference when we checkout at the grocery store or at a food truck. I unraveled the power cord of my vacuum and thought about how much copper I'd just disregarded and vacuumed up throughout my life, and couldn't help but wonder how many dollars I'd sucked up and thrown out with the trash. It seemed like the big joys were always worth savoring but the small ones weren't good enough until enough of them had been accumulated. The Saturday night before I had gone to a local wing restaurant and ordered a two piece whole wing and one piece catfish combo (it's always cheaper to get the combo). The restaurant was supposed to close ten minutes before I walked in. The cashier was irritated with my timing and I could tell—as was the cook. She was a plus-sized woman, and the sweat from working so close to the kitchen made some of her black hair stick to her forehead. The cook was tall, bald, and had a patchy salt and pepper five o'clock shadow. He was also missing one of his front teeth. My untimely arrival worried me. I assumed I'd get home, open my to-go-box and find my food undercooked. Instead, when I sat down on my couch with my salt packets and hot sauce, I discovered that the cook included two extra wings and an extra catfish. That was my shiny penny founds heads up on the pavement. The preceding Wednesday I got a call from a prospective employer offering me a job that paid me exactly what I felt my time was worth. That was the dollar bill that fell out of my dirty jeans pocket. Those two joys, both valid on their own terms, made me think about the change under my couch cushions, and the paycheck I got biweekly, and about which one made me the most excited to see. I had to admit to myself, between vacuuming and picking up items too big to be sucked up, that a well timed penny beats finding a dollar on all days, not just the good ones.

Change has also never been big—merely tiny steps in a different direction. We generally dislike coins, and our partners, parents and, well, anyone we've grown to learn truly does care about us, have a nasty habit of dropping pennies all over the place; and we, ever in search of that whole dollar bill (usually without the sense needed to understand what they tell us), spend quarters of our lives with an even nastier habit of throwing them away, only to stop on a dime and appreciate them once we needed a hundred cents. The currency of growth is indeed change—and my growth has only come in small, incremental steps. The pennies we get, I've found, seldom come as shiny, new Lincoln's, instead as the tobacco ash covered, sticky, rusted pieces of copper that are the criticisms we all disregard and deem worthless. The problem with only having eyes for the dollar bill is that we'll, all too often, throw out more dollars than we find and end up with a broken vacuum. All things considered now, I'm two cents short.

About the Author:

Christopher Major, a native of Birmingham, Alabama, spends much of his free time recording platinum selling Hip Hop albums in the shower and his car. Much of his work deals with race and class, and he's currently working on his book, "Porcelain Musings".

THE LANDLADY

by Robert Steward

Paris, France 2001

"I like your clothes," I said, before taking a sip of my *café au lait.*

"Thank you, Robert." My landlady touched her headscarf. "I make them myself."

Her silk floral caftan hung loosely over her large frame. It was burgundy, with purple spots, gold suns, azure swirls, lilac flowers and hints of mustard and antique rose; it was all held together with a silver brooch, set in the middle of her chest. She had a pale round face, puffy cheeks and a double chin; two large eyebrows hovered over brown eyes and black rimmed glasses, and her burgundy lipstick matched her nail varnish and flowery earrings. She looked bohemian, like an artist.

Behind her, stood café Zebra, with its French windows, black and white striped awning and blackboard, displaying the *plat du jour*. It was getting dark now, and the old-fashioned streetlamps lit up one by one, accompanying the neon lights of the boutiques, bistros and bars.

"So Robert, how are things at your school?" she asked.

She had a quiet, refined voice with a slight Spanish accent.

"Fine, thanks," I said.

There was an awkward silence. I didn't know what else to say.

A waiter weaved past with a tray of coffees.

"And the apartment?" she asked. "Is everything okay?"

"Yes, everything's fine, thanks."

"I hope the smell of paint has gone," she added.

"Oh yes, I hardly notice it now."

"Good," she said. "Good."

I took another sip of coffee and remembered something from our first meeting.

"So, you lived in Barcelona, then?" I asked.

"Yes," she replied.

"Whereabouts?"

"Sorry?"

"In what part?"

"Oh, in Gràcia," she replied absently.

"Oh, so did I!" my voice rose, as if now we had something special in common.

Suddenly, it all came back to me; the bars in Plaça del Sol, the smell of the Gràcia food market, the sound of children playing outside my apartment.

"Do you know Plaça de John Lennon?" I asked.

She pursed her lips and frowned.

"Yes, I think so," she replied vaguely and studied the back of her hand.

"So, were you born there?"

"No, actually, I'm from Bolivia."

"Really? So when did you move to Barcelona?"

"About ten years ago. Before that, I lived in Argentina."

"So, you've travelled a lot, then?"

"Well Robert, we had to leave Bolivia for political reasons," she said in a low voice.

Her expression remained fixed at the memory.

"Oh," I said, a little unsure of what to say next. "So, what made you come to Paris?"

"I've always wanted to come here," she said, adjusting her headscarf. "It has everything: art galleries, museums, classical music, theatre--every night of the week."

I nodded approvingly. Paris wasn't just a city, it was an education, in art, cuisine, culture; it was an education in life.

"And I just love art." She sighed, playing with her brooch. "I can spend hours and hours just wandering around an art gallery. Only last week I was looking at a painting in the Louvre and found myself completely absorbed by it. There was a half-naked woman holding the French flag in one hand and a rifle in the other, and the people from the revolution following behind; I must've been standing in front of it for over twenty minutes."

"Really?"

"Yes, it was so vibrant, so fiery that I even started to cry."

"Gosh."

"And then a museum guard approached me and asked if I was okay. I must say, it was all a little embarrassing." She smiled.

"No," I said softly, shaking my head.

"Finally, I just had to sit down--I was so... so overawed by it all."

"Amazing."

The word eccentric didn't come close to describing her; neither did the words odd, peculiar or unusual. But I liked her; she was fragile, sincere; she had a fascinating charm about her.

I sipped my coffee. She sipped hers too, with her finger and thumb pinching the cup handle, her other fingers in the air. When she put her cup down she rubbed her shoulders. It was starting to get a bit chilly.

"By the way, I've got the rent for you here," I said, reaching into my jacket pocket.

She lifted her hand.

"Wait," she said.

Her face became serious, her eyes watchful.

She took an envelope out of her burgundy handbag.

"Here," she said softly but firmly. "I'd like you to put the money in this envelope."

She slid it across the table and looked away.

I took the envelope.

"No, not here," she whispered.

I looked around, slightly confused.

"Go into the toilet." She nodded towards the café.

"The *toilet?*"

"Shhh!" She put a finger to her mouth.

"Oh, okay then." I found myself whispering.

I got up and went into the café. It was full of people eating, drinking, smoking. The bar was L-shaped with two red dome lights hanging from the ceiling. One corner of the bar was filled with wine bottles and spirits, and in the middle sat a silver coffee machine with La Marzocco written on the front. Behind it stood a barista, making some coffee. He was bald with a hooked nose and handlebar moustache.

He wore a white shirt and jacket with a black bow tie. He seemed like a caricature of himself.

"Où sont les toilettes?" I asked.

"Là-bas," he indicated with a wave of his hand.

Past the bar, the café looked cosier, with wallpapered walls, brown leather armchairs and felt covered chairs. On the wall hung a picture of a black cat, called *Tournée du Chat Noir*. It was one of my favourites.

The toilet was down a winding staircase, the cubicle small and dimly lit. I took out the French bank notes from my pocket, counted them out and put them in the envelope. It felt like I was doing something sinister, like doing a drugs deal or selling stolen goods.

If anyone could see me now, I thought, looking into the mirror.

I couldn't help but laugh.

I put the envelope into my jacket pocket and unlatched the door.

The café looked smaller now, the atmosphere more intense. I started to feel self-conscious; maybe my landlady's paranoia was becoming contagious. Eyes looked up at me from everywhere, the barista from behind the coffee machine, the waiter from behind his tray of drinks, the customers from behind their tables. It was as if they all knew. I tried to avoid their glances as I went outside and sat down.

"Ah, there you are," my landlady whispered. "Have you done it?"

"Yes," I replied.

"Okay." She looked over her shoulder. "Give it to me under the table."

I took the envelope out of my pocket and passed it to her under the table. She looked around again and put the envelope into her handbag.

"Wait here," she said out of the corner of her mouth and walked into the café.

I sat at the table and waited.

I wonder if I'll have to do this every time, I thought.

A waiter walked past.

"Er, l'addition s'il vous plaît," I said, catching his eye.

I waved my hand as if writing a cheque.

"Tout de suite," he replied, and walked into the café.

I looked at the other people sitting outside. Two women sat crossed legged at a table; they seemed to be gossiping about something. At another table a man sat alone, reading a book, and at another, a woman also sat alone, smoking.

Paris was a good place to be alone.

I stared into the distance in a pensive mood. I felt relieved to have my own apartment; no more living out of a suitcase, no more flea-ridden pensions in Gare du Nord, no more embarrassing phone calls enquiring about flats to rent. Now, I had my own place, my own bed, my own kitchen, my own bathroom, my own--

"Robert?" my landlady said, breaking me out of my spell.

"Everything okay?" I asked, scratching my head.

"Yes," she replied, and sat down.

She adjusted her headscarf. She touched her ear, wrinkled her nose and finally settled down to playing with her brooch.

She seemed more serene now, happy to sit in silence.

"It's a nice evening, isn't it?" I said finally, looking out onto the cobblestone street.

"Yes, it is," she said.

She moved her head as if she was looking at a picture.

"Oh Robert, what a wonderful tree!" she exclaimed.

I looked over my shoulder. The leaves were starting to turn yellow; in the lamp light they looked almost golden.

"Oh yes," I said, turning back to her. "It's beautiful, isn't it?"

"I never noticed it before." Her eyes glistened and her lips turned upwards into a gentle smile. "It's so small, so fragile, so... so *joli.*"

#

About the Author:

Robert Steward teaches English as a foreign language and lives in London. He is currently writing a collection of short stories, some of which have appeared in Scrittura, The Creative Truth, The Ink Pantry, Winamop, The Foliate Oak Literary and Communicators League magazine. You can find them at: twitter.com/theroadtonaples

ORANGE CAT
by Mark Jamieson

Orange Cat

Orange cat, orange cat, what is it you see,
From this where you have chosen to be?

Been off to visit the Queen, I've heard.
Duty and wisdom, a whispered word.

Fine foreign places, and heads of state,
Early rising, and staying up late.

Grand festive dinners, and caviar,
And fancy waiters, but here you are.

Just then to visit, or here to stay,
In my backyard, this warm summer day,

Where the tall grass meets deeply shaded,
And from my vision you have faded?

Years of travel, four legs and a tail.
Careful, measured steps, rarely to fail.

Cat of the world, and close to the ground,
Tell me truly, what is it you've found?

She Could Be

She would be the proof in the pudding,
Once beyond the should not or shoulding.

Ever always, that one stitch in time,
Willing and able, to save other nine.

Her manner, sweeter more pass, than fail,
Forever never an old wives tale.

Necessity, the best of intention,
Only truly, a mother's invention.

Ounce of prevention and pound of cure,
Lest ill wind, misfortune, there to occur.

Too much cook, for a soup to spoil,
And the better, of tears and toil.

Often silent, but all ways golden,
Picture perfect, like in days olden.

She would be the proof in the pudding,
Allow herself a, perhaps, coulding.

Mountains Yesterday

Mountains yesterday, western Virginia,
Into West Virginia turning.
Clutch down, lean, look, lift, clutch up,
And again. Interest every turn earning.
Excitement, adrenalin, exhaustion.
Riding at the edge of risky.
Providing for years of stories retold
Over steaks and bourbon whiskey.
Today looks to be calmer, quieter,
Good surface road, little more straight.
We're cruising Pennsylvania to Ohio
On the Highway Interstate.
A week of new places, hotels and maps,
This being the final section.
Now's a chance for silent trip in review,
Or some in general reflection.
Thoughts, situations, problems, notions,
Newly necessary to address.
Standing unresolved issues,
Which need more attention,
And which deserve less?
Enough gasoline till about Pittsburg,
Maybe stop, grab a sandwich, too.
So much for lofty mental exercise,
Just hang on, and absorb the view.
Low clouds follow. Been chasing us all day.
Gaining, looks like foul weather gear,
And our first ride in the rain, this trip,
Not, however, the first time this year.
Heading home. Couch, clock, conformity, shoes.
Work, chores, watching television.
Intermittent rain drops on my face shield,
Momentary indecision.
The adventure will continue when bikes
Are cooled, covered, and parked inside.
With our well-travelled leathers, and photos,
We'll have not finished with this ride.
Mountains yesterday, western Virginia
Into West Virginia turning.
Geography taught by motorcycle,
And other lessons worth learning.

From Motorcycle Stories

About the Author:

M.T. Jamieson and his wife, Susan, live in northeastern Ohio with their rescued dog and two rescued kitten/cats. He is twice a university former student, and a Viet Nam Era U.S.A.F. veteran.

Some of his poems have appeared in recent issues of "WestWard Quarterly", "Pancakes In Heaven", "Northern Stars Magazine", "The Poet's Art", "The Poetry Explosion Newsletter", "The Lyric", and "Fourth And Sycamore".

BOSTON, MASSACHUSETTS
by Emily Brummett

she steps off a twelve-hour ride
next to a stranger-
whose shuffled music playlist
and snores
didn't know personal space.

Footfalls and fast food stops
fill the train station
as she barrels through the masses
suitcases dragging behind
to hailed taxis and busy streets

where he waits-
a five-year, long distance relationship with
six months of separation:
her final months of medical school
and his overachieving investment schedule.

Her diploma and
vigorous job search landed her promise
where *they* saw a future, and where
a white picket balcony,
empty living room,
and bare hardwood waits for them.

Jackhammers, bulldozers, sunrises,
and dark roast fill the apartment:
the daily wake up-
no snooze setting.
Keurig's *Donut House* gurgles and brews
as his weekly suit rental is buttoned.

During his nine to five,
she finds the nearest wi-fi connection:
listed jobs and internships
to secure next month's bills,
because

a hand me down fridge, stained with old
motor oil and chipped stickers is occupied by
cheap beer, leftover pizza boxes and coffee
creamer-
not what she imagined for their future.

Monetary struggles among other disagree-
ments creates a strain-
no longer in the honeymoon phase,
a taste of reality.
a stressful and *out of love* reality.

And with not a word spoken
she slips off her interview black dress,
as he unbuttons his shirt, reaching into the
fridge- his nightly routine: throwing back a 6
pack until it puts him to sleep, as she sits in bed
and watches Real Housewives until he joins
her.

She thought Boston would solidify a future,
but a half drank light roast with hazelnut
creamer and 1 pack of sugar sits
beside a vacant folding chair atop carpeted
covered hardwood, inside their white picket
balcony, and waits for him to come home.

About the Author:

Emily Brummett is a young and aspiring international business entrepreneur who enjoys traveling and writing in her free time. She was published in the Adelaide Literary Magazine No. 14. and is greatly obliged to her friends and family for their endless support.

I DO NOT LIE IN 'T, YET IT IS MINE

by Dane Myers

If my dead grandpa, a kindly and devoted Republican farmer, were to visit the living

he'd first ask about black angus and alfalfa...

then the weather...

and then politics...

I'd first ask him about Adrienne Rich and Dante, Abe Lincoln and Hamlet...

then ask ha riddle: "Who builds stronger than a mason, shipwright, or a carpenter?"

and then I'd tell him how institutions such as universities, religions, and political parties were more intent on protecting their power and image over beneficence, truth, and children.

Perhaps he'd chuckle and say, "Oh? That hasn't changed."

"But now they separate the children from parents, brothers from sisters, and babies from breasts."

"Speaking of children," I'd say, "there's been an eruption of shootings, some at schools. One involved a kid with an AR-15."

"No," he'd reply. "We must protect the Second Amendment *and* agree on some common sense rules."

"The N.R.A. begs to disagree."

I'd tell him how Republicans had placed business, the present, and profit over climate change, the environment, and our future.

Maybe he'd shake his head and say, "Tough choices... How bad is it?"

"A hideous list of rising seas, storms, and smog... offshore drilling, droughts, and dying reefs... melting poles, fires, and extinctions..."

"Speaking of bad," I'd say, "the self-proclaimed party of fiscal responsibility has exploded the deficit and debt."

"No! Is there a war?"

"Only on the media, taxes, and trade. The tax-and-spend Dems have been dwarfed by the little-tax/ spend-a-ton Republicans."

"How much?"

"A gift of trillions for our grandchildren."

He'd laugh and say, "That much money doesn't exist."

I'd recall how my Grandpa, a kindly and devoted Republican, had once voted for a Democrat. "Jimmy Carter," he'd said, "was a good Christian... and a farmer."

Then he'd smile and say, "A grave maker." My dead grandpa was still good at riddles.

"I'd tell him how his party had supported a misogynistic, racist, and mendacious president. An orange peacock who'd said, "Grab them by the pussy." A man who'd described immigrants as animals and infestations. A man who'd described Haiti, El Salvador, and some of Africa as "Shit-hole" countries... The guy tweets like an adolescent chicken, splutters incoherent word salad, and exceeded a thousand lies during his first year in office. Perhaps I'd mention Charlottesville and Puerto Rico, Maxine Waters and the wall, Stormy Daniels, McDougal, *et al.*

"Oh?" he'd reply. "But my party has always sought the moral high-ground. Does he attend church?"

"The man has been given a pass. But he's religious about money, philandering, and golf."

"Speaking of scrutiny," I'd say, "he granted questionable security clearances and threatened to strip others. The President has alienated allies, saluted adversaries, and undermined our own intelligence. He howls "Fake! Witch Hunt! and Hoax!" His fans believe that their ruined 'Constitutional' makes anything so. Perhaps I'd mention Conway and Cohen, Giuliani and Gates... Papadopoulos and Porter, McEntee and Manafort... Flynn, Nunberg and Stone...

"No. Ours is the party of law and order."

"Now it is the slumber party of an averted gaze."

I'd tell him about the Mueller investigation, how Russia influences our elections, and how the inquiries and reforms are being thwarted by—oh yes—many Republicans. I'd tell him about the bewildering hell at Helsinki and how the slogan "America First" shall be laughed.

"Nonsense!" He'd stomp and proclaim: "Russia, and particularly Putin, are not to be trusted. My party would never turn away from any caustic manipulation and meddling."

"Gaze averted, with a dramatic turn. They are Diving into the Wreck of their not-so Divine Comedy... A house-divided, distracted globe, and unweeded garden filled with diseased wormwood and wit."

"Most foul, strange, and unnatural! Who is this feckless leader?" Grandpa would wail to the Commander-in-Chief who rules with changing recollections, evasive derangement, and a shriveled staff. "But he's a last-rate showman and con artist constituted of endless ego."

Then I'd frown and say, "His lemming-like followers would leap from a cliff if said to be a Hoax, Witch Hunt, or Fake. Drunk on power and prejudice, they might even drink cyanide-laced Kool-Aid that's said to be Constitutional and First."

"Oh no," he'd reply. "Either you jest, or America has turned upside down." My dead grandpa, a kindly Republican farmer, would leave the living and say, "I'd rather return beneath the earth as they make their own graves... I'd rather stay dead, rollover, and think of my children...

then their grandchildren...

and then their children's children

About the Author:

Dane Myers holds a B.A. in English/ Philosophy and a M.F.A. in Creative Writing from the University of New Mexico. He has published fiction, creative nonfiction, and poetry in Fresh Boiled Peanuts, Ascent, Willard & Maple, World Audience, The Evansville Review, Ginosko, North Dakota Quarterly, and Slow Trains. His short story, Respite, was nominated for a Pushcart Prize; his first novel, Siren's Red Light, was released in 2017 (Amazon and Kindle). Although he mostly writes fiction, Dane experiences an occasional itch to write poetry-- particularly poems with titles usurped and trumpeted from a Hamlet of Danish clowns. He lives in Albuquerque, where he continues his 30+ year day job as a paramedic.

I BARELY ESCAPED WITH MY LIFE

by Louis Gallo

"I BARELY ESCAPED WITH MY LIFE"

The lacquered reporters declare another miracle
as we now deem the merest rosy swerve from
doom
a glittering token of divine twitch.
Minicams pan the charred fuselage
with highly resolved devotion,
zoom slowly upon a shadowy figure
who emerges from the sizzling wreckage.
I barely escaped with my life, she exclaims,
the lone survivor, a Civics teacher,
early forties, dazed, someone you won't recognize,
always one of us, already losing the battle,
though she clings to her plaid overnight bag
and looks intact enough but for patches
of sooty rouge baked into her cheeks.

But who is this I who escaped and with whose
life?
Is "I" separate from the metabolic stew of hormones,
enzymes, corpuscles, protoplasm and pulsing
jellies?
Suppose she had barely escaped *without* her
life —
returned to Bradley High in the swank part of
town,
its antiseptic brick and quicksilver windows,
computers in every class, perfumed kids
with names like Misty and Sean, driving
Volvos and swollen with the yeast of good luck.
You know their elegant uptown mothers
who can't give up leotards or Merit ultra-lights,
an hour at the spa before cruising the coffee
shops
for lavender tea and heavenly cream puffs,
the boutiques and Langenstein's,
a sternly Caucasian grocery with exotic delica-
cies
like chocolated ants and rum bon bons
exquisitely priced to make one feel perfect.
So troubled their lives, what with Misty pregnant
and Sean howling as he shoots spiders in the
attic . . .

who could begrudge the Prozac, the martinis?
Lives worth escaping or heaven on earth —
that is, the best it gets in this hive?
Their children, languid clouds of resentment,
file into school corridors that reek
of puke, Tampax and leathery old sweat.
Moon-faced, they stare at the wonder
who stands before them with new assignments
—
Mrs. Xnitious? — on the civics of the soul,
the cartography of beatitude
and ecclesiastics of the bardo.
Will it be on the test? they want to know
before it's back to scratching emery boards
and blasting heavy metal into gray matter
that took a million years to evolve.

Mrs. Xnitious — we know her too now —
drifts from desk to desk with the glow
of a bodhisattva shorn of flesh and desire.
She is everywhere, here in room 202,
in Yukon forests she has always longed to visit,
hovering at the rim of the known universe
beyond which lies a sea of pure radiance.
She has side-stepped time and place, suckles
at the breast, slouched in study hall with *Cos-
mo*
hidden under homework, stands at the altar
as Mr. Xnitious slumps over a steering wheel
ten years later, feels the plane begin to vibrate
and rip to shreds before it crashes,
staggers out again to meet ravenous reporters,

I barely escaped with my life

wears the face of each student from birth to
death,
howls with Sean, lies with Misty on a cold
stainless gurney
as blood and a ghostly infant crawl down her
thigh,

squeezes into a leotard and giggles over tea
and brioche,
feels Mr. Xnitious penetrate, his breath la-
bored,
sweat dripping into her eyes until that final
shudder,
strokes his cheek in the open casket, no longer
merely wife
but mother as well and daughter, unsteady on
her feet,
on their feet, the feet of all who have barely
escaped
with our solitary, grievous, sundered, beautiful
lives.

WINDOW WASHING

The Mexican window washers banter
in Espanol while dangling five stories up
by two ropes each, buckets looped
to their belts, wash rags flaring
out of their pockets. I can't quite hear
what they're saying except for a word
or two. I've drawn my shades
and can see only their silhouettes
as they squeegee the glass—each window
(I have two) about ten by eight, five
stories of them on this wing alone of the edi-
fice.
They will be at it for quite some time.
At the moment, two of them sway
outside my shades. I catch the words
"Hernando" (Cortez? DeSoto?) and
"manana"—
Hernando, Manana! And Montezuma dead.

Inside I advise a student that she must,
despite her repugnance for mathematics,
sign up for the basic course to fulfill
General Ed requirements. Then I trek
to the bathroom. Then I write this
as the workers still sag off a side of our
massive office building. I wonder what
they're paid and hope it's a thousand times
my salary. I may be suspended from the edges
of my psyche, but you couldn't get me out
there, outside the windows, in the air
penduluming like a plumbob, for a clean million.
I remember long ago a drive-in movie
about Egyptian slaves being crushed
to death as they slipped while rolling
monstrous stone slabs on shaved tree trunks
to build Pharaoh's pyramid, an inert
triangle splashed with blood—such that
the mighty and the lowly commingled
in the afterlife.

The workers now sit cross-legged on the grass
eating lunch, laughing, bantering, good-
natured.
Soon they will return to risking their lives
to scrub clean a gargantuan rectangle of glass
for another kind of Pharaoh, an abstraction
cold as Tut and his eternal doodads.

THE NIGHT I WAS SAVED, ALMOST

Last night a band of squeaky, dusty angels
(which at first I mistook for gnats)
arrived with news of my salvation.
Ah, the splendid au revoir at last!
Their leader assured me that no strings
dangled from this package of good fortune.
I passed, he said, a test I didn't take.
How professional, mused I,
and called Marie at once.

Today, I don't know . . .
I'm still here, pale, destitute and sad.
I'd always thought great events happened elsewhere
and in different clothes. But see, the same
trembling hand wipes the same hardened
crumbs
off the same cracked table.
And the old sun spits a lethal dawn
right through my windows again.
If anything, I feel worse, more vague
in the throat, and my eyes have moistened
with sentimentality.
No yeast-like rising, no ballyhoo
among the relatives I've notified,
no telegrams, bouquets, no cabs –
and Marie, she's left me for a less righteous
man.
I'm betting, though, with my last dime,
there's more to this than redemption.

About the Author:

Louis Gallo's work has appeared or will shortly appear in Wide Awake in the Pelican State (LSU anthology), Southern Literary Review, Fiction Fix, Glimmer Train, Hollins Critic,, Rattle, South-ern Quarterly, Litro, New Orleans Review, Xavi-er Review, Glass: A Journal of Poetry, Missouri Review, Mississippi Review, Texas Review, Bal-timore Review, Pennsylvania Literary Journal, The Ledge, storySouth,   Houston Literary Re-view, Tampa Review, Raving Dove, The Journal (Ohio), Greensboro Review,and many others. Chapbooks include The Truth Change, The Abomination of Fascination, Status Updates and The Ten Most Important Questions. He is the founding editor of the now defunct jour-nals, The Barataria Review and Books: A New Orleans Review. He teaches at Radford Univer-sity in Radford, Virginia.

ART

by Aditya Shankar

Art

A bird
wove its nest
tirelessly

with
beak and wing,
twig and grass,
tweet and silence,

deep
inside the forest.

A nest, demolished
and rebuilt,

till it became
what the bird desired.

It did not matter

that the nest
was never titled
or signed,

spoken about

or adulated.

It hung there,

a perishable nest
sneaked in the shade
of a snag*

at the end of a
toilsome wild path,

ready to be abandoned,
even by the
fledglings within.

In believing
and trying,

the nest silently
performs the
true function of art.

Note: * - A dead tree

The Purpose

The oar is no friend, says
the ferryman

almost an amphibian
speaking in tongue,

the way it dips and bounces,
a lactometer replica
measuring human density.

The boat is no friend,
says the ferryman

envy of the local frog king
on a lotus leaf,

the croak-free stillness,
not a reciprocation of love.

The water is no friend,
says the ferryman

hidden nails stitch the flow
into ripples, touches gloves
with the ferry, à la fighters —

a partial referee, favoring
upstream stories, washed
away python and deer,

eroded time.

The ferry, oarsman, water,
the sunset at the river bank

in between being themselves,

tries to serve the purpose
and name you define.

About the Author:

Aditya Shankar is an Indian poet, flash fiction author, and translator whose work has recently appeared in Egophobia, Expanded Field, Armarolla, Ghost Parachute, MoonPark Review, Modern Poetry in Translation, and elsewhere. Books: After Seeing (2006), Party Poopers (2014), XXL (Dhauli Books, 2018). He lives in Bangalore, India.

SUNDAY COMING DOWN

by Jamel Hall

Sunday Coming Down

The slight shudder of newspaper
adds accents to the commercial break.
My mother in her meekest vestments
paces the house singing songs of jesus,
of better days, and inheritance.

His name pressed to the walls
like a cigarette stifled in ash.
In the kitchen, the cooker whistles softly
trying to hush the house as if it were
a child with a skinned knee.

Sunday morning descends, aging
like an expensive ale. I rise late
 noting the thickness of the room.
The ugly rumble of the washing machine,
and the subdued scent of ackee
a whetstone to sharpen my senses.

Humid hymns hold the air
as if they were passengers on a bus.
My brothers voice tangled in laughter
and TV sounds climbs the concrete steps
losing luster with each vertical bump.

I chase my stomach across the passage divide
halted by the haze of the radio. Crooning electric,
quaking with conviction; choir belting promise,
reward, and punishment.

She passes unmarked books in hand,
voice like a straw broom bound in iron.

My mother in her humble dress
tosses her church purse aside
and paces the house,
singing songs of better days.

Her husbands' car wakes at the gate.
Songs of Jesus.
The grand children may visit today.
Of inheritance.

Nina's Child

My body is no longer heavy with your loss,
you were much too good to it.
Every kiss cooling fever, fingers playing
my scalp like a tune. Palms a salve,
wrapped tight against life's meaner seasons.

Dear heart, I miss you like the sun misses
Its lover, wide berths and fraying shadows;
days spent plashing light across the stencilled
earth.

I still dream you in Paris sipping tea
at some roadside café, tattered dictionary
sleeping peacefully atop tattered novel.
Map tucking table like morning linen, juke Jazz
rising Fahrenheit in your bones, soft melodies
seeping Nina into your sediments.

Love I understood.
I bet the band will play your heart to rags,
thin strips of paint-soaked memories
no longer good for much.

The crowd will touch and shake and sway,
calling back to a place they never knew.

You will nod your head and sing
on nights that colour some kind of blue.

Salt

Your lips taste of salt,
nothing will grow here again.
My tongue dry and bitter
all that is left, is to leave.

The house without sound,
my footsteps on the cold floor,
wait I had almost forgotten my keys.

'I'll find them and go!'

Perhaps they are under the carelessly
flung robes of our morning,
maybe by the paper on the sun deck
where we whittled down days to afternoons.

I'll start, in the living room, penned in by
empty candy dishes, wickless candles,
and old photographs of people who only
smile when viewed at angles.

"I've found them, I'll take them and go."

My hat! I cannot find my hat!
"It is frayed and fading but it is mine.
One little look, that's all I need."

By the mirror, on that table with two tones,
one leg shorter than the other.
I always put it there.

"I see it, it's right where I left it!"

My voice echoes through the rooms.
I have collected myself.
I think it is time to go.

White Noise

Will you still look at me with
half-moon eyes when the feelings
That marionette-ed us in the small hours
Abruptly turns to ash? The siren sounds
of a receiver sparking tinder-ed air.

Will the memory of minutes past,
fingers etching skin be enough to call you
back to the comfort of these crumpled sheets?

A leapfrog of hours, the inevitability of dinner,
the world beginning to remember your name.

A loud lie from an all too quiet place.
The hum of a fan held close to ear
becoming bridge and tunnel static.

I will hear nothing over the search
for saucers and cups, over the whistle
Of punched steel; while you weight words
In the market of hearts.

Pot on tray, matched cups, biscuits beside
butter,
knives neatly crossed. A proper tea,
served at the table, while you finger curtains
and wait, for the sun to set fire to the sea.

Will you look at me then, head tilting in consideration?
Or will you again slip out the back, slide along
the house
and disappear into the darkness of a slightly
dozing city?
Will I finally find the right reasons for you to
stay?

This day and the Next

On a church morning sitting in the shade
of a fern tree listening to an old man
whistle to the beat of his god, I waited.
Patient breaths paced for some sign,
some grandiose gesture clothed in a
sheppard's humility.

From the pulpit a voice booms.
Vibrations made speech coaxed through
coaxials and quarter inch cables rise
and spill out into the street like a bar room
brawl. Pauls penning chase cars like hungry
dogs
passing people walking the sunned scene.

Light spills through the branches tattooing my
face;
in the church, children shift and shuffle under
thumb.
The old man rises like a bird leaving X's in his
wake.
The Noon day sun paints us all in a hue of gold.

...In the slow birth of light that marks the beginning
of a new day I packed, moving carefully
amongst the furniture that had sprung like a
stand
of trees drinking the carpet dry. Slowly searching drawers,
sweeping nooks and crannies for defining moments,
for something to name as important.

About the Author:

Jamel Hall is a writer, art curator, event organizer, occasional musician and freelance everything else living and working in Kingston, Jamaica. His poetry focuses on the small, complex and common stories that make up human existence. The work tries to engage all the sense seamlessly transporting the reader to small places and moments in time. Hopefully leaving a little piece of poetry with them each time as they come and go. As a Poet, he has won local competitions in his home country, performed on stages across Jamaica and taught workshops to adults as well as college and high school students. Jamel has had three poems published to date, Clash by Uk Journal Ink Sweat and Tears in October 2018, The Art of Falling also in October and White in November 2018 both by Jaipur Paris based magazine RIC Journal. He most recently completed a two-month Writing Residency in Bali, Indonesia on December 19, 2018, which was awarded to him by the Esirom Ltd. and the Sama Sama Residency Programme.

AND SO I BELIEVE

by Clark Holtzman

AND SO I BELIEVE

A stranger stood next to me at the city zoo. I had stopped at an exhibit of sand and boulders, limbs and brush. It appeared to be unoccupied. The stranger studied the exhibit intently, nodding his head back and forth as though trying to catch a glimpse of something. The stranger said that you had to stand very still and look carefully but still you might not see the inhabitant of that savannah-like world. He said few people had ever seen one, invisibility being its natural defense against predators, but it was always there. So if one looked hard enough . . . The stranger said the creature's scientific name was *Semper absens*, which made perfect sense to me. I stood very still, searching the recesses and the deep shadows for signs of the beast. Suddenly my mother, who had been listening nearby, said, "How cruel! Fooling a small boy like that! You should be ashamed of yourself!" She grabbed me by the arm and began to drag me away. The stranger, whoever he was, had vanished when I turned back to look for him. It was as if he had never been there. I thought I caught a glimpse of something among the boulders as my mother hurried me off to the next exhibit (of a family of gnus, I recall), a pair of bright eyes from out of the shadows. I thought I heard a voice whisper, *believe*.

UNCLE FRED, THE BARBER

When at the age of six, my Uncle Fred gave me my first haircut. He said to me, "Let's play barber. I'll be the barber." And that was that. He started in with shears that seemed too big for his little boy hands. But I didn't worry. My Uncle Fred's hands have always surprised people. When at the age of four, my Uncle Fred could hold me in the palm of his much smaller boy hand. He carried me around the neighborhood concealed behind his back and then sprang me upon anybody we met. Mrs. Parrott nearly had a heart attack. Before long, snip, snip, snip, one side was done, but once the bleeding stopped we lost interest in the barber game, and so the other side never got a haircut. The thing I'll never forget and for which I shall always be grateful is that first haircut. They don't give haircuts like that anymore.

REVERIE OF THE NOON HOUR

Everyone in the office has stepped away for lunch. Everyone in every office has. The restaurants are packed, it's payday for the pretzel vendor, the short order cook is beside himself with joy. The cloud that had anchored itself above our city shoved off for another locale. It's finally the warm day we've waited for and you can hear the sounds of chewing. As you read this, huge quantities of food are being consumed by people in the busy restaurants and out on the sidewalks, and this is something for the farmers and the butchers and the deliverymen to celebrate, for without a doubt this is why they do what they do for a living. As you read this, people are forgiving themselves and each other. And eating. Nobody feels bad about himself for an entire hour.

GOSPEL FOR THE DAY

I got into a heated argument and lost my head. It just separated and fell off, then rolled into a storm drain. The drain's iron grating warned DUMP NO WASTE. RUNOFF FLOWS TO JORDAN. I chased after my head but was too slow. I could only listen as my head plopped into dank darkness and was swept away. I thought I heard it still heatedly arguing the point before everything but the onrush went silent again. I can't help wondering what will happen in Jordan when my head is discovered in the fishing net and Simon yells to his friends, "Look! As prophesied, we've caught a man!" Try as I might, I can't remember what got me so worked up in the first place.

MY MOTHER'S WORLD

My mother was a handbag, or rather, the handbag that she carried with her everywhere, under an arm. Or rather still, my mother's world was the world she inhabited inside the handbag. The world of the handbag that was my mother always closed with a snap if I got too close. I can hear the snap to this day, a sound that said *private*, and to keep out. I've tried to imagine the world of the handbag that was my mother, its zippered pockets, its secrets, but I can't. Things would go into the handbag and disappear. Things would emerge, words, thoughts, tears and laughter, that gleamed in sunlight, but they remained mysteries to me. I can only guess at the world in which they existed. I suppose that's what I am doing now, guessing. Something was in there, a person, a life, an entire world, but I never knew it, and now I never shall.

About the Author:

Clark Holtzman performs as Lord Byron with the spoken word jazz band, Program for Jazz. You can find us at www.program4jazz.com. Thanks to the following journals for publishing my poems in recent months: American Poetry Journal, Shot Glass Journal, 34th Parallel Magazine (Paris, non-fiction), Visual Artist Collective-all roads will lead you home, North American Review (online), Antiphon (UK), Bangalore Review (Bangalore), Autumn Sky Poetry. He lives in Chapel Hill, North Carolina.

NEW WORLD
by Doug Sutton-Ramspeck

New World

Once, in California, I watched
two lovers wading in the ocean,

watched the black, consuming waves
wash over them—all mindless,

all dumb substance. We were living
separately that year, and I had flown

west to visit but had stopped in
the rental car before arriving

at the apartment. And from
the bluff's height, I could see

the moon rising free now of its
socket, see the sleeping clouds

floating captive and disembodied.
I imagined the waves growing

epileptic in the wind, some glossolalia
of tongue flashing up. And it seemed

I could hear something coming,
slinking and crawling and emergent,

some hollowed husk pressing toward
shore with the waves. And the lovers,
meanwhile, were embracing

in the shallows while the water

ghosted past. And their bodies
were like the hives of stars that soon

would appear above the sea.
And I knew, in that moment,

how darkness can begin
at the spine then work its way

out into the body. And why,
from the distance of the sky,

there is only the curvature of land,
the sea bottoms that open into doors.

Long Marriage (Omens)

It is winter here. Clouds brood
on the horizon. And because

memory is geography, everything
is pared down: our children

living far away, our parents
long gone, the hours crawling

forward on their bellies. We exist,
we imagine, in the hardness

of the mud, in the triangular
prints of deer. And sometimes

we imagine that our thoughts
are as old as wind over snow,

as the fingers of desiccated grass.
We think: *this is the life we have made.*

Or we dream of prayers growing
thick above the Earth, of a blade

of light cutting a jagged line
across a ridge where shadows

bisect the lowlands. And sometimes
we pretend that the mountains

are a ship slowly pressing its prow
into the sea. But now, today, we study

how dust collects on our windowsills,
how the elongated railroad tracks

reach out and out across the fields,
how there are six, maybe seven crows

in the tree line past the fence, and how
we carry each hour as prophecy.

Sacred Omens

After she lost the child
in the eighth month,

the sun was dull canker
along the fence where

an amanuensis of wind
sifted through the autumn

leaves and where fog clung
some mornings with priestly

devotion. And everywhere
there were signs:

pine cones arranging
themselves in unexpected

clusters, the long bones
of railroad tracks stretching

into nothing, the lingering
moon a desiccated tongue

or an otherworldly wheel.
And once, in broad day,

she saw hinged wings
half-hidden beneath the loose

skin of a shagbark hickory,
the bat trying to burrow

out of sight, and later she heard
crows calling their occultations

from the woods, some abattoir
of sorrow, the sky gesturing

in its mother tongue of day
then night then day.

About the Author:

Doug Ramspeck is the author of six poetry collections and one collection of short stories. His most recent book, Black Flowers (2018), is published by LSU Press. Individual poems have appeared in journals that include The Kenyon Review, The Southern Review, Slate, and The Georgia Review. He teaches creative writing at The Ohio State University at Lima.

ILLUMINATING POETRY
by Judith Simon Prager

Illuminating Poetry

A candle, held up to the unknown
    to fathom, or to pray against, what darkness holds.
A lighthouse searchlight,
    reaching out to assess the terrain
    and find, in all that is, the similars that only seemed
        by dint of matter, separate and apart.
A shard of jagged lightening
    The quickest flash of truth, so naked you cannot stand
    to stay and watch for long.
And in the heart of a song-drenched lover
    that moment
        the curtain of clouds relents
    and, just before it sets, the sun is freed to nearly blind us and
        certainly to dazzle us, long enough, this time, for the
        senses to stir, for the echoing heart to reverberate,
for the rich, orange spell-glow of late afternoon,
    the day turning the corner and,
    almost unwillingly shifting to a dark blue
        in which the waters blacken
    and the celestial lights, always there,
        become visible,
A poem can be that moment,
    that golden light that keeps us warm
    through long and lonely nights.

Portrait of a Man Lost in Love

I once knew a man so in love with his woman
      that he carried her photo,
      with her and without her.
Whether she was near or far, the prize never vanished
      but held dear, by heart strings, kept close to his sight.

Even when jointly they went on their travels,
      the same trip, the same train,
      the plane with the arm rest up, holding hands,
      she was never
          out of his mind,
          you might say.
Sleeping together in a bed far from home,
      he'd prop up her portrait on the night stand beside him.
So that facing toward her or away from her
he was always seeing his love in the flesh or in a frame.
And in his sight she was his treasure.

I knew this man and his odd, sweet secret.

Did anyone else guess that the attaché case
      he carried with him to dinners out, lifting a glass to toast
          the host
          or to offer an anecdote to cause delighted laughter among his
          own friends and admirers
          Did any of them guess—
          as his elbow touched hers reaching for the bread,
          as he allowed his glance to fall on her face mid-story or between the salad and
      the flaming dessert,
or when she excused herself to go to the ladies room and his eyes followed her
      like a calf half-desperate for his mother,
      —that the framed trophy never left his side?

I wonder, now, what he's done with that
      artifact.
Now that they've gone their separate ways.

In Good Taste

Like the loud clash of cymbals that stuns the ears,
Words in the mouth began to burst with raw flavors.
And people began to notice that the act of speaking produced
      A new medical condition,
      Instant Verbal Reflux.

True words tasted clean, a bouquet of herbs, perhaps. Minty, cool.
Kind words tasted sweet, a treat to tongue and ear.
You know the rest, of course,
      why it is a
      threat to have to eat your words if they are
poison darts not cupid's arrows
if they come from the bowels instead of the heart.

And so in the days of that followed
Some people began to walk from here to there, hand over lips
  Lest what they say might fill their mouths with bile.
Some became wiser, some more silent, some growing accustomed to
      Bad taste.

About the Author:

Judith Simon Prager is an award-winning instructor in the UCLA Ext. Writers' Program, author of several non-fictions books, most notably co-authoring The Worst Is Over: What To Say When Every Moment Counts and most recently the novel, What the Dolphin Said. She is an international speaker on the protocol, Verbal First Aid, training medical professionals across the US and around the world in how to speak in medical emergencies and crises to set a course for recovery. She is married to the poet, Harry Youtt, and has a private therapy practice in Los Angeles, CA.

KELP LASER

by Daniel King

Anyon Ethos

So I will Preserve; so I will Destroy
An anyon is my soul; and as a boy
Honeyed is your clay
My plan is advancing dharma
Those times I am hailed as Rama. Pray.

So I will Destroy; so I will Preserve
Mere oats you are to me. Grant you deserve
The fields I will burn
Stalks reduced to letter N's. Cry
"Warrior!" to me, Kalki, and learn.

Kelp Laser

Swell is roiling far above my head
Wells of sand are spiraling below
Kelp extends as far as I see
So my central standpoint may be the key.

Pearls like prase are glistening in clefts
Thoughts they stir are bubbling, but burst
Somehow spheres are shown as a draft
They are spheres tomorrow's lasermen craft.

What is the answer I seek?
And who is the weeper I am?
And why is the future so velled?
And what is the leap I must take?

Visions slowly form within the rips
Tidal easels show themselves to me
Royal figures rise from a reef
And they plot to be our Destiny's thief.

Stealing Time, they fabricate a sphere
Seeking oneness clearly is their goal
Keepers peer from shadows, and wait
For Kaldog to load the infinite Eight.
This is the answer they seek
And that is their exile's extent
And that is the leap they must take
To gain for us praise of Kalki.

Nightwheels

Here I stand on this desolate world,
Far removed from the glow that I left.
Stars Nubecula Major unfurled
Stab like these, but my mind's cleft:

Twinning galaxies blaze on the ice,
Fused to form an infinity sign.
No description can ever suffice;
No amazement transcends mine.

Brother bonded, those seething nightwheels
Heighten thoughts of the Twins within me.
Every chant was to make me more real;
Every sign was for Kalki.

Expeditions like this underline
I as well am enabling the real.
Vishnu's son, I create with my mind
Shiva's son, I demand steel.

Secant Lads

You are monads, loved for a moment
Attached to me as acolytes
Chords but not diameters, bowmen
Who chant my mantra, solstice nights:

Secant lads, secant lads, secant lads, secant lads
Secant lads, secant lads, secant lads, secant lads
Secant lads, secant lads, secant lads, secant lads

You are nomads, castle encircling
As venomous as aconite;
Tiger moths from Saturn, checkmating
With darts or arrows, sound or light;

You are comrades, Diaz in daring,
As dear to me as ammonites;
Sand from Sagittarius, blasting
With chords of Ø, you topaz knights!

Sonnet: Be Redfish Which See

White horse waves, khaki-swirled, chase the fish that flash
Making surf glint as though *Devadatta* slashed.

Such red shoals make me think every soul can join:
All we Twelve, Tower-born, share the bond. The cache,
Sphere-enclosed, spreads from Mind, plain to coast to groyne.

Shuka's beak, topaz red: now it's dawn, a gash
Day has dealt. Seeing more clearly points the way
Being drew me, Kalki, close to those who cry,
"Just a few days ago I was like a cay

Sea-enclosed; fences shut out November's sky".
Far behind, horses foam, shoreline bound; I dry
Board and hair. As on day twenty-seven, high
Insights surge, wave-like. *Tell my eleven why.*
Make them weigh Vishnu's name fifty-eight: Red Eye.

About the Author:

Daniel King is a prize-winning Australian writer. His poetry collection, Amethysts and Emeralds, was published by Interactive Press on May 15 2018. His hobbies include surfing, skateboarding, following the latest developments in space exploration, and listening to the music of Mike Oldfield and Project System 12.

EYELASH

by Glen Armstrong

Eyelash

It is not strange enough.
Nor beautiful enough to discuss.
At length in the museum's coffee shop.
I'm remembering it differently.
The bees both threaten.
And reinvigorate the landscape.
The sky looks like paper.
Another skinny girl.
Makes a wish on an eyelash.
And the wind takes them elsewhere.

I see them both again.
But this time the eyelash makes the wish.
And the girl floats away.
This is my life.
An endless introduction of replacements.
And delays.
I start to see the loose change.
And its random patterns.
Against the palm of my hand.
As the main event.

Funhouse

There was a time.
That I would walk right through.
The clown's grotesque teeth.
And enjoy the poorly recorded.
Laughter and polka.
Now I only have fun ironically.
And never as much.
As the elderly who have conquered.
Incontinence in the ads.
It's all about pills and charcoal.

Linings.
It's all about cola.
And being playfully sprayed.
With the neighbor's hose.
It's all about crows that smoke.
Cigars and teach.
The ingénue to fly.
I wouldn't say.
That this has been a particularly bad day.
But I somehow expected more.

To the Sky

I have no time to float.
In you slowly.
Like a rogue constellation.
Or to make a spirited year-long return.
As if I were a comet.
Caked with ice and alien DNA.
Outer space is none.
Of my business.
I can imagine nothing beyond you.
My kismet plays out amid anthills.

And poisonous eggs.
I have no time for dandelions.
That whiten and fall.
Apart and take to you.
Because some Russian weed might.
Get to you first.
I have no needs.
That you have left unfulfilled.
No notion that a sexier world.
Surely exists.

About the Author:

Glen Armstrong holds an MFA in English from the University of Massachusetts, Amherst and teaches writing at Oakland University in Rochester, Michigan. He edits a poetry journal called Cruel Garters and has three recent chapbooks: Set List (Bitchin Kitsch,) In Stone and The Most Awkward Silence of All (both Cruel Garters Press.) His work has appeared in Poetry Northwest, Conduit and Cloudbank.

OLD SALT

by Christina Petrides

Old Salt

Flushed from alcohol, wind and weather,
And grooved from age,
The woman clutches her fishing rod and glares
at the sea.
It twinkles back at her
And crashes unconcerned into the rocks below.

Barista

There's a pretty man behind the bar.
"May I help you?" he inquires,
Ready to make a drink to our design.
We flock in to order, to admire
The careless scruff on his chin
And the high black bun from which his thick
hair escapes.
He resembles some classical character in an old
romance
When heroes were roughly muscled,
Gently mannered,
And yet somehow had perfect teeth and no
stink of sweat
After battling bandits and dragons.
In the aroma of freshly roasted beans we
dream
That he could be as dashing as he looks.

Precaution

Watch where you tread
For what seems stable will
Disappear.
You will drop like a whole cherry
Falling between
Ice cubes that collide
In a fresh glass of bubbling soda.

About the Author:

Christina Petrides is an expatriate American living on a small Pacific island where all the palm trees and the magpies are imported, but the rice wine is indigenous and delicious.

CHARLEY BOND

by William Schoedel

He came upon me suddenly
Before I could retreat
His long lean figure
Wrapped in an abused overlong grey coat
With a shock of nearly pure white hair
Tumbling from beneath
The confines of a tattered woolen cap
Like just so many flecks
Of windswept cloud
Or snow.

A quick nod of his head
Was all he offered me
By way of greeting
Yet managed to convey
Without the waste of a single word
How he truly wished to share
Much more than a silent hello.

"Bond's the name," he began
Charley Bond.
Know the store in Boston by the name?
Brother owns it
I once worked there
'Fore my eyes gave way."

"Glaucoma," he explained
In answer to my gaze.
"Don't mind it much
But it makes my walkin' hard."

"She's born in Phoenix." He informed me
As I reached to pet his dog
A frisking small white poodle
Like a fragment of his hair
Transfigured.

"Fourth in a litter of six she was
Born a purebred. Got good blood
Say her daddy was a champion
She's good to me. I like her company."

He jabbed a bony figure at my camera
"Used to live in Dallas
'Fore I went to Nashville
Had a camera shop there
Man what owned it
Ran on hard times
Owed me money
So he give me the shop instead
Used to work that shop alone
Knew all the rigs by name."

"Started on the Dallas Times
So's they called it then
My first real job as pro
They sent me on assignment
As assistant
Coverin' a high society weddin'
Remember it like yesterday
Ol' head man I was workin' with
He had them all lined up

In their white suits
And dresses there before him
And dropped two packs
Of number two Apex in the slot
Didn't have no flashbulbs then
Used a powder charge instead
Well, I knew right then
It was way too much
And I told him out my mind
But he just said
You're bein' paid to help, not criticize
I'm the head man, you're my aide
And he flashed it off
And covered them all
With thick black soot
From head to toe
Like tar babies all!
Ol' headman
Didn't keep that fancy job
Too long.

From this here twang I got for accent
Bet you'd never guess
I come from round these parts,
But course I do!
Got my roots sunk here
Up New Hampshire way
Way on back to Revolution days
Once belonged ... brother still does
To the Keene New Hampshire Legion.
Used to dress up fancy
In full parade regalia
March in all parades
And town occasions
Fine group we was!
Too bad I don't meet with them no more."

Charley's dog, impatient, tugged its leash
Went nosing into flowers
Sheltering by a shed.
While Charley stood there
In melting snow
His hair tossed gently by the wind
His feet in tattered boots untied

His face unshaved
His flesh all red and puffy
His eyes set far away.

When suddenly
He shook himself
Or shivered.
"Guess it's time we was gettin' home.
Ol' Donna must be gettin' hungry.
Aren't ya girl?
Never smart to keep a good girl waitin'"
And he winked to show his humor.

At the corner
Charley stopped
And glanced back once.
Then raised a hand
In half salute
 ... to say good bye.

About the Author:

William J. Schoedel is a 73 year old married man with an unwanted Bachelor's Degree in Electrical Engineering from the University of Pittsburgh, who loves to write Poetry and Short Stories, and has several poems and 13 completed stories with 6 more in the works, a few of which have been read by friends and family with enthusiastic feedback. He had never been published, except for one small article in a Muskegon MI newspaper.

HOPES

by Alexa Tirapelli

"Hopes"

His name was Bud Hopes, or Lou –
something like that, or what-have-you.
They found his journal in an abandoned barn
among dusty knick-knacks and next to his body,
to which he had done some harm.
They took his book and spilled its guts,
opened it up, invaded a dead man's thoughts:

I.
  I could go into the Abyss
  or to a therapist.
  I've been told these are the two options.
  It's not much, but it's not nothing.

II.
  I go to this coffee place
  damn near every day
  sometimes to the counter guy
  (a nice Australian type) I say:
    TWO SMALL BLACK COFFEES
        To stay?
    NO, TO GO.
  I pay.
  I bring them home
  where it's empty and wholly my own
  (no one lives here but me).
  But I really fool that Aussie
  sometimes into thinking i have
  another half to me,
  or another place to bring this extra coffee

  (i pour both twelve ounces into each other
  and make it twenty-four).

III.
  we all pretend we're going to live these long
  lives,
    but maybe we won't
    and we all say we're happy when we're prob-
  ably not
    say we'll push on and put on a brave face,
    but we don't

    what makes me less important, for the love
  of god

IV.
    there's something crawling around inside my
  head
    I'M WELL AWARE OF HOW LOST I AM, BUT I
  THANK YOU
    is what I told it, the voice – The Crawly.
    I've burned some bridges to ash, I am sure.
    It's not like it used to be.
    i am right here but i never say it
    open another bottle of bourbon
    another
    another
    okay,
    last one.

"Lacuna"

Shoe repair!
Shoe repair!
Neon signs curved into words
in bar windows and store fronts
Technicolor lightning strikes along the streets,
we're east of the Hudson and west of the East.

After the fourth low-end canned beer,
I start to taste apple skins
and begin to straddle a timeline
between kidhood and being adult
Living in a catch-22 city
(by that I mean
I can't stand living here
but feel I can never leave).
We talk about not having it all figured out
on flea market couches and across coffee tables
covered in ashes and empties.

A yellow taxicab pulls to the side of the street
The snow is wet and heavy
It is March, the lion,
and everyone carries umbrellas for protection.

YOU KNOW WHERE CHERRY LANE THEATRE IS?
the taximan screams out his open window at
a man, mid-50s, in a puffy black jacket
(no doubt worth more than renting my apartment)
IT'S ON GROVE STREET, ISN'T IT? IT'S ON
GROVE!

The scene is New York, late winter, bleak
Fat flakes swim to and smack my cheeks
I roll my eyes, I smile, I carry on.
I remember now, I remember why I live here
though I couldn't explain it again or any better.

"Monday"

I spent the morning masturbating
and playing guitar,
sloshing reheated coffee around
in an old yellow mug,
letting smoke escape
my lungs,
and eating chocolate by the handful.

You ever feel like you're dying?
I don't feel much,
but I feel that.
Confused little girl.
Confused little girl.
I touch my face, it grows thin,
I fall into the psychedelic,
melt to music,
then to pale blue tangerine tie-dye sky.

"Dinner Table"

Cold pizza, flat soda.
Mom's drunk and alone
passed out on the sofa.

Wait.
Let me paint the rest of the picture
of the way the kid in me lived
when everyone else was looking the other way.

The small crystal vial of vodka
greasy finger marks on the cylinder's waist
bones gloved lightly by skin
pale and effervescent in morning sunlight.

She bubbles somehow
like something brewing;
something Macbethian.

An evil monster stirs at evening.

Turn to the cabinets, bare.
She is barely there.

I'll have cold pizza
and flat soda
until someone notices something.

"Recoil"

Turn a handstand on the highway
and headlights become stars in the sky
(when we were younger
we called it the way-high)

The pitch-black slick pavement
of nighttime after a rainstorm
like wet painted walls
or concrete scuffed and worn

I think of you, of that house,
while staring between the tiles
at the yellowing grout

Soap, skin
The shower curtain licks my shoulder
I cringe

Clocks tick in every room
to different downbeats,
Curtains hang at jagged lengths
Chain locks fend off enemy fleets

Baskets rest on cabinet tops
a set-aside, forgotten space
filled with empty woven things,
bug carcasses, and dust cloud lace.

Surfaces like this rip me apart
peel me backwards, bone from flesh

Cut me open with a
smooth-handled hunter's knife
Peel me away from
the textures of this plain life

About the Author:

Alexa Tirapelli is a bartender in the West Village of Manhattan. She grew up in the Catskill Mountains and currently lives in Brooklyn with her boyfriend and two cats. She is working on her first novel and writing poetry from home. She has been published in Bitterzoet Magazine and the Hudson Valley magazine Chronogram.

TALK RADIO

by Sugar Tobey

Tang Dynasty Poem

She looks twenty but she's about
twelve hundred years old now
the tang dynasty was a long time ago

she still waits for a young man
to come and dig her a carp pond
I have dug her this pond so many times

Shooting

A lot of people here get shot
grown men old women
children everybody

if I got shot I would want
Clint Eastwood or
Lee Van Cleef to do it

then I'd fall backward into my own
freshly dug grave
on tenth avenue

Peaceful Lovely Beautiful

The afternoon sun light slowly crosses the bed
her head on my arm as she sleeps
a beautiful face so close to mine
her breath in quick but gentle rhythm

I won't disturb her rest
she has been through so much
leaning forward I can't help but
kiss her ear

happy that she wants to stay here
I rest my head lightly against her side
and listen to her as she
purrs so sweetly

Talk Radio

It's gotten late again
way down the AM radio dial
her voice so gentle
so sexy

she's not speaking english
I don't understand her
she talks all night
deep into my night

I fall asleep
only to wake hours later
to static
the universe speaks

About the Author:

Born Coney Island, Brooklyn. **Sugar Tobey** is the editor of Modern Poets Magazine. His own work has appeared in many publications including Bangalore Review, Indiana Voice Journal and Coldnoon. His new book, "Two Girls Make the Train" with artist Hiro Kurata has recently been published by Biondi Books. He currently lives in New York City over a pizza parlor.

OUT OF THE BLUE IS TRUE

by Tim Suermondt

DEAUVILLE

The morning comes like movie stars,
movie stars in sailboats.

I'm no star in any configuration,
but I acknowledge Beauty's pecking order
and I gladly give her a pass on my behalf.

On the beach I talk to an old man
who's searching for coins to give to his
long lost son--"He will need money, Qui?"

A Question: Will any of us ever be found?
But...no, that's a story for another day
or poem—like the dogs dashing over and rolling
in the sand, I'm happy

and when my wife arrives any complaints
I might have will garner zero defense.

Beside a water level pole red as lipstick
the old man waves and I wave back--
with all my might.

POINTE du HOC

In a small Normandy town
my wife and I enjoy
a fine, economical dinner.

The bright lit full moon has anchored itself
slightly slanted near a rather big cathedral,
as if looking down,
concerned for us all.

On the way back to our hotel
my wife and I stop and kiss
across from a house locals say
held its share of the wounded and dying.

I sense the soldiers who came by sea
don't doubt we came there for them,
to show that the world *is* beautiful
despite history's attempts at making
this sound foolish, obsolete.

Beautiful as my father sitting on a hard chair,
analyzing his maps, lost and saved
everyday in the suburbs of Valhalla.

WALKING ON BOYLSTON WHEN IT STARTS

The jazz player who said "Open the windows

or we'll all get sophisticated" leads to the re-mark

about the ballplayer who was so fast "that when

he turned off the light switch when he went to bed,

he was under the covers before the room got dark."

And Oscar Wilde coming right out and saying "Give

me the luxuries of life and I can do without the necessities"

and Kenneth Patchen defining hopelessness better than

any other when he wrote "I feel like a carpet in a cathouse."

I could go on and I will, but it's time to duck into this

small café/diner, a clean, fairly well-lighted place where

it's quite felicitous to utter "All men eat, but Fu Manchu."

OUT OF THE BLUE IS TRUE

Things supposedly difficult often
turn out to be simple, easy to the core.
I thought of this, standing by myself
in front of the pizzeria, eyeing the oak
tree nestled behind the garbage bins.
Sausage, pepperoni, toppings galore
and since the world and I are friendly
again to one another we walked in with
grandeur, ordering the biggest pie to share.

About the Author:

Tim Suermondt is the author of four full-length collections of poems: Trying To Help The Elephant Man Dance (The Backwaters Press, 2007), Just Beautiful (New York Quarterly Books, 2010), Election Night And The Five Satins (Glass Lyre Press, 2016) and The World Doesn't Know You published by Pinyon Publishing in late 2017. His fifth book Josephine Baker Swimming Pool will be released in 2018 by MadHat Press. He has poems published in Poetry, The Georgia Review, Ploughshares, Prairie Schooner, Blackbird, Bellevue Literary Review, North Dakota Quarterly, December magazine, Plume Poetry Journal, Poetry East and Stand Magazine (England), among others. He is a book reviewer for Cervena Barva Press and a poetry reviewer for Bellevue Literary Review.

SLICK

by Mia Condic

#1
SLICK

I knew a guy in college
he listened only to classical music
a psychology student
you could tell he was destined for a future in
philosophical monologues
the way he orchestrated the words from his
classical mouth
but a terrible character
the one that demanded the supper on the
table
at precisely 6 p.m.
just as warm, not too hot
so he could go to bed at 9
despite the differences in our
lifestyles
I enjoyed talking to him
even now I cannot explain it
but he was a pleasant person
from afar
I'm sure he still is
somewhere
while composing his stilted music
or orchestrating his patients
with his long thin fingers
classic slick outfit
ironed monochromatic shirt under a sweater

a look not a lot of guys tried in college
carrying his briefcase from class to class
while others carried loose scripts under their
armpits
eternally asking for a pen
in their neighbor's pencil case
thinking how many familiar faces will be in that
cheap cocktail bar after class
but our classical guy always went straight
home
alone
he despised sharing his living space
where he held his baton up high
while listening to Mozart
I bet he'd enjoy being my therapist today

#2
WEATHER

they have been falling all day now
fingertips on typewriter keys
sprinkles on a fairy bread
cinnamon on milk foam
randomly and nimbly
hitting your forehead and eyelids
melting on your cheeks
divine white sparks and trickles

#3
PLAYING DEFENCE

This is home
You are the front door
and all the windows and our hanging photos
This is home you give me
on a good day
when my voice isn't high-pitched
my muscles relaxed
I don't have to stop to inhale air
You're the light breeze and the calm
I'm the earthquake
I shake and I rattle
I cause disturbance
I fuss and I rebel
Even when our bed is not a battlefield
I still have my shield on
I still defend myself
I still charge
dreading
at the same time
you will change
or perhaps already have
I look for defects
justifying my early way out
I don't like myself for that
but I don't know who the aggressor is
anymore
is it me
is it you
or is it the society we feed with our discord
Only we ate from their hands first

About the Author:

Mia Condic is a 27-year-old girl from Split, Croatia. As a huge travel aficionado, she's constantly daydreaming about her next trip. She's a University graduate with a Bachelor's degree in Spanish, and a Master's degree in Russian language and literature. Shy, and a complete geek when it comes to good books, movies, and music. She likes writing better than speaking, and it has been her good companion for the majority of her life. She currently resides in The Netherlands.

WHAT XERO OFFERS
by Mark Young

What Xero offers

The leading online storage &
file delivery service is envied
for her use of the tropes she
keeps in a secret gulag of
unique art forms. Her young
adult ministry is a global
provider of real-time product-
based symposia that encourage

our youth to buy pharmaceuticals
& pirated DVDs. All asymmetry
& angularity, she writes in an open-
access article that the feminist movement didn't actually help women. She
is set to earn millions from her app.

expands the now posture

The high price of fuel means
that the last Mexican will soon
be selling signed jerseys &
music action figures in an
attempt to break the blockade.
Maybe I haven't been paying
proper attention, but it seems
a well designed authenticity

dilemma, & comfortable for your
small dog. No doubt has been
discovered by the Arabs through
a body of research. Now ready
to be transmitted, & poised to
tear apart our modern paradigms.

to elucidate

A little Turkish Delight
is the perfect medium to
strip a heavy vessel of its

lining. It's a remedy from
the old west, particularly
useful for hospitals, cities,

schools, but moved side-
ways & into the closet
so the stains don't show.

the / use of / the hands especially

Revision of the Dublin regulation
has combined malformed blood
vessels with obsessively detailed
itineraries to create tax exemptions
on fund earnings & insider access
for as little as $15 a day. We are
now able to easily track the time
spent on individual jobs, explore

the rôle of 'real life' experiences,
embed the critical so that the
two main charcters can sit up &,
at length, move about. Still, one
must explore with caution & beware of exorbitant cover fees.

A line from Debbie Harry

Fulfillment Daily tells
us the stress of urban
living is more than
an abstract trace on a

map. Is a breeding
ground for psychosis,
is reflected in each &
every boat that leaves

the UK's only licensed
cannabis farm. From
the isolation of Guan-
tánamo it may seem a

trivial thing; but as a
socially disadvantaged
ethnic minority we are
completely vulnerable.

OUT OF BED

by Penney Knightly

Out of Bed

Slow to serenade, wispy, extending
arms and legs, a jungle heap.
Moss-fern overgrowth.

Dew on cheeks and inner limbs,
I blush in dark places
hiding against sky light, and crunch of air.

I slither back, move like Eden;
a dream ghost.

A Letter Leaves

Little square holding so much heart,
bursting of seams, some stitching
needed for a stamp.

Scrapes to paper. Carrier of so much weight.
Athletic eyes, perky and bouncing;
love-muscle conditioning

Mesh

in this dream there was a screen
pressed over my face, an impression
and I couldn't feel anything but a smile
but I wasn't allowed to have it

my face felt strong from your hands
more homely and becoming
I could feel your eyes on mine
straining through fingertips, lonely

aching cheekbones and dry lips
I blend into the cushion of a lie;
this is not my jaw,
I am holy exclusion

Grief Bone

I imagine it smooth
the polishing of ache
as important and trivial
as a rib bone, or a clavicle
but more lengthy,
think femur
that sort of dimension
with fractures like a child's drawing—
marks that often leave the surface.

About the Author:

Penney Knightly is a survivor of sexual abuse; themes about that are often found in her work. Her poetry has appeared in Eunoia Review, Dead King, and elsewhere. She lives with her family on a sailboat in the San Francisco Bay, where she writes and creates art. She tweets @penneyknightly and shares on her blog http://penneyknightly.com.

BUDDY

by Jonathan Andrew Perez

Burn, Barn, Burn

What remained couldn't be salvaged from
the shipwreck of my immobility.
Climate change. Father warned me don't
dive deep:
Wake before you go to sleep, migrate in the
afternoon
Read Borges, Neruda, mostly maybe *Los
Cantos* de Lorca,
we migrate. Don't own a little nest-infested
barn,
Don't sit all day, writing spiritual poems,
like a Barn Owl, while the barn burns,
ambiguous as a lung, lost like a bleached
Ghost.

Speak, memory: I do not speak Spanish,
but I am Spanish. I maintain the right to not
be forgotten. A twilight I own despite my
own
secrecy. The danceable tapestry: fiestas,
community,
in the garden of joy imagined far-off
within the untimely, the dead lose no blood,
the untimely are kept in corners, cut-off,
wakening, in me sits a mud jar of empathy
for others who have lived the opposite of
fuel

and entropy. There is no justice for fourth-
generations
white ceiling meets the late bloom of light,
familiar as the progression of longing,
here is the opposite of love, the sharp shrill
of hate,
the imagery: olives in my pocket, a mule,
valiance and folk songs of death, in Andalu-
sia,
for those mired in the hours of love and bal-
lad of light.

After the divorce, my father returned his
books
to the library, in Spanish, left His-Panic, a
terrible leap
across the country, a grace to change the
white ceiling,
and leave behind no history, a homeland of
books like a wound,
only meager beams of light from his car: his
vehicle
could never pass the emissions test of time.
Little Barn Owl, fire or not, it was rude to
ignore you,
What remained after the smoke cleared: all
shades of music rung.

Buddy

The land is a swash of monotone:
cobwebs against yellowing barns, seed pods
off rusty fences. Being a magician the setting
dulled the senses. Nothing to pin the astound-
ing.
No image to bind the glue that made life from
Death. Pulled a parent fox family survival from
The carnivorous sleeve of stripe ribbons of
roadkill.

Give me: dog ripping leg on gravel road,
Give me: wolf on fire trail that circles a valley.
You see I heard dogs travel in packs, at night.
You see I heard undomesticated baying at
the rough horizon, voyagers of mongrel order,
they plunder the uninhabited, they live somehow
without our living, like a hound on the trail of a
hare.

They tear a shrew from its hole, or like an Orca
flip a seal pup, head-over-heals in the supple
light.
Buddy, the black lab, has proudly returned
home,
And proudly struts along the avenue, gangster-
like,
Head cocked, half-awake and half-asleep
down the avenue, jaw clenched over a wet
mouse.
Buddy, listen up, predatory dogs are not welcome here.

Buddy, only mate at night and do not disturb
any of the familiar faces that make up the
townsfolk.
Buddy, you are not a regular visitor. Lower
your music.
Buddy, each year I have come here, you are
not here

but wandering the harbor less hills: drinking,
cheating, killing
in the lot behind the high school gymnasium
near the torn-up mounds to the north.

Buddy, I saw you once. You and I are some kind
of undead,
like mutts washed up in some quarry to the
north
up a peak, behind the back of the sun, no help
from Mother Earth:
You see, Buddy, sooner or later a rumor will
start
that you or I may have come back
as a mountain lion.

The Broken Ivory Tower

1.
*Tower (v.) to passively stare in awe like rever-
ence*

Of a white pastoral: all is invigorating
And crystal at the lake, two boys back float
prone
the reflective depths: from the eye's blue zen-
ith,
past the lake-scapes, there is no color, nothing
fowl

Just two brown trout, and the snap associated
With a turtle nipping at the under-toe
From divers, white like the monotony of bone,
Sand at the lake's edge, salted and blue,

The last of the vacationers have made a nimble
Rift with the water, chilled the vibrant shone,
You don't belong here, the beach umbrellas
cracked,
A band that flaked in the sunlight, hauls beers
home.

Self-portrait in an othered landscape,
At noon the swimmers sprint, curling fingers
and wrist,
Piled up in the dune high, brackish brown
catfish
Accumulated in the sun and silt, shored against
skeleton.

2.

Tow-her, (n.) to make believe to feel, not steal

All is crystal and invigorating at the lake.
Across the beach I don't belong here. In shal-
low sport,
An osprey laments the lack of deep dive by
shiver
In the wind sheer for an impossible fish.

A while back the sunlight entangled the brown
land,
Someone invested in an abstract perfectionist
portrait
The spotted bejeweled damselfly, mistaken for
a bloodstone
Jasper stone, the grueling violent survival just

Beneath the clean flows, the coldest darkest
sprouts,
Like fuselage from the seams, the surface
brims
With the sounds of police cars at night, high
rise city,
And watch out the window for a wisp of wind

Welcome back the pastoral sophistication
As music is to the cold eye without pity,
These filaments are not corner dealers, kids
wanting
No more than to plumb depths of life upward
to the sky.

3.
*Broken tower (v.): to careen, newer usage,
leave behind*

Of a white pastoral: all is not white pastoral.
nothing is crystal and invigorating at the lake,
we watch as the kaleidoscope became bity
a simple careen of fuselage in the elastic tide.

But there are crustaceous things: pink oyster
half-devoured,
Feral cats sing propelled by refuse in swelling
tide,
The brackish water is a public works experiment,
An urban gift to the cascading highway projects
out the city.

I have no use but for granite, or inert signals

But a morsel remained in the dry sweep, a music will echo it
*it is I that have made it out of existence, no
pity,*
*I am not a blip, a blemish, a confusion on the
white scape*

Indeed, this crack will become a more serious
fissure
Mounted on the angelic weather, white cascading
Puddles mistook for cloudlessness –swiftly
Clouds exist: they are recorded in the broken
tower.

The hand that fell the trees, which ripped up
gardens,
and at the same time assuaged me from late
bills, evictions,
came home empty handed with holes in its
shoes, was not bought
by doctors on cape cod or made by fireplaces
on wall street –

it felled when we recognized its false conviction: the sea unsounded gave peace.

Men

To head out at daybreak
to make the rout easier
hunters, maybe men, grizzled
and huge, abolished maps for

large steel tents, deep in petrified
forests in the North, calloused hands
hung onto the rifles and gun powder
and stood on cliffs that protruded

out into the abyss. They have hunted
in despondency, with sorrow over lost
wives and sons, they have lost money
on football games, by the crescent moon

and smelled of cigarettes and plaid, to poke
heads into the rabbit-run, by love
and fear whistling for the first rabbit
of spring to stare out of the confusion

neither to suffer or die, but to see
the twitching of ears in the eyehole
and wait beyond duck blinds and share
stories of conquests and lies in Polar

Ice Caps, jumping between volcanoes,
High school knee surgery from lacrosse
And not the least part to keep a record of
Rabbits shot, in the vanishing green

For them, standing on the threshold,
The hardest part, is how small and pure
That feeling is: to spoon a bunny and kiss him.

Alien

About Lobster Rolls and Creamsicles: they
resembled a dinner party drive-thru,
an everlasting purge for little children
a permanent vacation
the scarab-beetle-black Harleys

the out-of-towners, the fried shrimp boats
with onion rings, rhubarb crusted cobbler,
a clam burger with tartar,
you could have called it: *yuppy
postcard, Lobster Shack and Root Beer*, Cape
Cod, circa 1999.

Unto you, fried rolls are not sin.
I let Puritan friends locate my origin.
I used to tell them: I cannot locate
my origin. A red-headed teenager (pimples)
blasted orders from the mollusky balcony,

we were all visitors back then.
Gulls carried the scent of fried-smelling,
Rough-sounding, wearied, like tortoise-
Rimmed doctors on vacation, patrons
Of the symphony. *Does your family speak Span-
ish?*

The caws in the parking lot
was the riff to *She's Got Legs*.
We went from one weekend to the next,
the secrets we kept, I could not fit in,
from a movie like *Uncle Buck*.

Let me know when your parents get back.
I will write to them, on a postcard
I found chasing other postcards
through the parking lot.
I will exit by spaceship, side-scrawled,
Not from here: and make my way back

To an unassailable place.

About the Author:

Jonathan Andrew Pérez, Esq. has published
poetry in Prelude, The Write Launch, Meniscus
Literary Journal, The Florida Review Aquifer,
Panoply, Paradigm, and was featured in Silver
Needle Press's poem of the week. He has
forthcoming poems in Yes Poetry, The
Westchester Review, Watermelanin Magazine
(for writers of color), Cold Mountain Review in
the Justice Issue, and Swimming with Elephants . He was a finalist in the Still Journal
Poetry Prize and for the Raw Art Review's Walt
Whitman Prize. Jonathan is selected at Cave
Canem for the Fall 2018 poetry workshop. Jon-
athan is in the process of completing a chap-
book, "Dispatches from Flight Calls Over White
Pastoral." Jonathan started his career as a
"poetry-editor intern" at the Atlantic Monthly.

MANOR

by Ann Pedone

Manor

Particles of light
Strain to the seen
In the shadows of his heart.

He knows her face
Taqstes her lips—
Sun wrenched in the sky of her longing for
The sight
Him
Inside—the inside of her
Growing upon t he sight of him

Induces a fear.

To release the time apart.

It was then that he held her
Dense in the Spring.
Grasses surround the pale-ness of her
Face up to the moon's
Shadow.

Without the climbing rose, the walls are bare
Of fruit in her
Eyes
Blue
The moon said.

On Sappho

To kiss between
Words—in spaces
There lie ages.

      "You'll lose your soul
      In pockets of rain."
Trailing behind her
To find.
Blindly, he falls.

To piece together
The light that shines
Behind her eyes
      In danger of forgetting
I call to the girls weaving
The remains of
His heart, he said
Is never to be.

It is circling always in
Broken voices to her
His call.
To know the
Words
He told me
That came before the rain.

On William Carlos Williams

Flower
Into me-
Slip from the darkness of
Petals
End
Rose-hipped
By the weight of love.

Read between the edges of
Paper flowers-
Take me
Figured in silk
Fireflies.
Nights-light onto the shore of
Roses.

Somewhere I read
Your name
Petal-spread,
Rose-
Touched by the palm
Of my hand.

A line starts between you and me.

Come-
Press me into the
Figure
Of
Your eyes'
Blooming
Rose

Down to the shore, she cried.

Find me before the rocks are
Cured
By the
Salt air-

Break the
Sense of me
Into the sand I feel
Between your toes.

About the Author:

CITADEL

by Keith Carver

CITADEL

You teeter on the wall, that *that*
that keeps the ancient world

ancient, and talk
as though to rid yourself of helium,

Your voice is a rumor in the smog the semi-
circle
of tourists dangle their feet into.

The smog is just the dust
of construction yanked from the old city ruins.

A blanket of noise tosses itself
over the flames of another explosion.

On these Roman shards history strolls
without noticing the hundred-foot drop

to wrecked mansions picked apart by CAT exca-
vators.
The neighborhood children know one word

in English, and it's *money*. For once, I did not
arrive
at the mountaintop following prophets.

We left before the minarets burst with
chanting
and descended into the green of a dead August.

Maybe death clings to borders like static electricity.
The children here have that same metallic
smell.

I remember my hometown, like a money booth
where I ate dollar bills, how it sent me away

chewing on presidential likenesses.
America, this girl begs at my feet for coins

she carries back to her father,
who holds up the walls

all these centuries.

RICHIE

Even you felt sad sometimes
after a night of waiting tables.

I'd left town already,
so I have to imagine your years
at the FireKeepers Casino,
the sonic ascent of slot machines,
the weightless perfect fifths
of jackpots ringing four hundred
thousand square feet
on our town's frontier.

Richie, I'm the tender spot
somewhere below your ribs.

I'm Anatolia
at the ambassador's mansion,
a chain-smoking attaché,
a girl who flicks the corners
of her headscarf like pigtails and rings
the ambassador's Himalayan singing
bowl with a wooden mallet and poses
beside the ambassador's
third-world props, a fine American dust
settled on everything.

Elderly waiters carry sliced beef on
toast with pickles, smoked salmon,
goat cheese mousse with roasted pear,
seltzer and saison and rye on ice
in immaculate dinner jackets.

This is a civilized world, Richard,
opposite that Partello tree
you gave your name to,
that buds picture frames
and crosses now.

I've been in barrooms
with you, excising
with a scalpel your best,

doling it piecemeal when you knew
we were starving.
When you told us
you loved us we believed you
because you needed us to believe you,
your face lit by the jukebox nights
that killed so many of us already.

May your ashes float
atop the hundred million
gallons of oil that make
the Kalamazoo River
something really special.

You know I won't be back to visit
anytime soon.

SAMSUN

Where do the Laz live? In Egreli,
the Laz live east of Egreli,
in Zongulduk, east of Zongulduk,
in Trabzon, east of Trabzon.

In the extreme eastern villiage of Kazimiye,
population 220, strung in a series of hamlets
along the Georgian border,
the Laz are said to be extinct, but
they are revered nonetheless.

And what a complete heaven, Samsun
after the Amazons, with Russian frieghters
waving at the Laz, said to live
on anchovies alone.

But, there is always another
earthquake. All at once
the rocks move because the rocks
were really warty crabs resting.

You kneel toward Mecca.
Your father is in this city somewhere.
Looks like you in photos,
woman's face, cheeks preserved
with anise liquor, boyish in the habitual
drinker's manner, then all
at once infirm.

Those aren't shadows,
those are crabs,
eriphia verrucosa,
in camoflauge, the color
of Black Sea haze.
Those are the ants
of the sea. You pushed
a dead jellyfish
back into the water
with a stick.

Of course, the real Laz still exist.

You can Hellenize some,
and you can bring some to Mohammed,
but Lazuri remains,
in spite of banishment.

We count crabs under this cliff edge.
We wander the shoals
until you're afraid of thunder.

The tracks run all the way past
the bazaar now, three city blocks long.
The fakes are good, the Gazelles look like
Gazelles,
the Superstars like Superstars. The leather
leathery,
the suede with a nap, Arabs and Russians and
Germans,
the smell of butter and flour.

Your father tests the nap
on a pair of bootleg Nikes. Your father
pulls a gun on a guy who catcalls you
and pistol-whips him until he's
jellyfish.

Butter and sea water and plasma,
dirt weed and cracked white leather.
Three miles outside the city
and still you say I smell just like him.

HEAVEN

Sorry I haven't written you
these many years,
and that I changed my name
so you'll never find me.

I have lent the sea my voice.
I am no longer the foremost
authority on my life.

Humdrum existence here is fine.
Braying horses and garbage, both,
in these pastures, just the sort of thing
that breaks into song with you
as you ride past.

There's an empty lot where refugees
sort plastic bags. They are not
a treatise on my mistakes
or an illustration of my tenacity
so I won't belabor them
any further.

I watch a wrecked man,
alone near the sea, kicking stars
on a swing set.

You must remember when we almost
burned down your father's barn
and laughed about it, between the swamp
and the river, in Marengo Township.

The man's laughter
reminds me of yours,
lit by a blaze.

Poor boys pay a few lira to become
their favorite soccer player
in the shabbiest PlayStation café
in Anatolia.

The world doesn't end
past Pearl Avenue
like you said.
Sometimes the Shepherd's crook
has shit on it.

A staircase on his handmade
brick home
leads to the roof,

where he watches, drifts in
and out of sleep, counts
his derelict flock.

READING ALICE COLTRANE'S MEMOIR IN A
WALMART TIRE SHOP

In astral projection, Alice
hears sub-contra bass
under the floor of this world
for whose sake the Creator
sustained Himself on thought alone
for one bored eternity.
Alice contacts the supreme
consciousness and sleeps
two hours a night for months.
She buries her eldest then sings
at his plot. She suffers
a night so dark
she nearly disappears,
ninety-five pounds
of piano wire and shale,
a handful of sand. She survives
on the soot left
of childhood. She walks
the embers of the cremated.
She has become,
in deprivation, those holes
you call hands
and hold out to eat
and carry to serve
everything that slips away.

About the Author:

Keith Carver, of Michigan, is a transnational educrat with a DHS file and big-boy striver debt. Ex-Fulbight/Cub Scout. His work has appeared or is forthcoming in Rust + Moth, Black-top Passages, armarolla, and Your Impossible Voice. He lives near the Black Sea with his wife.

PARISIAN PHOTO BOOTH

by Mary Shanley

Parisian Photo Booth

In the metro station,
she was playing a saw
like it was a cello.
It sounded like a theramin.
The photo booth was
just feet away. Lisa and I
crammed into the single
space and popped Euros
into the machine and began
mugging for the camera, all the
while accompanied by the
other-worldly, weird and wonderful
sounds being produced by the
spacy musician wearing a black
leather jumpsuit. She owned
the local airwaves and captivated
the crowd surrounding her.
A slice of Parisian magic,
everyone tossed money into
her black fedora.

Everything Shakes

1.
My heart opens.
There is no sound, yet I hear the wild,
undefined rhythm underlying all.
Every move that I make, everything
shakes.

My heart shakes
a rhythm that sets
my life's course
for the day.

Sometimes my entire
body shakes from the
effects of atomic spinning
and excess caffeine.

What spinning holds
a hummingbird in mid-air,
quietly shaking.

When I leave this body, I will
still be shaking. And held
in mid-air for all eternity.

2.
I'm on the couch, writing;
attempting to capture
free-floating moments
of joy. I want to save
them for when my spirit
falls, fast and deep.
The abundant universe
may impart vibrant energy
to set all life a spinning;

but I'm not always able to
access this grace and to
feel welcome in the world.

3.
Ancient French cave paintings
in Lascaux, provide the mystery
and Paul Klee's Moroccan
paintings provide the back drop
for my visions.
They are projected onto a screen
I can't stop watching.
The cave paintings tell a story
I can't crack. I'm too modern.

Rimbaud turned his back on
the encroaching world and instructed,
"Go Back." No modern world
for him. He refused to be civilized.
He refused all of societies attempts
to control him.

All around, he witnessed:
The spectacle
The substitution
The pretense
The facades
The inauthentic.

Like a painting you pass every day.

Beautiful, but not so much, after
awhile. Predictable colors. Predictable
patterns. People living symbolic lives.

Rimbaud aspired to live archaically.
To live by his spirit map. To listen
to illuminated voices. The only rules,
his own. He contained journeys that
were his alone to take.

His young soul dwelt elsewhere;
deeper than the messages he received
at home, in church, in school.

He plunged into an exploration
of ancient belief systems. He traveled
back to the time, "Before civilization
made criminals of us all." (Francis Picabia).

The ragged punk was launched into
an illuminated state where he recorded
a wild explosion of winged words. The value
of his young defiance was misunderstood
at the time. Rimbaud spoke about resistance
in a language I understood, "Don't let yourself
be one of the captured."

St. Mark's Place

Lisa leant me Reshad Feilds's book, The Last
Barrier.
I read it long into the night. The story follows
an
English healer whose spiritual journey led him
to
Turkey. He wanted to meet the dervishes.

As I read, I continued to return to one particular
passage, "It is important to remain spiritually
awake,
so, you don't miss the moment." My memory
echoed
back through the history of my soul, and I recalled
the many times I received messages about
awakening.
I re-read the passage, reflecting on how much
loving
instruction and wisdom, I had forgotten.

When I awoke the following morning, I sat quietly
and reflected on my desire to remain awake to
the lessons I had been taught: compassion and
kindness,
the true aims of my life.

It was early, and I was going to work. As I
walked
across St. Mark's Place, I noticed a woman with
long
black hair walking parallel to me on the other
side
of the street. I was in front of the Dojo Restaurant,
when the woman with the long black hair
crossed
the street and stood in front of me. I stopped
and she
asked me, "Well, are you awake yet?" and she
crossed

back over to the other side of the street and
resumed
her journey west, walking in tandem with my
gait.

At first, I was a bit shaken, but, ultimately, I did
not find
the message from the woman all that surprising. I
inherently knew this was not an uncommon
occurrence
in the spirit world, where we are all connected.
I did
continue to ponder the woman's question, as I
descended
the subway stairs, boarded the train and went
to work

Truth

One lone bulb
hanging from a tin ceiling,
in the tenement
where I used to fly blind
around the corner
to the bodega
where I never received
any change from the large
bills I often paid with.
I knew I was getting beat,
but I was too high to calculate.

I tap danced on the loading dock
on Broome Street. I visited
Stanley in his macramé shop
on Thompson Street. He fought
in the Spanish Civil War, but
rarely spoke of it. This day,

he was making chicken soup
with apples on his stovetop
in the rear of the store. He invited me
to share dinner, as he often did.
.
Later, we went to the Back Fence,
where Jill Freedman breezed
in with a brand-new copy of her
latest book, Circus Days.
Her photographs of elephants
became a topic of discussion
in universities across the country.

I was in the wind for many years.
I had a hole in my head where my brain
used to be. I filled the hole with
fictitious stories and ignored tugs
toward truth.

At times, my life was split between
spiritual growth and breaking the law.
By day, I worked a mail fraud; at night,
I went to healing meetings.

I ran the con job until my legs gave out.
And, as my dishonesty faded, a collection
of wall hanging masks crashed to the floor;
and there I was, crawling around, desperately
looking for a face to wear.

Always a windy being, my thoughts
flow in, out and through my head
so fast and far out, I have worried
I wouldn't make it back.

When the drugs wore off,
my friends welcomed me back.
"You've been gone longer

than any of us.
Gene didn't make it back,
John didn't make it back,
Jamie didn't make it back,
But, somehow you returned."

My mind was sound, and,
in moments of reflection,
I wondered how many spirits
and prayers assisted my return?

Back in the tenement, the bright
morning sunlight reflected off the maple
kitchen table where I sat drinking a fresh
brewed cup of Gillies Ethiopian coffee.
I drank it slowly, practically meditating
on the deep, rich flavor of the African blend.

Rastas began dancing in a hypnotic moment
that was mine, alone.
I may improvise my life for a moment
or a lifetime; depends on how good
the coffee is.

About the Author:

Mary Shanley is a poet/storyteller living in New York City. She has had four books of poems and stories published and frequently contributes to on-line and print journals.

BEFORE THE INK WAS DRY

by Kevin Keane

Before The Ink Was Dry

He would take a razor blade from his desk and a make little slit
On his hand and use it as an inkwell
Then signed the letters he so carefully composed to her
Placed them in the mailbox on the side walk
Beneath the elevated train in Cypress Hills so long ago
When he still believed in poetry, still believed her vicious smile

Walked his bicycle along the boardwalk
The seagulls screaming in the terrible wind
Walked out on the jetty and search for that same starfish
The one washed away when he still believed she read his letters
Signed in blood and sealed with his tongue in that dark building above the street
Where the train no longer woke him as he slept

He no longer used a razor blade for he no longer bled
Signed off one last time with a cheap red pen substitute
And a brief explanation of his betrayal
The creaking of the mailbox never to be heard again
Drowned out by the train overhead
Now taking him beneath the river and gone

Stasis of Soul

Angry like hornets
Your death comes at me
 I don't even cover my face, my thoughts swell
Unlike the hummingbird
With its sweet buzzing that follows my life

Like the geese overhead I cannot reach you
Your death comes at me
I am red, bloated, under water
The sun can no longer burn me
I am sinking past bindle stiff puppets dressed in rags
Bathed in brine

Your death comes at me
Angry like hornets and sharp as the ice
Forming on my lips
Transparent as the flies' wings buzzing around this mound of dirt
Comes at me fast and blinds me
Turns me into an unresponsive monolith
A reeling corpse

The Lugubrious Mannequin Self Portrait

Late under a velvet sky
Across my bottle neck
Howling
Pumpkin leaves blow and freckle my evening moon
Blinking eyes over the hunchback bough

Lugubrious parasol of emptiness
Crustacean of my look alike
A four cornered yellowing self- portrait under a velvet sky
Across my bottle neck
Howling

Periscope to the evening wilderness
Frozen starfish in rectangular frames
Empty headlights gaze through passages of terrified deer and staggering trees
Leaping over glass monuments in the pumpkin wind
Pumpkin leaves blow
And freckle my evening moon

About the Author:

I was born in New York City and currently live in Arizona in an eighty year old house that I share with two kittens. I am currently working on an autobiographical novel that I hope to finish before I know the ending. I run a small bicycle shop out of my home and build custom bicycles as more of a hobby than an income. Last year, 2018, was the first year I decided to begin submitting my work for publication.

I have always considered my poetry a private thing but over time I have come to realize that this is perhaps a selfish assessment of my work. I have been editing several hundred poems over the past two years with the intent to complete a full volume of poetry this year with work that dates as far back as 1976 and up to the present day. I have been heavily inspired by the work of Lorca and Don Van Vliet.

FLY FISHING THE RIVER STYX

STORIES WITH AN ANGLE

By Richard Dokey

Paperback: 174 pages

Publisher:
Adelaide Books (December 11, 2018)

Language: English

ISBN-10: 1949180492

ISBN-13: 978-1949180497

Product Dimensions: 6 x 0.4 x 9 inches

"Dokey is a writer who can take common people and ordinary places and make them resonate with meanings that suggest themselves to the reader long after the book is closed." San Francisco Chronicle

"He is able to tackle enormous themes (birth, love, marriage, old age) and successfully incorporate them into relatively brief, carefully tailored stories. The author should be commended also for his ability to move effortlessly among a range of narrative voices." Publishers Weekly

"Readers will be taken aback, too, by Dokey's candor and eloquence" Chicago Tribune

"The complexity of Dokey's fiction creeps up, unveiling striking layers of humanity to quietly reward the patient observer" The Sacramento Bee

He speaks to us in a solitary, moving language that only writers as skilled as Dokey can record. We are transported to the highest levels of human experience." Milwaukee Journal

Richard Dokey's stories have won awards and prizes, have been cited in Best American Short Stories, Best of the West, have been nominated for the Pushcart Prize and have been reprinted in numerous regional and national literary reviews and anthologies. Pale Morning Dun, his collection of short stories, published by University of Missouri Press, was nominated for the American Book Award. His writings have appeared most recently in Adelaide Literary Magazine, Alaska Quarterly Review, Grain (Canada), Natural Bridge, Southern Humanities Review, Lumina and The Chattahoochee Review.

QUEENIE'S PLACE

By Toni Morgan

Paperback: 300 pages

Publisher: Adelaide Books (December 1, 2018)

Language: English

ISBN-10: 194918059X

ISBN-13: 978-1949180596

Product Dimensions: 6 x 0.8 x 9 inches

QUEENIE'S PLACE, set in rural North Carolina in the early seventies, is the story of an unusual sisterhood between a thirty-something white woman from California and a fifty-something black women from the south. From the moment Doreen Donavan sees the "Welcome to Klan Country" sign outside Goldsboro, North Carolina is one culture shock after another. She thinks the women she meets on the military base, where she and her family now live, are the dullest, stuffiest, most stuck-up women she's ever run across, and frankly, they don't think much of her either. She's hot, miserable, and bored. Then one day, BAM, her car tire goes flat, right in front of a roadhouse outside the town of Richland, near where MCB Camp Puller is located. Inside, Queenie is holding forth at the piano. The place is jumping. Besides the music, there's dancing and the best barbecue in North Carolina. Doreen's husband, Tom arrives and must practically peel her out of the place. Queenie doesn't expect to see Doreen again, but Doreen comes back and their unlikely friendship begins. Without warning, Queenie's place is closed, the women accused of prostitution and bootlegging. A born crusader (she cut her teeth demonstrating against the Vietnam War—yes, even with her husband over there), Doreen quickly dons her armor and saddles up. Things don't go quite as planned.

Born in Alaska, raised in Oregon, where she studied history at Portland State University, and married in Hawaii, Toni Morgan has lived all over the United States, from California to Washington, D.C., and the world, from Denmark to Japan. She now makes her home in southwestern Idaho. She is the author of six novels: TWO-HEARTED CROSSING, PATRIMONY, ECHOES FROM A FALLING BRIDGE, HARVEST THE WIND, LOTUS BLOSSOM UNFURLING, and QUEENIE'S PLACE. Toni's articles and short stories have been published in various newspapers, literary maga-zines, and other periodicals.

Forty-six-year-old FABY GAUTHIER keeps an abandoned family photograph album in her bottom bureau drawer. Also abandoned is a composition book of vaudeville show reviews, which she wrote when she was nineteen and Slim White, America's self-proclaimed Favorite Hoofer (given name, LOUIS KITTELL), decided to take her along when he played the Small Time before thinking better of it four months later and sending her back home to Vermont on the train. Two weeks before the son she had with Louis is to be married, Faby learns that Louis has been killed in a single-car accident, an apparent suicide. Her first thought is that here is one more broken promise: Louis accepted SONNY's invitation to the wedding readily, even enthusiastically, giving every assurance that he would be there, and now he wouldn't be coming. An even greater indignity than the broken promise is that Louis's family did not bother to notify Faby of his death until a week after the funeral took place. She doesn't know how she can bring herself to tell Sonny he mattered so little in his father's life he wasn't even asked to his funeral...

TELLING SONNY

By Elizabeth Gauffreau

Paperback: 340 pages

Publisher: Adelaide Books (December 1, 2018)

Language: English

ISBN-10: 1949180514

ISBN-13: 978-1949180510

Product Dimensions: 6 x 0.8 x 9 inches

Elizabeth Gauffreau holds a B.A. in English/ Writing from Old Dominion University and an M.A. in English/Fiction Writing from the University of New Hampshire. After a misbegotten stint teaching high school English and Latin, she has spent her career in non-traditional higher education. Her fiction and poetry have been published in literary magazines, including Rio Grande Review, Serving House Journal, Soundings East, Hospital Drive, Blueline, Evening Street Review, and Adelaide Literary Magazine, as well as several themed anthologies. Telling Sonny is her first published book.

PIVOT

Poems by Debbie Richard

Illustrated by Ashley Teets

This collection of poetic works articulates turning points that result in drastic change, realization, and understanding. From an Olympian ice arena to the cool cement floor of an Appalachian cellar, "PIVOT" takes the reader on a tour of poems spanning a broad spectrum of people, places, events, and time periods. From simple household chores to the emotional discovery of a mother's precious heirloom and "going for the gold," turning points channel, challenge, and change the course of our existence and clarify our purpose.

"Debbie Richard explores the beauty and honesty of love, regret, loss and the feelings that come after all of it. There is a delicacy and maturity in her frankness." (CARRIE McCULLOUGH JENKINS, freelance editor/publishing consultant)

"Delicately written and illustrated, these short poems are truly gifts from the heart. Richard's deep love of family, friends, home and Nature shines here. In her careful words, she captures loss and betrayal as movingly as affection, pleasure and joy." (CYNTHIA HODELL DYER, Poet and Songwriter; Past President of S.C. Writers Workshop; Founding Director, Long Bay Threshold Singers)

"Debbie Richard, in her poems, poignantly observes the values and needs, the pains and joys, in the human and natural worlds. She meshes all with the spiritual, her appreciation showered with grace, honesty, and love, and, finally, acceptance of what she cannot change. I love her poems." (DAVID SELBY renown actor and the author of My Mother's Autumn and Promises of Love.)

Debbie Richard is listed in the Directory of Poets & Writers as both a poet and creative nonfiction writer. Her poem, "Between Two Worlds," was selected as Adelaide Voices Literary Award for Poetry FINALIST for 2018. Her poems have appeared in Torrid Literature Journal, Adelaide Literary Magazine, Scarlet Leaf Review, WestWard Quarterly, Halcyon Days, and others.

Award winning illustrator, **Ashley Teets**, specializes in children's art, illustration, graphic design, and mural work. She has illustrated multiple award winning children's books that include 14 Mom's Choice Awards, four Indie Book and an Indie Excellence Award, an International Book Award, a USA News Best Book Award, and four Creative Child Magazine Awards.

"Marina cut her small ration in half, sharing with the sick (possibly dying) young girl she had been trying to look after. The girl was too weak to leave the cramped, dirty sleeping quarters to work in the camp. Marina feared the girl would be sent to the gas chamber if the guards deemed her incapable of labor. Marina was beginning to think this might be worse than Auschwitz, where she and many other women and children had come from in the fall of 1944. She had hoped the transfer would have improved her chances of survival, but it appeared now there wasn't much difference between one labor camp or another. Hope was in short supply, but not totally eradicated. Marina had heard rumors recently in the camp. Rumors the war was ending and the allies had won. Rumors of liberation. But she, like the other prisoners, had heard about liberators coming to save their lives before and it never seemed to happen." - from the Angels of Stockholm

Neil D. Desmond was born in Boston and has lived in Vermont for twenty years. He has a daughter who lives in Massachusetts. His mother is an artist and his uncle is a published poet. Mr. Desmond enjoys creative writing, traveling, as well as watching his share of independent and foreign language films. He is the winner of the 2018 Adelaide Voices Literary Award for his short story Angels of Stockholm.

ANGELS OF STOCKHOLM
Short Stories

By Neil D. Desmond

Paperback: 166 pages

Publisher: Adelaide Books (December 6, 2018)

Language: English

ISBN-10: 1949180549

ISBN-13: 978-1949180541

Product Dimensions: 6 x 0.4 x 9 inches

Donny Barilla, a poet covering the realms: human intimacy, nature, mythology, theology, and man's relationship with death and the departed, has been writing for over three decades. He writes daily and strives to renew himself as an artist from page to page and body of work to body of work. Very seldom does he take a break from writing as he views it as a full-time job. He lives a reclusive lifestyle and finds himself clinging close to nature and all her elements. His home state of Pennsylvania strikes chords of poetic depth about him as he finds loveliness from cornfield to meadow. Whether it's feelings of love, intimacy, or a special closeness, he maintains the feeling that death does not take these with him/her to the grave. Emotions and feeling outlast the flesh of the human body. Human intimacy draws near an enigmatic spiritual passion which conquers all on the prismatic scale of experience. When speaking of mythology Donny says, "myths were created to make sense of feelings which are complicated by very nature. They are perhaps more easily understood through persons greater than oneself. As for theology, a disciplined aspect, incorporates quite finely with passions and secured poetic comforts.

https://twitter.com/BarillaDonny

GALAXIES IN THE RAINDROPS

Poems

By Donny Barilla

Paperback: 274 pages

Publisher: Adelaide Books (December 6, 2018)

Language: English

ISBN-10: 1949180557

ISBN-13: 978-1949180558

Product Dimensions: 6 x 0.7 x 9 inches

www.ingramcontent.com/pod-product-compliance
Lightning Source LLC
Chambersburg PA
CBHW080719020726
47502CB00009B/2477